Alice
to
Prague

Alice to Prague

to

The charming true story of an outback girl who
finds adventure—and love—on the other side of the world

TANYA HEASLIP

ALLEN&UNWIN
SYDNEY·MELBOURNE·AUCKLAND·LONDON

First published in 2019

Copyright © Tanya Heaslip 2019

Allen & Unwin
83 Alexander Street
Crows Nest NSW 2065
Australia
Phone: (61 2) 8425 0100
Email: info@allenandunwin.com
Web: www.allenandunwin.com

A catalogue record for this
book is available from the
National Library of Australia

ISBN 978 1 76052 976 5

Cover design: Nada Backovic
Cover photos: Arcangel (Prague); Alamy (Trephina Gorge, Northern Territory)
Set in 12.5/17 pt Minion Pro by Midland Typesetters, Australia
Printed and bound in Australia by Griffin Press, part of Ovato

10 9 8 7 6 5 4 3 2 1

The paper in this book is FSC® certified.
FSC® promotes environmentally responsible,
socially beneficial and economically viable
management of the world's forests.

Contents

To three generations of wise, wonderful women who believed in me:

Nana Parnell—who led storytelling by example
Mum—who bought me an orange typewriter so that I could start
M'Lis—who loyally read every page that rolled off that orange typewriter

Prologue

The muster

Central Australia, 1972

Out of the inland sky roared the sun. It flattened the land with its intensity and turned the horizon into lines of mirages that shimmered along the distant foothills. Above those silver illusions a range of hills rose abruptly, curves of purple smudged with dark valleys and rocky outcrops. Below, where the red earth had once cracked and heaved, it now collapsed into ancient and misshapen forms as though exhausted. It was an ancient place woven with Aboriginal stories, hundreds of miles of emptiness, largely untouched by Europeans.

And in that particular spot of nowhere, on a Tuesday afternoon in November 1972, a group of stockmen, including three children, drove several hundred cattle from the scrublands of the north towards the mirage-dotted hills of the south.

I was one of those children. My skewbald horse Sandy and I were on the tail of the mob—the lowliest role and the one I hated the most. It meant pushing up the slowest of the cattle, usually cows and their calves, as they called out mournfully to one another in a cacophony of unceasing bellowing. The air was red with thick, choking dust, the smell of sweat and shit, and the powdery taste of dirt. The ochre colours of the hard land underneath billowed as hooves rose and fell, generating waves of crimson and yellow-brown that covered Sandy and me. That was the worst thing about the tail. You were always in line for the bulldust.

On the western wing of the mob rode my nine-year-old sister M'Lis, her long brown plaits swinging out the back of her hat. We could have passed as twins except I was one year older and my plaits were long and blonde. On the eastern wing rode my younger brother Brett, eight years old, his freckly face dwarfed by a hat pulled low over his ears.

We three were all small, tough and wiry, with freckles; we were little men among big men, doing big men's work, and we knew no other way. But there was always a rush of happiness if Dad ever acknowledged we'd done a job as well as any man. Praise from Dad was rare and we gave our all for those tidbits.

Everyone called Dad 'The Boss'. Hard, determined and stoic, he walked fast and rode fast, stockwhip looped over his shoulder, boots crunching over the ground, stock hat pushed low over his eyes. Whatever he said went. One of his many mottos was: 'There is no such word as *can't*.' He and Mum were living proof of that. They'd arrived from the south during the 1960s drought to make a go of this station when everyone had said it was too small and drought-stricken to be viable. They'd put in fencing, they'd increased the herd, and they were still here.

But Dad wasn't with us this afternoon. He was at the homestead preparing for the drafting and trucking in the morning. And so in the heat I drifted off . . .

'Tanya! Stop yer daydreamin', girl, and push up them bloody calves!' The shout of Head Stockman Mick brought me back with a start.

A dry, wry bushman, Mick was a natural with horses and stock and kids. He could plait belts and bridles and stock-whips like no one else—and spin a long yarn while doing it—but when he yelled we all jumped. Especially as he was in charge today.

I looked quickly down at the tail. The cows, calves and I had all slowed down to a crawl, probably because it was so hot. No doubt the cows and calves still wished they were under a tree, as I did. Hours of interminable boredom lay ahead as we faced the long trek through the hot afternoon.

'Sorry!' I shouted back to Mick, all the while thinking of the word *interminable*. I quite liked that word. It sounded like it meant 'forever', which is how this part of the day—the droving part—felt to me. M'Lis and Brett, on the other hand, relished every part of the day and were 'born for the saddle' (a perfectly apt expression I'd read in a pony story recently). Me? I wished I was home curled up under my favourite pepper tree with a book in my hand and the dogs panting happily at my feet.

It had been a long day.

As with most musters, this one had begun before day-light, where we'd saddled up in pre-dawn shadows, our horses snorting and fidgety, everyone full of anticipation, edgy. We had swung up into our saddles and ridden to the end of Orange Tree Bore, a misnamed paddock if ever there was one; it was dotted with spinifex and its one gnarled tree rarely bore the sweet bush fruit it was named after. We'd mustered that day because the winter rains had not come. It was dry, feed was short, and the cattle had to be turned off before they lost condition.

The Bore was miles from the homestead so we'd camped the night before to get an early start.

The start of the muster, any muster, was the best bit of the day. As the sun rose, the distant hills would turn to mauve then rose-pink and finally golden brown, and the air would be crisp and our world beautiful. We'd canter along, looking for the first mob, then the second, and then another—and it was on. Shouts would ring through the clear morning air: 'Bottom of the gorge!', 'Down on the creek!', 'Up on that hill!' The cattle were often hiding out in gullies, some cresting the top of rocky ranges, others inside thick mulga scrub, and the minute beast saw man and horse it would break into a run. Then the chase would begin. There was the thrilling sound of stockwhips cracking, the rush of air over hot faces and sweaty heads, the leaning over the necks of trusty steeds as we wheeled the beasts towards one big mob with shouts of: '*Ha hup* there, cattle! *Hut hut*—walk up!'

'We are adventurers, one and all,' I'd whistle through my teeth as I crouched low over my saddle and raced towards the flat, although I wasn't sure where I'd learnt that from. I loved the rush of danger, of being one with my horse as we sprinted across rocky creek beds and up flinty hillsides and into the grey thickets. There was the thrill in my body of being truly alive, the sound of thrumming hooves and thumping hearts, and the drive for a successful outcome. Dad had drilled into us that nothing was more important than getting the mob together and heading home without losing a beast.

But now the rush had subsided and all I could think about was the dust that lay thickly in my mouth. It coated my throat and made me desperate for water. I wanted a drink so much it hurt like a bellyache. The first drink had been at the dam earlier that morning and I'd taken a swig from my water bag about once every hour since then. The hessian bag hung off my saddle on Sandy's withers, temptingly close but already half-empty. The rest had to last all day. And I knew the rules: drink as little as possible to train your body to be tough and strong, to go on as long as you can without water. 'Drinking makes you thirsty—makes you want to drink more,' Dad had instructed us from as early as I could remember.

I also knew the rules of nature. We lived on a dried-out former inland sea where you could perish on a summer's day, especially if you got thrown off your horse or lost during the muster.

But all I could fantasise about now was wetness in my mouth and the trough I would put my face in tonight, swishing my head from side to side, lapping the water like a dog. I screwed my eyes up under my hat and took in the miles of empty flat that lay ahead, then swivelled in my saddle to look at the mulga scrub I'd left behind.

The only way to survive the *interminable* was to escape back into my imagination. Daydreaming got me into a lot of trouble in the schoolroom (and with Mick) but right now it was my saviour. It was the place I hid in to endure the heat, thirst and boredom. It lived inside my head and was drawn from the books I read and the stories I heard.

My dreams were about a different world, another place, a contrasting landscape.

I had never seen this other world but it was as bright as day to me. There were rolling meadows of golden daffodils, moonlit lakes, fields of green grasses, shady woods, trees with delicious names like *oak* and *beech*; there was softness and coolness and endless water. In those lands there were children who played and had adventures and didn't have to muster cattle in the stinking heat. Well, Heidi did have to walk with some goats up a snowy mountain, and the children of the Famous Five and the Secret Seven and *The Magic Faraway Tree* had to do jobs for Mother and Father. But once those children had finished their jobs, they cycled on bikes up gentle hills and down gentle dales—just for fun—and ate delicious-sounding 'ices'.

Once I entered those magical places, like one of the children who fell through the wardrobe into Narnia, I could mostly tune out the unrelenting heat that pressed down upon me and forget the hours still to go; I could momentarily forget my cracked and blistered lips, my hunger and my swollen tongue. These fantasy lands pressed themselves upon my heart and I loved them. They were precious to me, my own mysterious hidden treasure.

Mum knew this. Once a month she drove through boggy creeks and along corrugated dirt roads to Alice Springs to get stores for the station, and always went past the School of the Air to collect a big box of enticingly musty books from their library for me to devour. She understood my hunger to read and lose myself in stories.

'Oi! Tanya! Whaddya think yer doin', girl? Head in the clouds agin? Move those bloody cattle along!'

As I pushed my chin up from my chest, to which it had sunk deeply in my trance, Mick's yells drifted into earshot. To my horror the tail had carried on without me and was now beginning to spread out into two groups, each heading in a different direction. Even worse, during my time away in fairyland all the stockmen, and M'Lis and Brett, had rotated positions. All except for me. I was still stuck with the tail.

'C'mon, Sandy!' I hissed and broke into a trot, hollering, 'C'mon there, you mob, move along, get back there, *ha hup* there!' But the breakaway group had moved such a distance it took a while to pull them back into the tail. Sandy and I then resumed our weary plodding.

As I gazed out to the west I saw the sun had moved lower in the big broad sky. I knew the heat would lessen as the afternoon pushed on, lengthening the light and shadows along the plain as we got towards the yards.

I thought about the ritual that was the second-best part of the day.

Once we reached the cattle yards, we would herd the mob in through the open gates, always a tricky and tense moment; nobody wanted to lose cattle right before the end, having got them safely there. Next was the job of getting the snorting, thirsty beasts to water. It was important not to let the cattle hurt themselves in their rush for the water. Once the cattle were safely drinking, we would water our own horses, unsaddle them and let them out to graze, loosely hobbled to ensure they were nearby in the morning.

Finally, the animals cared for, we would fall onto the water ourselves and drink until our bellies were swollen, light the fire as darkness fell, and eat steak cooked on the coals. We'd lean against our swags, numb with tiredness. The dirt and grease and red dust would make grotesque masks of our faces in the firelight. There'd be jokes, maybe a guitar and some Slim Dusty tunes. We kids would beg Irish stockman Ray to play 'Nobody's Child,' and he'd always oblige. My heart would ache for the loss and loneliness of the orphaned boy who nobody wanted, as Ray's mournful, lilting tones delivered the tragedy of the song across the dying embers of the fire. I'd think about my baby brother Benny, at home alone with Mum; he lived on my hip when I wasn't on a horse. Ray's songs always made me miss Benny more.

Then we'd roll out our swags and crawl in, fully clad, boots tucked carefully at the bottom to keep them away from snakes.

The sky would sparkle with stars and we'd fall asleep under a sliver of moon, listening to a dingo howling in the distance and the comforting clink of the hobbles as the horses grazed nearby.

The next morning Dad and the young stockman would arrive at daybreak in the old Land Rover, bringing branding irons and a fresh tuckerbox packed by Mum. We kids would rush to see if Mum had included the coveted tins of apricot jam and creamed rice, along with the essentials of corned beef, damper, tomato sauce, tea and sugar.

Then we'd all begin the yard work, with several days of hot, sweaty and equally boring work ahead of us, drafting the entire mob, branding the cleanskins and castrating the young micky bulls. The cows and calves would then be returned to the paddocks through the bush gate, and the weaners and fat bullocks kept aside for market.

Finally, the huge double-decker road trains from Tanami Transport would emerge like huge prehistoric perenties crawling through the dust. Into these giants the weaners and fat bullocks would be loaded and trucked off to their destination miles away down south.

That was my life.

But I knew there was another life. And I'd decided that when I grew up I would go and find it for myself—overseas, in those lands of magic. Until then I would think about it and imagine it and tell myself stories about it.

And so, once the evening came and the ordeal of the day was over, I knew I'd drift off to sleep, my head filled with dreams of running across a snow-capped mountain, arms outstretched in the joy of the moment, dancing with my prince, our eyes shining, our voices singing, and living happily ever after.

1

The Berlin Wall

Seventeen years later: November 1989

It was six o'clock in London on a cold November evening. The streetlights cast a pallid glow across the street as my friend Michael and I scurried towards the entrance of an old pub. I wrapped my coat more tightly around me, the chill biting my ankles as it seeped up from the flagstones and through my boots.

'Welcome to the local!' Michael pushed open the door and led me inside to the warmth and chatter and clinking of glasses. I followed him to a table in the corner, a good distance from the throng of people gathered in front of the bar.

'Glass of wine?' Michael didn't wait for an answer but pushed his way through the crowd.

As I watched him go, touched as I always was by his kindness, I had a moment to reflect. My year in Europe was almost at an end.

Yes, my dream had come true. I had made it come true. I was a bush girl who had finally made it to Europe. I'd backpacked alone and turned twenty-eight along the way. Admittedly, I was a late starter—most of my friends had 'done Europe' much earlier—but my life had been a rollercoaster since I'd been dispatched to boarding school at the age of twelve. After that came law school, which led to practising law, and my childish dreams had been put on the backburner while I built a career. In fact, it was a miracle I'd made it to Europe at all, but a love affair gone wrong that left splinters of my heart from one end of the Territory to the other was the motivator I finally needed to shriek, 'Enough! I'm out of here!'

Once I'd finally made it, I dived into every experience, longing to recapture those early dreams and recreate the magic of dissolving into another world.

I had travelled solo, which was lonely, but it had given me time and privacy to nurse my broken heart back to health. I'd also been lucky enough to spend time with my darling friend Michael, who had taken me into his tiny flat every time I passed through London. He'd made me Vegemite on toast and offered much-needed hugs when I was homesick for red earth and blue skies.

Michael and I had met at law school in Adelaide many years before. He'd moved to London and now worked for Oxfam, and he was very funny. Straight blond strands of hair fell in his eyes; he wore little round glasses and still enjoyed a student's propensity for beer. 'The only way to see a city is to walk it,' he'd told me, and he'd walked the length and breadth of London, and tried many of its pubs, to prove his point.

In the bar, Michael returned with a glass of white wine for me and a Guinness for himself.

'To your year here. Great effort.' We clinked glasses.

'I'll miss you so much, Michael.'

It was true. He'd encouraged me on every step of this trip. But there was something I hadn't shared with him, or with anyone for that matter. My endeavour to recapture my childhood hadn't been exactly what I'd hoped for and I knew I'd have to return home unfulfilled.

If I tried to pinpoint the exact reason for this, the closest example I could give myself involved oak trees. On arrival I'd longed to feel firsthand the sense of magic and mystery I remembered so vividly that oak trees represented for me: the Secret Seven hiding in their thick, green leaves, protected from the rain and the robbers, and the *Magic Faraway Tree* children climbing them to reach swirling lands at the top of the branches. Oak trees had seemed a wondrous part of England, as far removed from my childhood world of dry gums and spindly mulga as you could imagine.

But when I found oak trees, there were no children in them, no ladders to enchanted lands, and no magic. I spent hopeless hours gazing at the landscape, willing my heroines to emerge, wanting to have adventures and cycle down dales and eat ices. But all I found were a lot of cars on a lot of freeways, ugly fast-food outlets on the sides of roads, polluted skies, and no children who matched my daydreams.

Sitting there with Michael, it dawned on me that the journey back to my inner childhood had always been doomed to fail. Time had moved on. The world I looked for belonged to the 1930s and '40s. The world I'd arrived in was the late 1980s. The sacredness of the places and the stories of that time had gone. The sense of timelessness, of history, of beauty, seemed lost.

Clearly it wasn't possible to transcend the gap between the girl I once was and the dreams I had, and the reality I was now facing. Perhaps twenty-eight was too late to go hunting for childhood dreams anyway. The fantasies in my imagination simply slipped further away the more I searched for them. My fingers grasped at emptiness; my heart remained hollow. Like a clumsy lover who'd been away a long time, unaware, insensitive, I'd simply expected that by being in these places my imagination would spark back into life and the stories would write themselves afresh. But the stories I'd made up to transport myself there could not be revived.

That realisation was deeply confronting. While I had spent the last decade trying to become a professional lawyer, deep inside I'd continued to carry the innocence and hopes of that young girl on the horse. My stories were precious, like silent, secret companions, and their very existence nurtured and sustained me through the rigours of law. The daydreamer had never truly gone away. I truly believed the Magic Faraway Tree existed somewhere. But despite searching high and low through English woods, I had not been able to find it.

I couldn't tell Michael any of this. I could barely admit it to myself. I'd started out the year feeling like a loser and a failure and was ending it feeling like a loser and a failure.

So what now?

'Will you go back to law?' asked Michael.

I sighed. 'Probably—I'm pretty broke and my firm's expecting me back.' But as I said that, my heart sank.

'The sooner you leave law, the better,' said Michael. 'Like I did.'

He looked cheerful at that memory, as well he might.

'You once wanted to be a foreign correspondent,' he reminded me. 'Look at this year. If there was ever a time to strike out and cover world events, it's now.'

He was right about the year. My trip had coincided with an unprecedented upheaval in Eastern Europe, the world behind the Iron Curtain. I didn't know a great deal about that region, other than that it was a dark place, oppressed and cruelly controlled by the Soviets.

The Cold War had been a hot topic throughout my whole life. I'd never known life without it. In fact, it had comprised a large part of conversations at home with Dad and my studies at school. Mrs Howe (Modern European History, Year 11, boarding school) and John le Carré's books gave me more detailed insights into a bleak, grim and unforgiving regime. Even the highly fictionalised James Bond movies depicted the communists as pure evil and we all believed it. To give this context, I was born the year after Fidel Castro's Bay of Pigs fiasco, during which the Soviet Union nearly blew up the world, so communism was considered in my family to be the greatest evil, ever.

But by 1989, the year of my travels, Soviet President Mikhail Gorbachev had decided to create a new era of restructuring (perestroika) and openness (glasnost) throughout the Soviet Union, and some of the Eastern Bloc satellite states were taking their own steps towards freedom. Poland agreed to open elections and Hungary dismantled the electrified barbed-wire fences along its border with Austria. However, hard-line regimes elsewhere, like East Germany and Czechoslovakia, refused to budge and there were riots. Hundreds of thousands of East Germans flooded the Alexanderplatz in Berlin, calling for basic human rights. People were beaten and incarcerated but the demonstrations grew.

I observed these developments with fear and fascination as I travelled around Western Europe. However, to be honest, the quest to recover my dreams took precedence over visiting a part of the planet I didn't want to visit. Nothing about the Soviet states of Eastern Europe made me wish to experience a daytrip to grim East Berlin or a week of thin borsch soup in Moscow where I might disappear and never be seen again.

On the other hand, the US President, Ronald Reagan, had been optimistic about the Soviets' intentions. He'd focused on the place where the Iron Curtain was most starkly represented: the foreboding Berlin Wall that divided East and West Germany. The Wall in question had been built by the Soviets in 1961, the year before I was born. Overnight, the Soviets divided streets, families and communities with forty-three kilometres of steel, concrete, barbed wire, watchtowers and gun emplacements.

The Wall was a symbol of tyranny and fear, a raw gash through the heart of Europe. It was perhaps the greatest symbol of the Cold War.

So in June 1987, Ronald Reagan had stood in front of the Brandenburg Gate in West Berlin and, in front of thousands, called out, 'Mr Gorbachev, tear down this wall!'

US President Bush subsequently came into office. But the Wall remained firmly in place, despite ongoing international political pressure.

———⟩●⟨———

'Well?' prompted Michael, raising his voice. 'Madame Foreign Correspondent?'

The pub was really noisy and it was hard to hear. I leant forward. 'I like that idea!' Michael always found a way to perk me up. 'Perhaps I could stay here and write stories about developments in Eastern Europe and not go back and face reality.'

'You can stay in my garret,' Michael said with a grin, 'but you and the rat would have to fight for the cheese.' He swivelled in his seat. 'What is going *on* here?'

A large roar erupted from the bar. We strained our necks to see. A television had been set up on the counter and people milled about in front of it. On the screen were flashing images of something—people, darkness, spotlights. What was happening?

Michael got it first. 'My God, it's the Berlin Wall!'

We rushed forward to join the chaotic crowd around the screen. Images of a huge, graffitied wall bore down upon us. There were thousands of people in a square; enormous black gates were opening.

'East Berlin tonight is a city in chaos,' a journalist shouted to camera. He stood against a backdrop of barbed wire and towers and piercing lights. 'The East German government appears to have collapsed, people are escaping into the West and no one is stopping them. Are we seeing the fall of the Berlin Wall at last? The end of the Cold War? Whatever the outcome, history is rewriting itself before our very eyes.'

The bar was overflowing and the place was in uproar. People were glued to the screen. More pints were pulled; Michael and I ordered another round and watched, agog. Before I knew it, my words were out, breathless, rushed.

'Michael, we've got to get tickets. We've got to get to Berlin—we've got to see this ourselves!'

Michael pushed his glasses up his nose and, uncharacteristically, shook his head. 'We'll never get tickets—'

'—but we can try!'

'I've got a conference tomorrow, in Manchester. It's really important. My boss is expecting me . . .'

Really? The greatest antidote to misery was action and I'd had enough misery. No one had ever thought the Berlin Wall might fall and the Cold War might end. Certainly not Mrs Howe, who in Year 11 predicted that Stalin's evil legacy would live on forever. I was driven by a force greater than me.

'Michael, come *on*! We're here, we're so close. It's meant to be. Your boring old conference can wait . . . and besides'—this was the clincher—'this is my chance to be a foreign correspondent. If we go together I'll write a story about it for you!'

Michael looked at me as if I was mad. But I was on fire. I'd had enough of travelling alone for months, looking for something that no longer existed. Now I had the chance to share something extraordinary that *did* exist, something that in fact was taking form and shape as we spoke. I wasn't going to give it up.

'Alright, alright.' Michael finally capitulated like an exhausted parent with a pesky child. 'Better find a phone box and ring my boss.'

———————

The next morning we caught a flight to Berlin, scoring two of the few remaining seats. As Michael predicted, the entire world's media had the same idea, and the flight was abuzz with the uncontrolled energy of the first day on a school bus trip—just without the singing.

We landed in fog. Berlin was icy, dirty and unforgiving to physical extremities. My feet, fingers and nose froze. But I didn't care. The scenes down at the Wall were everything the TV journalist had reported, and more. My eyes worked overtime, soaking in the expressions of thousands of bewildered, ecstatic East Berliners flooding to freedom through the Brandenburg Gate.

It was the euphoria of the end of a war.

Germans from both sides drank champagne and shouted victory on the top of the hated Wall. Men and women danced. At Checkpoint Charlie, a girl with laughing eyes clutched flowers and kissed a man in uniform. Did she know him? Nobody knew, nobody cared, because the unimaginable, the unthinkable had happened, and journalists now predicted we would see the rest of the Soviet Bloc states fall like dominoes across Eastern Europe.

When an East German soldier in hobnailed boots with nowhere to go and no job to do hacked me off a piece of the Wall, I knew that one day I would return. I would find a way to get behind the Iron Curtain and learn firsthand what the world of the Cold War had really been like, what our history books had never really told us, never been able to tell us: the story of forty long, brutal years of communism and a decade of Nazi occupation before that, of the evil things that Mrs Howe could only hint at.

I knew it was ironic. A day earlier, nothing would have persuaded me to undertake such a venture. Now I was fuelled by a hunger I could barely comprehend. After a year of indecision and dithering, the purpose of my trip had come into focus; shiny, sharp, clear and thrilling. I might not have found what I was looking for in Western Europe but in Eastern Europe, who knew what might happen? In the adrenaline rush of the moment, I was a risk-taker and an adventurer again, a horserider and pioneer from the wildness of the outback. I'd been given a miracle to pursue. Real magic had broken through and I intended to honour it.

Of course I had to go home and return to my law firm for a while. That was a promise I also had to honour. There was a more prosaic reason too. I was broke.

'Always a couch here if you come back!' Michael grinned, hugging me before I boarded my plane at Heathrow. 'Just don't take me across any eastern borders.'

I arrived back in Australia clutching my bit of the Wall, while euphoric commentators declared, 'This is the greatest event of the last five decades, if not the century . . . thin edge of the wedge for countries like Czechoslovakia and Romania . . . only a matter of time before their socialist governments secede to the masses . . .'

Now I had to find a way to get back.

2

Adventures, ahoy!

November 1993

Back at my old law firm in Alice Springs, bit of Berlin Wall on my desk, I started rebuilding my bank balance and planning my new life. At night I dreamt of crossing the Iron Curtain to hear the stories of the people who'd been freed. I dreamt of learning what their lives had been like and writing it all down. That dream kept me going through divorce cases, contract arguments, contested wills, criminal matters, and the endless stream of angry people who turned up at my desk, hating someone or something, unable to resolve a dispute themselves and wanting me to fix it for them.

That dream kept me going for the next four years, which was how long it took me to extract myself from law again and find a way back to Europe. It also took a spot of divine intervention in the form of international lawyer and barrister Peter Barr, who lived in Darwin. 'He worked in Eastern Europe after communism fell,' a mutual colleague told me during her visit to Alice. Stunned at what seemed like such an extraordinary coincidence, I begged, 'Would he meet with me?' Yes, apparently he would, if I could get to Darwin.

Once again I was driven by an energy akin to fire, just as I had been that night in the London pub. I wangled a court case in Darwin and boarded a plane in Alice Springs to fly north, all my hopes flooding back.

Darwin was sweltering and cyclonic when I arrived, thunderclouds circling. I made it to court and, when I finished with witnesses for the day, I discarded wig and gown and rushed to the Hotel Darwin to meet my fate. I arrived in a state, trembling, with perspiration pouring down my back.

Peter Barr was waiting in the bar, wearing a pressed linen suit and Panama hat, looking cool and elegant. He stood to meet me and ordered gin and tonics in a beautifully cultivated accent. We sipped them under the leisurely *thwat-thwat* of an overhead fan (well, *he* sipped; I sculled, fingers unsteady), while he told me his story and I listened, dizzy with the possibilities he was outlining.

'I taught English in Czechoslovakia, in a country town called Sedlčany. I wanted a break from law and it was a fascinating time over there. You ought to go.'

The thoughts that rushed through my mind were as fizzy as the tonic in my glass. Peter himself was fascinating. Very few people that I knew were particularly aware of Eastern Europe or indeed interested in it. I gazed at Peter like he was the Messiah and slowly repeated the name of the town: '*Sed-dool-char-ny.*' Peter nodded approvingly.

'Tanya, I've still got contacts. I could find you a position. Three months to start with, and if things work out, maybe six months, or even a year? I loved it—I'm sure you will.'

Teaching! Such a thing had never occurred to me. Yet I remembered the teaching style of my School of the Air teacher, Mrs Hodder, from many years before. Mrs Hodder spoke to us every day on air and she had the most beautiful voice. Growing up I was surrounded by stockmen who barely spoke, and when they did it was usually to swear or shout at cattle (or at me, for daydreaming). But Mrs Hodder had sounded like the Queen. She spoke graciously to her subjects. She brought lessons alive. I waited every day for my half-hour lesson like I'd wait for water on a muster. If I could channel her, I'd be right. I just had to inspire students the way she inspired me.

Peter Barr read my thoughts. 'Obviously, I wasn't a teacher either but the school is always happy for assistance, to give their students new opportunities not available under the old regime. They will call you'—he paused—'a "native speaker".'

The stormy evening air was fragrant with frangipanis and I was intoxicated by the thrilling prospects that lay ahead. I pummelled him with questions. Peter answered in his cultivated voice like a British agent in the exotic East, or a spy in *Casablanca*. I felt like I ought to have a tape recorder hidden in my bag.

'The country is now called the Czech Republic. It is made up of Bohemia, Moravia and a slice of Silesia. Slovakia split off during my time there. The Czechs consider themselves more connected to the West and the Slovaks to the East.' He paused, smiled boyishly. 'The Czechs are the original bohemians.'

Free-spirited people in cheesecloth, free love and lots of music? *Really?* Perfect.

'Mmm, what else? Okay, Václav Havel—from prison to presidency!' he quipped. When he saw my expression he explained further. 'Havel was the greatest dissident voice under communism, a writer and poet. He was elected president after the fall of communism. Once in power, he pardoned his jailers and those who'd persecuted him. He is known as the Nelson Mandela of the East.'

My head whirled.

Peter added, 'He lives in Prague Castle now but meets journalists and diplomats for a cigarette and a beer at his local pub!'

I momentarily thought of Michael in London and how much he'd love the sound of that.

'Prague is the most beautiful city imaginable, Tanya—music, literature, culture. It is still largely hidden from the outside world. You must catch a bus from Sedlčany one weekend and visit it.'

Bohemians dancing through a beautiful city, a poet who became a president, me soaking it all in—I was in heaven.

'Three pieces of advice.' Peter folded one perfectly pressed trousered leg over the other. 'Read *The Unbearable Lightness of Being*, a small masterpiece about, among other things, the 1968 Prague Spring. And anything Kafka.'

'Er, right.' I had read some Kafka but not enjoyed it.

'And you must learn about the Velvet Revolution, which is the term used to describe the collapse of communism in 1989. *Allegedly*'—he paused, as though addressing a jury—'there were no deaths then, hence the term *Velvet*. There was plenty of brutality though. Hundreds of students beaten, hospitalised. The history of Czech occupation is appalling.' He paused again and tapped his finger on his knee. 'But the resilience of the people is extraordinary.'

My throat was dry. 'The third thing?'

'Yes. Learn the language while you're there. It's complex, similar grammar to Latin, but will enable you to talk to people and make the most of your time.'

Yes, yes. I kept nodding. Books and talking—two of my favourite things. How hard could it be?

There were, however, a few crucial facts about Peter Barr I hadn't factored in.

Peter was already fluent in many languages, including Latin. He enjoyed numerous international diplomatic connections. He was the Honorary Consul for Belgium. It didn't occur to me to be concerned that I was fluent in no foreign languages, especially not Latin, and enjoyed no international connections, diplomatic or otherwise.

Nor did it occur to me that Mrs Hodder from School of the Air and I spoke the same language, and that channelling her into Czech might be slightly tricky. No, instead I was filled with blind optimism. In 1989 I'd lugged around a trusty pink backpack and *Let's Go Europe* as talisman and guide. That had worked then— why not now, in the East? After two gin and tonics, what seemed like an answer to a prayer meant that anything and everything seemed possible. In my mind's eye I could see myself sweeping into a picturesque village nestled in rolling hills, arriving like Julie Andrews in *The Sound of Music*, full of hope and encouragement and even some song.

Peter stood up, his linen suit crease-free, his Panama hat held loosely between his graceful fingers. 'I'll put in a call tomorrow for you. Then I'll be in touch. Good luck!'

———

I flew back to Alice, dizzy with excitement. Peter called me within a few days, confirming the school was happy to take me on in the new year and looking forward to my arrival. I resigned immediately and wrote off to Canberra for the relevant visas.

Not everyone was as enthused. 'What are we going to do with all your cases?' my boss demanded. I apologised repeatedly, my face hot and pink (crushing eldest-child guilt invariably loomed large at those moments), but there was no turning back.

Mum was horrified. 'Please don't go,' she begged when I told her, crossing her arms with the conviction of one who'd lived through the Petrov Affair and 'Reds under the Bed'. 'Those Cold War countries are dangerous. They won't have changed overnight.'

The concerns of well-meaning friends and family poured in alongside hers, ranging from security and logistic issues— 'We've never even heard of this place; how do you even get there?' and 'You mean you can only be contacted via a *fax* at the school? No phone at all?'—through to concerns about my career: 'You know this time you really will fall off the ladder and not be able to get back up. You *know* that, don't you? You *can't* keep running away from work for a year at a time, Tanya.'

Oh, but there's no such word as 'can't', I thought, channelling Dad.

Dad was slightly pacified by the fact I was at least going to work somewhere else. He was also curious about my destination. He was a self-taught historian with a huge interest in the world wars. It was in his *Encyclopaedia Britannica* that I found a small dot on a map that told me where Sedlčany was located: south of Prague. The paper of the map was smooth under my fingers; I doubted whether this page had ever been opened. I was proud to bring it to life. Dad nodded brusquely as I showed him and told me to keep good records. He even suggested I should visit Moscow, home of the Cold War, if I had the chance.

I worked right up until the weekend before I left, finalising file notes and farewelling clients, so there was a complete lack of preparation for my trip (other than packing a bag and receiving my visas only two days before departure). But I didn't care. There was nothing I could really do until I got there so I had to trust it would all work out.

The exception was hunting down *The Unbearable Lightness of Being*, the book Peter had recommended. I couldn't find the novel but borrowed the video. I put it on excitedly, keen to see the bohemian city of Prague that Peter had described.

To my surprise the movie was about an oversexed surgeon named Tomáš, his long-suffering wife Tereza and his long-term mistress Sabina. As I was wondering what Peter Barr was getting me into, I saw the references to the Prague Spring, and thought it must be some sort of lovefest in the sunshine. Er—no. The movie included real footage of what was in fact an invasion: Russian tanks rolling into Wenceslas Square to crush innocent people. Massive steel tanks mowing down screaming students. Communist soldiers firing into the crowds. I could hardly believe my eyes. Terror trickled down my spine.

The movie depicted life after the invasion too: fear etched on people's faces, ordinary men and women vanishing in the night never to be seen again, people's occupations stripped from them. (Tomáš, refusing to bow to the regime, goes from being an acclaimed surgeon to a window washer. He still manages to have a lot of sex with the women whose windows he washes but I'm not sure it compensates for losing his brilliant career.) My skin crawled at the faceless men in low hats and long coats who moved in and out of shadows, directing people's lives in some sort of Kafkaesque plot.

After watching the movie I spent several days in high anxiety. Was I making a mistake? Peter had said the transition to freedom in the Czech Republic had been slow.

But something deeper and unspoken was pushing me forward. It overrode my apprehension. And it wasn't the fear of a political system. It was something worse. It was the fear of my own social system, my society's expectations, the expectation that a woman of a certain age (say, thirty-one, for example) was expected to have both a ring on her finger and a bunch of children. All I had to show for my many years was a long list of unsuccessful relationships while all my friends were busily married, having babies, cooing and delighted.

The unspoken text was 'What is wrong with *you*?'

At this rate I would be left on the shelf and run the risk of becoming a spinster (a word still bandied about in 1994, and the worst possible outcome for any young woman in my society, it appeared). I cringed every time someone raised an eyebrow at my lack of a suitable suitor, and every time someone tried to sound encouraging: 'Oh, it will happen for you, it's all in the timing!' My beloved grandfather said mournfully, 'It is a great pity a rose like you should be left on the vine'.

Sure, I wanted love—didn't everyone? But I was like a nervous filly, shy of being controlled, longing always for the openness of the plains. If anyone tried to tie me down, I was off, galloping wildly, nostrils flaring. I wasn't sure of the cause of this unhelpful affliction but early years of bush freedom followed by teenage years of boarding school imprisonment were in the mix. As a result, good men didn't stand a chance, while cads and commitment-phobes came and went in droves. Going to an unknown country would give me a chance to escape those scenarios and expectations I could not seem to fulfil, did not know how to fulfil—and a chance to start again.

My sister M'Lis, my much-loved soulmate, was the one person who truly understood me. We went for a long horseride out through the hills before I left. We talked about our futures as our horses picked their way along the narrow trail.

It was dusk when we returned and I took in the beautiful colours as they deepened into apricot and deep golden hues along the ridges of the ranges. 'I'll be back, Lis. This is my country, but I need to get away, to do this first.' I stroked my horse's mane and breathed in her sweet scent.

M'Lis reached out and touched my hand. 'I know you do.'

———⟫•⟪———

'We'll miss you terribly,' Mum whispered to me at the airport, her eyes brimming with tears.

I hugged her, struck by that same sickening feeling of being twelve years old again and saying goodbye to her at the boarding school gates.

M'Lis held me tight and we clung together for a moment. Dad, Brett and Benny gave me a last hug. Then the flight was called.

I headed across the tarmac. All around me were the huge blue skies of Central Australia. The sun shone hot on my bare shoulders and the light was intense. In the distance, the mountain ranges shimmered purple under the midday sun. Catching one last glimpse of my family standing close together at the gate, I swallowed down tears.

But I knew there was more to life than what I was experiencing at home and I felt driven to discover what else was out there. A whole new world was waiting to be explored, and if I didn't take the opportunity now, I might never do it. And I didn't want to live with regrets.

There would always be time to return and be a conventional girl later.

Perhaps.

Breathing in a last deep gulp of clean, fresh air, I waved my final goodbye. The scent of eucalyptus from the flowering gum trees lining our path drifted to me and felt like a good omen. Even with tears on my cheeks, I couldn't wait to get on that plane.

3

Maruška and Zdeněk

March 1994

'Taaaarnya?'

A young, slim woman with high cheekbones and short, dark curly hair disentangled herself from the crowd in the arrivals hall of Prague-Ruzyně International Airport.

My legs wobbled and I was flooded with relief.

I'd just endured three hours of wrong queues, wrong box offices, and interrogations by passport and immigration officials that I couldn't understand—and undoubtedly never would. What had I been thinking? I'd had to sign documents I couldn't read. (Nothing terrifies a lawyer more than signing documents they can't read.) My head ached. Nothing in the previous three hours had made sense to me, not the signs covered in words made of letters with hooks on top of them and dashes either side, nor the officials barking instructions meaningless to my untrained ear. I'd had no expectation it would be this difficult. After all, when I'd travelled in 1989, the romantic-sounding languages of French, German, Italian and Spanish were filled with letters and words and phrases similar to those in English, and I could usually work out the gist of what was meant. Not here. I might as well have landed on Mars.

What had I been thinking?

There was something else equally confronting. My joyous memories of shared love and elation and freedom and dancing at the bottom of the Berlin Wall had vanished in seconds of landing. The airport shrieked 'Cold War prison camp!' to me. Barbed wire and chain-link fencing stretched across flat land. Soldiers with guns watched us silently as we crossed the tarmac. Then they barked orders inside. I'd never seen guns at an airport before. Maybe this country hadn't moved on from the bad old days after all. I felt crumpled and dirty and exhausted, like a prisoner myself, my joie de vivre dissipating with each step.

But now a woman smiled shyly and extended her hand.

'I am Maruška, English teacher at Gymnázium Sedlčany, and this is Headmaster Zdeněk.'

A swarthy, muscular man with a mat of light-brown hair pumped my hand. His face creased into a grin that lit his eyes as he thrust a cellophane-wrapped pink carnation at me. At this unprecedented show of welcome and graciousness, not to mention the pleasure at seeing a burst of colour in this sea of grey, my knees sagged. Swaying slightly, I gazed, stupefied, at the shiny wrapping around the carnation.

Zdeněk said disarmingly, 'I do not speak the English,' picked up my bag and led us out of the building.

'Welcome to Czech Republic!' Maruška spoke softly and slowly as we walked, her English punctuated with rolled 'r's. 'It is custom to give flowers to men and women at times of arrival, departure and celebration. We are happy to welcome you here today.'

I was unbelievably grateful to Maruška and Zdeněk for turning up and saving me. Throughout the passport and immigration process I thought I'd end up being shipped off to a gulag in Siberia, or worse. I was equally grateful that Maruška explained things as we hurried through the icy afternoon towards the car park. She told me her name was pronounced *Mar-oosh-ka*, that the cars were Russian-style Ladas or Škodas, and that Zdeněk was here to collect me because he was one of the fortunate few at the school with a car. That was a sign of great status, although she did whisper that *škoda* meant 'it's a pity'.

The Ladas and Škodas were teeny-tiny, like toy cars. They squatted around the car park like beetles, in shabby shades of brown and grey. There were even smaller toy cars too—Trabants, boxes on wheels run by two-stroke engines, like lawnmowers. The car park was full of smoke and the din of revving and vrooming, exhaust pipes blowing hard into the chilled air. In my jetlagged state, I had trouble remembering where I was.

'*Tak!*' Zdeněk shoved my case inside the bonnet. The bonnet? He slammed that down, walked to the back of the car, and opened the boot, revealing a tangle of wires and tubes. He checked something, shut the lid and shouted, '*Tak, jdeme.*'

Baring teeth through a frozen face, I hopped into the back seat and we set off for my first back-to-front car ride. The engine throbbed under my bottom, sending painful vibrations up and down my spine. Derelict buildings, ringed with washing hung high, lined the airport road. Little old cars like Zdeněk's puttered along, blowing smoke, occasionally overtaken by large black Mercedes and windowless cars.

'Russian mafia.' My hostess's face contorted. 'They have taken over from the communists.'

Mafia? Peter Barr hadn't mentioned anything about this. I thought the bad old days were over?

But Maruška and Zdenĕk had more pressing matters in mind. 'So now, we would like to know—how is our Peter Barr?'

Recovering, I quickly updated them as best I could.

'We all loved Peter Barr,' Maruška said.

Then she added, in devout homage, 'Peter was a wonderful teacher. He played football with all our men and students in Sedlčany. He made all the girls laugh. He learned our language. Became fluent in Czech. Very difficult language, of course, but he was so clever. He walked around with Walkman and head-phones listening to Pavarotti. Very cultured man.'

I sat in silence, swallowing hard. There was not a chance I would meet that standard. As I was contemplating this new dilemma, blocks of identical grey concrete buildings came into view. The effect was of one enormous prison that stretched for miles, obliterating the horizon.

'Oh my God!' The words burst out of me as one anxiety was quickly replaced by another. What were they used for? Torture chambers, factories? Why were there so many of them?

Maruška pointed out, matter-of-factly, that I was looking at one of communism's enduring architectural legacies: the *paneláky*. 'Housing estates for hundreds of people.'

'People *live* in them?' Australia was a country of bungalows and backyards, with seemingly endless space for people to live and move in. I'd never seen a housing estate before, not like this anyway; I didn't even know such things existed. Why hadn't Peter Barr given me the heads-up, suggested I steel myself?

Maruška set me straight. 'You are lucky—you will have own *panelák* apartment and will not have to share with anyone. Peter Barr had to live with families when he was here.'

I quickly tried to look grateful, and in an effort to distract myself started gabbling. 'Peter told me Prague was beautiful. Will we see it today?'

'Yes, of course! We call Prague the city of one hundred spires. Survived all wars. It is the most beautiful city in Europe. Wonderful concerts where you can listen to our famous musicians.'

My spirits lifted again, emotions yo-yoing through me like I was a hormonal teenager.

Maruška then tapped the windowpane and pointed. 'Below you can see our River Vltava, and in it the colours of the Old City.'

A river twisted away below us like a serpent, swathed in ribbons of shimmering silver and gold, curving between the hills.

Maruška told me the river was so famous it was celebrated by all Czech composers. 'Smetana, Dvořák and Suk. Do you know them?'

I did not and cursed Peter Barr, yet again, for not briefing me. Fortunately, I was saved from answering as Zdeněk swerved around a corner; fortunately, I also caught my first glimpse of the fabled city, far below.

A jumble of turrets and towers and spires filled the sky. I glimpsed an ancient bridge, then another one. Fairytale palaces and red-roofed shapes crowded down to the riverbanks. Presiding over it all was a huge castle, Gothic and grand, with even more spires rising up high into the clouds. Ohhhhh, it was so beautiful.

'Is that where your President Havel lives?' I burst out.

Maruška smiled, nodded, and I pressed my eyes with my fingers, blinked, and looked again, to make sure the scene was real. Three days ago I was in Central Australia. Now I was in Central Europe. Three days ago I was surrounded by the ancient lands of the Southern Hemisphere and now I'd arrived in the ancient lands of the Northern Hemisphere. So similar, so utterly different. The word *surreal* kept buzzing through my brain.

Vaguely, I heard Zdeněk changing gears, turning a corner. A large hill loomed, and as quickly as Prague had arrived, Prague was gone. For one terrible moment, I wondered if it had been a figment of my imagination. All I could now see was a wide highway overflowing with smoky trucks and little cars hooting and chugging. I cricked my neck looking back, feeling like a child whose birthday present had been ripped away. There was a hollow crater where my stomach had been.

Maruška lapsed into silence too. Perhaps she felt the same sense of loss.

Zdeněk drove and drove and drove. The little car strained its way along roads increasingly pitted with holes and surface cracks. Each time we went up a hill Zdeněk changed into first gear to ensure we made it to the top. On the way down, he slipped into neutral and slid down the other side. When I asked about this, Maruška explained, wearily, that the neutral-gear approach was 'special-Czech-petrol-saving-device'. Zdeněk put it back into first as we hit the bottom and chugged away again.

Small villages started to emerge like cut-outs before us. Crumbling buildings lined the road, drab in the late evening drizzle, all signposted with strings of consonants I couldn't imagine ever being able to pronounce, just like the names of those three Czech composers Maruška had mentioned. I'd already forgotten all of them.

After an hour, we pulled up outside a long, low building running the length of a street. The evening shadows had lengthened. Maruška told me this was a former communist headquarters and that we would eat here.

I stumbled out, stiff, the feeling of dislocation growing once again. Three days ago I couldn't have imagined entering a room where Czech secret police once plotted against the enemies of the state. I represented those enemies, or at least I once did. I wondered if it all still felt strange to my hosts. I wondered if there was a chance I'd be strip-searched or arrested.

But no. Ex-communist headquarters or not, it was now just a noisy bar, full of people eating and drinking and smoking at small tables covered in red-checked tablecloths, and no one noticed us. The air was thick with cigarette smoke. We took a table and Maruška consulted the menu.

'You can have pork four ways here, some prepared now and some prepared earlier today. Boiled, roasted, fried, in the pot, with and without dumplings, which can be made with the flour or with the potato . . .'

Zdeněk interrupted. Maruška translated. 'And you will have some beer, yes? Zdeněk says to you: Czech beer is best in the world!'

I wasn't much of a beer drinker—more of a bubbles or G & T gal—but it didn't seem the right time to refuse, so I smiled politely as a waiter with greasy hair plonked down three enormous glasses of beer.

'In our pubs, waiter brings you beer when you sit down,' Maruška explained. 'If you do not want beer, you need to tell the waiter you want something else and he will take the beer away. Okay?'

I learnt that beer was cheaper than water—such was the devotion to beer, especially for the men—and for a panicked moment I wondered if I'd spend most of my time dehydrated and drunk. Excusing myself, I headed for a door marked with 'WC' and a lady's hat.

The room offered three cramped cubicles, each with a bowl almost overflowing with water and a weird-looking handle on the side. A small box attached to the wall provided squares of brown, cardboard-like paper. They were rough and barely did the job. The floor was filthy and wet, and the drains stank.

But worst of all, a horror-film image stared back from the mirror when I washed my hands: green eyes now bloodshot; short, mousy brown bob bedraggled; mascara caked. Not the look of an inspiring teacher-in-the-making. Nor of Julie Andrews, her shining face alight with confidence, on her way to the von Trapp household. Nor of my beloved Mrs Hodder, for that matter.

In desperation I splashed my face with water and reapplied my lipstick, but my shirt simply got wet, and no amount of blusher could help my face. I blocked my nose, grabbed my bag, and rushed back to the table, trying to look like the relaxed, happy traveller I'm sure Peter Barr was.

Back at the table I drank my beer and smiled to show I was enjoying it very much, all the while wondering how much I could drink before I collapsed and lost all feeling in my body. The beer—a Pilsner Urquell—came from the local town Plzeň. Pilsner ... Plzeň ... piss. Weird neural connections were rewiring themselves in my brain and I hoped my hosts hadn't guessed I was falling apart inside.

A sour-faced waitress in a short skirt arrived to take food orders, returning shortly with enormous plates of pork schnitzel. Maruška told me it was called *řízek*. The glistening meat fell over the edges of the plate. Exhaustion swamped me as thoughts of constipation, scurvy, alcoholism and serious weight gain loomed. But my hosts ate quickly, undaunted.

Before long we were back in the car, and to distract myself from the *řízek* and beer churning in my stomach, I asked Maruška to tell me about Sedlčany.

'*Tak*, Sedlčany is industrial town. It has approximately 8000 people. Many people come there to live because they need work. In the factories. And also because there is cheaper housing.'

Industrial town? Factories? Cheaper housing?

I sat back and tried to breathe deeply, feel calm. I'd seen factory towns at a distance during my 1989 travels through Europe but never been in one. I'd sought out places with light, space and clean air, as I was wired for that kind of thing from growing up in the bush. Had I missed the fine print in Peter Barr's descriptions?

———❦———

It was dark when we arrived in Sedlčany.

Blocks of the grey concrete *paneláky* rose up before us through the blackness, hung thickly with washing lines from each window. I pushed back in the seat, squeezed my eyes to shut it out, then I choked. A putrid stench swamped the car. I wrenched my eyes open again, gasped, couldn't find air, croaked, started coughing.

'Ah yes,' Maruška sighed once more and Zdeněk tightened the window. 'I am afraid the pollution in Sedlčany is very bad. We have two furnaces in the town. Everyone in winter uses brown coal which gives out a lot of—how you call—sulphur?'

Sulphur? I was allergic to sulphur. It made me swell up, choke and go to hospital. The last time it had happened, my throat had caved in and I'd thought I would suffocate. A stern-looking doctor warned me to never go near sulphur again—and that time it had just been an ingredient in a prescription drug. Now I was about to live in a town drowning in it?

I tried to focus on breathing as Maruška kept sighing. 'It is made worse because our town is in this valley.' She pointed to the hills rising on either side of us. 'So, the smog gets trapped here all winter. But'—she finished hopefully—'when spring comes, it will get better.'

Zdeněk drove into an old cobbled square with a fountain in the middle. 'The Old Town Square,' said Maruška. A group of old men stood outside a pub, no doubt enjoying their beers. They were the only signs of life.

She pointed to a demountable building on one side. It was long and low, like an Australian mining donga dumped in the wrong place by accident.

'Tanya, this is supermarket. You can get your food here.'

Out of the supermarket roof grew a Gothic tower and dome.

Maruška said, matter-of-factly, 'Former regime put this supermarket in front of the church.'

Seriously? In my increasingly overwhelmed state, I imagined the conversation: 'Comrades, let's stick a supermarket in front of a church, so the workers can't see the church. Then they won't be tempted to go into it, unsupervised, dreaming up incendiary ideas and threatening state control. Hurrah! What a plan! Instead the workers can quickly buy necessities from this hideous supermarket and get back to toiling in the fields and factories.'

'It is okay,' shrugged my hostess, as though the architectural, spiritual and political barbarity of the former occupiers had long ceased to move her. 'You can still find a way into church through some side door on side street. It is fourteenth-century, very nice to visit.'

Zdeněk drove out of the square and up a steep hill until we reached what Maruška called 'Panelák Block Four'. I swivelled my neck up to see a high, soulless building staring down at me. Zdeněk motioned me out of the car: 'Tak, jdeme!'

I stumbled, coughed. My eyes stung. Then the back of my neck crawled. It took a moment to realise what had unnerved me, and when I understood my stomach twisted.

I'd arrived in a ghost town. Everything was silent.

But it made no sense. This town had 8000 people. And it was only seven o'clock at night. Where were the snatches of conversation floating out of windows, babies crying, children playing? Music, even the sound of television? The town was silent. Had everyone been locked up and forbidden to talk?

'Maruška,' I blurted out. 'Why is it so quiet?'

She looked sideways at me and said, 'This is normální.'

I followed her, confused. Had the whole town been kidnapped? Were we in some sort of Kafkaesque nightmare where no one acknowledged what was happening?

The fact was that this was a normální state for Sedlčany. Over time, I began to call it the Silence of Sedlčany—the fear-induced silence of people who had lived for decades under domination. And it was a fear so deeply ingrained that people couldn't bring themselves to start talking openly, even at night, even after the occupiers had gone. The shackles may have been officially taken off but, as one elderly man later put it, 'You could never be too sure who could hear you speak, at any time, what might be reported, how it might be misunderstood. You could disappear at night and never be seen again . . . how can we trust it to be different now?'

Survival habits, self-preservation and silence lived on.

It briefly occurred to me that this was what I'd come for—to learn what it had been like for the people under communism, to discover firsthand what they'd gone through. But now I was here my courage deserted me like a traitor. As my hosts pushed open the door to a tiny entranceway, I felt like the next inmate being delivered to prison. The air was foul, the floor littered with rubbish and cigarette butts. To the right-hand side sat a concrete staircase. In front of us loomed a tiny antiquated lift.

Zdeněk opened the lift door like we were at The Ritz and motioned me inside; not even the irony of this could cheer me up. One stark light hung down above our faces, as if we were in an interrogation cell. I kept my eyes down, kept trying to breathe. Vaguely, I heard Maruška speaking.

'We go to floor seven, the top floor, but in the morning, you may wish to go up and down these stairs because there are many people in this *panelák*, and only one lift.'

The lift was also very slow. Finally, it disgorged us into the middle of a narrow concrete corridor, with more cigarette butts on the floor and many doors around us. Zdeněk headed to a heavy door at the far right, produced an enormous key and turned it.

'Your new home,' Maruška said kindly, leading me in.

4

First night at boarding school

My new home was a tiny bedsit.

It reeked of the same stale cigarette smoke as everywhere else I'd been that day. It came with a couch bed and a filthy bolthole at one end that passed as a bathroom and toilet. Its sole redeeming feature was a set of large windows in both rooms. I immediately tried to open them but they were locked; Zdeněk shook his head, frowning. Windows were kept shut to keep out the cold and pollution, Maruška explained.

I bit my lip—it was freezing in here anyway. But how else would I get rid of the cigarette stink? As Mum always said, 'All houses should have fresh air!' Having grown up under the clear, empty skies of the outback, I found myself (wherever I was) rushing to open windows and bring in outside air. Only then could I feel safe, breathe properly. *Breathe anyway*, I told myself, *breathe anyway. Don't let them think I'm worried, not coping.* The worst outcome would be for me to fall below Peter Barr's standards.

Maruška walked into the tiny kitchenette next to the windows and opened the door of a small fridge. She pointed to a hunk of cheese, some salted butter, several winter apples and a loaf of dark rye bread.

'This is good.' She was pleased. 'Some teachers have left you food. We will see you at *gymnázium* tomorrow. It will only take you about twenty minutes to walk. Go down the hill the way we came up.'

I took a deep breath. 'Thank you so much for everything today, Zdeněk and Maruška.' I hoped I sounded as confident as Peter Barr would have been on his first night. 'I look forward to becoming a teacher at your school.' I also wanted to apologise for talking non-stop all day and asking so many questions, as I'd already worked out that wasn't *normální*. Now we were here, though, I couldn't find the words.

The heavy door banged behind them, the lock clicking shut on my cell. My pretence at confidence collapsed and I sank onto the couch bed, staring numbly out the window. For a long time I sat unmoving. I felt like an aeroplane coming into land, unable to work out how to put down its landing gear. I was stuck circling blindly in no-man's-land, waiting for a word or a light or a direction that would not—could not—materialise.

In my heart I was twelve years old again, arriving at boarding school in Adelaide to start a new life behind high stone walls, leaving behind all I knew, a thousand miles south of my home and another world entirely. I had been clueless about how to inhabit it—a concrete wilderness without reference points or markers. That was 1975. This was 1994.

Not much felt different.

In 1975, I was put into a dormitory of twenty-four girls. On my first night I climbed out of bed, up into a large bay window, and peered into the night sky. If we had stars in common, I thought, I might be able to see home somehow. Outback skies were smothered with stars—the Southern Cross, the Saucepan, the crowded Milky Way. Now I remembered the paint on the wooden window frame flaking under my small fingers as I tore unsuccessfully at the latch; the foreboding shadow of a large, locked iron gate below; and the hard sob in my chest when I found no stars at all, only blackness. What was this boarding school? Who was I, now that I was in it? How would I exist, confined to buildings in which I could not run and walls through which I could not pass, and no stars or sky with which to commune?

It occurred to me, as I rocked on the Sedlčany bedsit couch, that 1975 and 1994 had two things in common. Both involved arriving in strange and scary places, miles from home and from anything I knew, and both involved a school. Perhaps it would have been useful to have thought this through before leaving Australia. Perhaps I could have saved myself a lot of heartache before inadvertently reinventing 1975. After all, I hadn't been forced to come here, not like I had been back then. Boarding school was the hell that had instilled in me a terror of entrapment, a fear of being controlled by others, panic attacks if I thought I couldn't escape from someone, something or somewhere.

Eventually, I realised I was stiff all over, and cold, and I dragged myself to my feet. No one was coming to save me, no one could help me, and no one could erase my past. Nor was there any point looking out the window for stars here. Even if I could see them through the pollution, it was a different sky— we were on the other side of the world. And there was no use trying to rip open the windows. Zdeněk had checked, for good measure, that they were firmly locked.

To distract myself, I headed to the kitchenette. There was a little old electric stove operated by a black switch on the wall. There were no knobs on the stove, but it came with a tiny hot-plate covered over by a tin lid. There was no sink, but a plastic bowl was positioned under two taps, which presumably would fill the plastic basin and provide drinking water. What would I do with the water when I was finished with it? Down the toilet, I supposed.

There was no kettle or mug to be seen, but there was a saucepan, a glass and some unrecognisable tea bags, so I dribbled water into the pan, put it on the stove and turned it on. I stared at the stove maniacally, willing it to show life, to demonstrate normality. After a good old-fashioned cup of tea, I'd surely feel better.

But it took twenty minutes for a bubble to even appear in the water. Frustrated at its slowness, I ripped the saucepan off and poured lukewarm water into the glass over the tea bag. But the tea tasted strange—local herbs or flowers, perhaps—and I felt nauseous so poured it down the toilet, despairing, ashamed. I wished I'd had another one of Zdeněk's beers.

Eventually, I could no longer delay the inevitable. Time to pull down the landing gear. Time to unpack.

There was one tiny chest of drawers but no cupboard, so in the end there wasn't much unpacking to do. Most of my stuff remained in my case, which I shoved under the table near the window. I used the one small chair to arrange a few photos of family, and toiletries—brush and comb, moisturiser, lip balm. It was like the first night at boarding school all over again. I was too paralysed inside to do anything but stumble about, going through the motions.

That included braving the bathroom again.

Blocking my nose, I entered into an area so small I could barely turn in it, much less imagine having a proper wash. It featured a small, grimy tin bath with an attached nozzle and basin at one end. I guessed that was where I would also have to wash my clothes. I would soon learn the art of crouching in the tub and sluicing myself with a trickle of water that always seemed as grubby as the bath itself. There was very little water pressure.

There was also no towel. I dried my hands and face with my shirt.

The loneliness was deafening.

I wanted to scream. But then I'd surely disturb the neighbours, and the faceless men in trench coats and felt hats would arrive, inject me with a drug, bundle me into a car and take me to Siberia for experiments. The only two people in this entire country who knew me, Maruška and Zdeněk, would be none the wiser.

Perhaps I could escape. But how, and where to? I was totally vulnerable, trapped. I had no sense of direction here. Ironic, really: I could spend hours alone in the bush; I knew the miles of emptiness like the lines on my palm. I could look to the sun to determine the time. I could identify north, south and east from the peaks and rises of different hills, and I knew that where there were no hills, it was always west. I could work out which way to go by the lines of the scrub, the different shades of the red earth, and the curve of the creek beds. I was never safer than when I was in the bush. Here, however, I could be eaten alive and die a long, lonely, miserable death—and no one would know. Someone from the school might come looking eventually but it would be too late. Desperation rose in my chest like a mad, trapped bird.

What had I been thinking? I'd devoured stories about Europe and been lost in fantasies about it for as long as I could remember.

I'd longed to know these places and people firsthand; they often felt more real to me than my own reality. Now I'd landed in a reality as far from my dreams as I could have imagined. Shivering with cold, I thought about Peter Barr. What had made me think I could go where he went, carry out what he did? That was the problem, of course: I didn't think. I hadn't thought at all. I'd simply leapt into this void with lots of hope and precious little planning.

Rage at my own naivety and stupidity rose in my gut, uncurling like a vengeful genie. I started punching the couch bed, fist on fist, sobs coming in between jagged breaths. I ripped off the covers. The smell of the flat had permeated the linen and my shoulders jerked back as my stomach heaved. *This is it!* I thought. There was no way I was going to sleep in that vile stench.

Sobbing wildly by now, I grabbed my precious bottle of lavender oil out of my case and threw almost the entire contents onto the couch. Then I collapsed into a foetal position, body convulsing as waves of tears drenched my face, the sheets—the tears of a child on her first night at boarding school. There was no way I could survive in this place.

This was no longer an adventure I wanted.

It was a huge, humiliating, ridiculous mistake.

5

Gymnázium Sedlčany

It didn't really look like a school. A squat, featureless, four-storey grey building with large windows, set back from the road between the main square and the regional bus stop, it looked like all of the other Soviet-designed buildings I had seen since arriving the night before. A lone tree on the green square of lawn in front of the school shivered, unclad, in the half-light of morning. A drooping flag over the front door represented a stab at formality. There were no grounds, sports fields, students in uniform or anything else to suggest it was a school.

But inside, it felt like one. And to my relief, I liked it immediately. It was big, clean and airy. There were long halls with polished floors, wide flights of cement stairs, large classrooms and, best of all, lots of students. As I walked in through the front door, I could hear them and see them everywhere—young, excitable, noisy teenagers, gazing at me with unabashed curiosity. Some smiled and giggled. Their fresh, vibrant energy gave me a lift. Despite the long, cold and polluted walk I'd just had, I felt better in myself already. I'd awoken with the optimism of a new day. If I could put my fears aside and focus on doing the job I'd been given, everything would surely work out. I just needed to spend time with people so I didn't feel lonely.

Of course, there would be a few challenges. It had been a while since I'd been a teenager like these students. I hoped I'd know what to talk to them about, assuming they even spoke English. And I was barely four feet eleven (150 centimetres) tall, while most of the students swarming around were lithe and leggy. But we did have something in common. We were all attired in faded jeans and scruffy sneakers and worn coats, which suggested a cheerful sense of equality.

'Hello, Taaaarnya!'

Maruška arrived with her kind and patient smile, and relief flooded through me. A familiar face! She told me that I would soon meet all the teachers, receive my books and settle in. Tomorrow I would start teaching. New opportunities, a chance to learn, new people and a new life—what had I been worried about?

We headed to the office of the school's Deputy Headmistress, Lenka, which adjoined the staffroom.

'*Dobrý den* and welcome to Sedlčany Gymnázium!' Lenka beamed. She wore her auburn hair swept up in a glamorous beehive, and looked far more energetic and elegant than I had imagined a Deputy Head to be.

'I don't speak English,' she continued in a strong Czech accent as she served me *Turecká káva*—the Czech version of Turkish coffee—in a small glass. 'Well, only a *leetle*. How is our Peter Barr?'

I couldn't answer as I was choking. The coffee was a black, bitter sludge, made (I was told) by boiling ground beans and water together in a saucepan in the nearby kitchen. Once boiled, it was then poured straight into a glass, resulting in a concoction of frenzied bean froth on top of black, gritty water. I spent the next five minutes sucking bits of coffee bean backwards through my teeth while covering my face with a tissue to mop up the black mess that had spread from one end of my mouth to the other. Maruška politely averted her eyes.

The coffee wired me for the day. After exchanging pleasantries about Peter Barr, Lenka beamed me out of her office. Maruška then introduced me to her husband, Franta, who was next door. He was in charge of the school's computers. Embarrassingly, I didn't even know computers were taught in schools, even back in Australia, and I certainly didn't know how to use one. Franta politely refrained from suggesting we were behind in the West (or that I was, at least) and smiled.

'It is no problem. I teach you how to use computer. And now, how is our friend Peter Barr?'

Next stop was the staffroom. Maruška introduced me to a stream of teachers arriving to start lessons. People spoke rapidly and shook hands. No one spoke English. But it didn't matter. I had some wins up my sleeve. I had got through the night, managed a hair wash and shower (having improvised and used my pillow-case as a towel), and made it to school. I'd seen some students who had smiled at me and I'd downed my first *Turecká káva*.

'Here now is our Head English teacher, Jindra.' Maruška took me across to meet a dark-haired, bespectacled teacher, who was marking papers at a big table. She had high cheekbones and an oval-shaped face, the fine and elegant features I was starting to associate with Czech women.

Jindra stood up and shook my hand gravely. 'We have heard from Peter Barr about you. Welcome. I am in charge of your duties here.'

'Thank you, of course.'

'At *gymnázium*,' Jindra went on briskly, in fluent, accented English, 'we now have English classes for all our students. We want to be progressive with English. Everyone here knows that you are not a teacher but, like Peter Barr, you are advocate, so you can help with our program.'

I nodded, anxious to be seen as useful.

Jindra started piling textbooks into my arms, briefing me on the background of the school and what to expect—a lot, as it turned out.

There were between nearly four to five hundred students, depending on the time of the year, split into classes of about thirty each, often at different education levels within the same class. I would teach children aged eleven to eighteen, all hours of the day (and sometimes night), and assist the six English teachers, none of whom were trained to teach English, and three of whom were not teachers at all. They had been brought into the *gymnázium* to help with staff shortages. At least I wouldn't be alone in lacking teaching 'quals'.

Jindra led me to the other side of the room and introduced me to three of my English-teaching colleagues. First was Old Maruška, so-called to distinguish her from Young Maruška, who had picked me up from the airport, then Blanka, an ethereal-looking, blue-eyed version of Juliette Binoche. Last was Staňa, tall and imposing; I couldn't work out whether she spoke much English but apparently she was very good at maths and science. All three had high cheekbones and oval-shaped faces too. I kept mixing up their names, but did my best to smile winningly with the kind of confidence I imagined they were expecting from their new incumbent.

'And now,' said Jindra with a slight frown, looking up as a young woman burst into the room carrying an armful of books, 'this is Naďa, our most recently appointed English teacher.'

Naďa shimmied towards me and I caught my breath. With her make-up, her short blonde-streaked hair, her stylish and tight-fitting clothes, and her blue eyes sparkling behind groovy glasses, Naďa looked like she had stepped straight out of the pages of a Western magazine. In a rather old-world atmosphere, this goddess shone forth like a beacon.

'Hello, hello,' she greeted me, as though this was the happiest day of her life. She shook my hand enthusiastically. 'I am so very glad to meet you! It is great you have come to our school.' Her voice was accented but clear, her grasp of spoken English fluent—the best I'd heard yet. 'It is wonderful for the students to have you here. They will enjoy you very much. And it is wonderful for me and for other teachers to have the opportunity to study with you. This is really, really great for us all.'

I wanted to throw my arms around this beautiful woman and hug her. She was fun, and early thirtyish—about my age.

'And how do you like our school?' Naďa asked, and without waiting for an answer went on, her words toppling one over the other. 'I want to talk about how to prepare the good English lessons with you . . . we will have a *very* good time teaching our students together. Please, come to my table, yes?'

We started chattering excitedly like two schoolgirls, both of us delighting in the chance to speak English and in the thrilling, instinctive knowledge that a friendship lay before us.

Jindra watched me with pursed lips and crossed arms. For a moment I paused, met her eyes, but Naďa's energy drew me in like a magnet and I couldn't let go.

Within seconds, however, the noise level within the room had dropped. It turned to murmurs and then, finally, there was nothing. The back of my neck prickled. The room had become oppressively quiet. We were encircled by a kind of watchful, wary silence.

I looked up slowly. Faces that ten minutes ago were benign and friendly now looked—well, not so benign and friendly. I could tell we'd broken the rules. But which ones? Too much noise? Too much English? Too much of a language almost no one in this room spoke, a language that not long ago represented the Western enemy? Too much fun, too fast? I felt the same uncertain feeling I'd experienced last night outside my *panelák*.

Crash!

Behind us the door banged loudly. A rotund man with limp hair entered, carrying flowers and a bottle of Cinzano. Mercifully, he broke the unnerving energy that had built up. Recovering her bounce, Naďa then introduced me, but I missed the man's name completely, focused as I was on the bottle in his hand. I felt like ripping the top off myself.

'Now we have Name Day celebration,' Naďa whispered.

Each day of the Czech calendar year a Czech name was celebrated. A name-day was equivalent to a birthday, and recipients received flowers and gifts—men included. In return, where possible, the recipient provided drinks. Because there were 365 name-days, celebrations fired up workplaces all over the country on a regular basis.

The door opened once again, and Headmaster Zdeněk and Deputy Lenka walked in. Their presence seemed to give the 'morning recess' proceedings the official stamp of approval. Teachers lined up rows of small glasses on the desks and the newcomer poured liberal doses of Cinzano for everyone. Other teachers pulled out plates of tiny open sandwiches topped with potato salad and thin slices of dried red meat. The desks were soon laden with food, including caraway seed rolls, plates of butter and small containers of yoghurt. The man whose name I never managed to catch passed around the glasses and was toasted with shouts of '*Na zdraví*' ('on your health'). I was handed a drink, which I threw back like a local—I didn't want to cause any more cultural faux pas—and it caught the back of my throat, stung. I spluttered. Admittedly, it was the first Cinzano I'd ever drunk at 10.30 a.m.

'And now, we will have the music!' Naďa was all good cheer again.

Two teachers pulled out guitars: Čestmíre, a tall, dark-haired pacifist who I learnt was escaping national service by teaching physical education; and Lidka, a tiny, blonde-haired chemistry teacher whose desk was almost obliterated by a rye loaf and a pot of honey. I stood back, clutching my second glass, watching in disbelief as they kicked off a staffroom singsong.

The room filled with voices that rose lustily and joyously and with an obvious familiarity that came from having sung these songs forever. I recognised the three-part harmonies; they were the same in folk music and country music the world over, and I'd grown up with music like this. Slim Dusty and Charley Pride and every other country musician I could think of revelled in harmonies; M'Lis, Brett and I sang them whenever we played our guitars together. But at recess time?

Listening to these practised experts, I suddenly wanted to join in, to be like them. But I didn't know the lyrics or the music; at best I would only be able to mumble something and look ridiculous trying to pretend I knew what I was doing. Instead I stood separate and alone in a moment that bound everyone else together, bringing light and laughter into their previously closed faces. I felt a pang of sorrow that I couldn't be part of the jam and just hoped there'd be more tomorrow.

Eventually, the singing stopped, the guitars were put away and I was introduced to more teachers, in particular 'the two Jiřís' (the two Georges). They were two teachers who didn't speak English (and apparently argued daily) but they welcomed me with hearty handshakes. They had played football with Peter Barr and wanted to hear all his 'latest news'. More teachers crowded around to hear about Peter and our exotic *Auuu-strahhh-lee*. My words rushed out and Naďa translated them for me. Nobody appeared to speak English except for the English teachers, and I wasn't even sure how well some of them spoke it.

Zdeněk, on the other hand, was full of surprises. '*Tak*! On your health, for new teacher, Taaaarnya!' he said, in his best chivalrous manner, surprising me yet again with his grasp of English.

I beamed back, soaking up the welcome, filled by all these connections.

Suddenly, the school bells rang, heralding the end of the morning break, and as quickly as the festivities had begun, they ended—abruptly. The room emptied. A glass or two of Cinzano appeared to have no effect on the teachers, and they were now off to class. It was business as usual. I was left sitting at my desk in an alcoholic daze, wondering how I was ever going to remember people's names, much less pronounce them with their strange sounds and unbroken consonants.

Jindra, who sensibly did not drink, organised the rest of my morning.

The first task was to arrange my finances at the Czech National Bank. As we walked out into the square, the grey, putrid-smelling smog hit me like a peasant tractor, and I started coughing again. I coughed all the way to a large, almost empty building in the Old Town Square. If the bank was anything to go by, trade and commerce were at an all-time low in Sedlčany.

Jindra and I were the only clients. I had to produce all my visas, in triplicate, and Jindra had brought a wad of documents from the school. She negotiated for nearly half an hour with a humourless man in dark glasses behind the counter, after which I understood an account had been opened for me, into which I would be paid a total of 4000 Czech koruna each month. That was approximately A$200 a month, or $50 a week, representing a standard teacher's wage. In good socialist fashion, all teachers were paid exactly the same amount, even newcomers like me with no experience whatsoever. If I needed money, Jindra said as we walked back outside, one of the teachers would help me withdraw it from the bank. *Thank you, thank you*, I kept repeating to myself; I was sure I wouldn't dare return on my own.

As we walked across the square a huge voice suddenly reverberated around us and instinctively I jumped, and then froze.

'What is *that*?'

High above us sat a loudhailer, positioned at the top of the Town Hall, and from it a voice had started booming. It boomed and droned, robotically, on and on. People in the square stopped and listened, their faces guarded, watchful. None of it made sense.

'The town microphone is former regime way of giving messages to us all, every day. It is so loud it can be heard all over Sedlčany. It was used for May Day parades and management of people.'

My God. This was George Orwell's *1984*. It was Big Brother.

'*Why* is it still used?'

Jindra shrugged. 'It is part of our daily life now. We've had it for thirty or forty years and it just keeps going: telling people what is happening, advising about rules and obligations, letting people know what will happen. It is useful.'

But I knew in that spine-crawling moment I would never get used to the sound. It was alien to anything I had ever experienced. It sent a chill through me every time I heard it. It was designed to penetrate the furthest corners of Sedlčany, even inside the walls and locked window of my little *panelák* high on the hill. I started coughing again, frantic to get back inside, away from the chill and the evil-sounding, disembodied voice.

Jindra obliged with lunch. Many students and teachers ate at the school; lunch was payable by voucher, and Jindra kindly gave me some vouchers to use. We descended down stone steps into a large, stuffy basement room. Inside it was complete bedlam. Over a hundred students and teachers were eating together at long tables.

'We have main meal in middle of day,' Jindra advised as we approached three old ladies ladling out watery, greasy soup from massive tin pots. The soup—a Czech favourite—was made from the lining of pigs' guts. The main dish was pork drowned in gravy, with dumplings and soggy cabbage. I stared, mesmerised, at both dishes, unable to bring myself to dip a spoon or fork in either of them.

Jindra finished her soup at top speed and then tackled her main course. Like Maruška and Zdeněk the day before, she ate fast. I turned my spoon around and around in my dishes, trying to do them justice, and was thankful when Jindra headed off to teach a class and left me to my own feeble devices.

'I think it best,' she said as she departed, in the tone of one who had done more than her duty for the day, 'you should go back to your *panelák* when you have finished the lunch. Unless there is anything else you need, I will see you tomorrow.'

I watched her retreating back disappear up the stairs and the optimism I'd felt at the start of the day slipped away like a Soviet deserter in the darkness. My only company now was the voice in my head that said I did not belong in Australia and I did not belong here either, and that I was a fraud—and it was only a matter of time before people here found out.

Perhaps Jindra already had.

I desperately wanted to invoke my childhood skill of disappearing into a fantasy world. But that skill had also disappeared and I was left, firmly and clearly, with a reality from which there was no escape.

How Kafkaesque.

6

Stake in the leg

I couldn't stay in the school basement any longer so dragged myself to my feet and trudged back up the hill to my *panelák*. It was bitterly cold. The stench of brown-coal sulphur ripped into my nostrils like pliers and I felt even sicker. My legs were like lead and my shoulders ached under the weight of so many books. From door to door took about half an hour and I puffed and panted and wheezed and coughed. It would take some adjustment getting around without a car. I was already missing my little brown Mazda back home. It might have been old and rusty but it had got me everywhere I needed to go.

I wasn't the only one without a car. Apart from one little smoky vehicle in the distance, the scene was like one from a retro B-grade movie, set in a time before the automobile industry had even begun. It wasn't surprising, I supposed; Sedlčany was barely four years out of communist control. I saw no evidence of a new world emerging here yet.

Men and women trudged past me, carrying bags of shopping or slowly pushing carts that held their goods and possessions. Their faces were grey and closed against the afternoon chill, their coats shabby, their hands worn. Decades of communism had palpably paralysed this place. It was bleak and crumbling and falling apart. Everything along the street smacked of hard work and poverty.

As I passed people, I smiled at them. I thought that's what a well-mannered foreigner should do: smile politely, sincerely, shyly. But no one smiled back. Some stared at me, their faces blank, as though they were looking right through me—as though I was invisible. Others looked away. Perhaps decades of distrust and fear had bred a closed, suspicious attitude to anyone new? And I was patently not a local. With my tatty pink back-pack, I stood out like a bright, sore thumb. How had Peter Barr managed it?

For the rest of the afternoon I hid inside my *panelák*. It was freezing and stank of sewage and stale cigarettes, but it beat the alternative. The sky and buildings of Sedlčany were a bleak grey outside my wide windows. I stood and watched people below moving slowly, like ants. I longed to contact Naďa but had neither phone nor any idea how to find her.

How had Peter Barr coped? He hadn't told me it was diffi-cult here; on the contrary, he'd said it was great. I was obviously weak, a wuss, a miserable ingrate. But I reminded myself that Peter hadn't lived alone. He'd been with families. How would I survive alone? *Alone. Loneliness.* Those bleakly interlinked words swirled around my brain. But I doubted either would have been an issue for Peter as he was such a socially competent chap. By day one I expected he'd have been off playing football with the blokes, with plans for drinks at the pub afterwards.

I continued to cough incessantly, the sulphur smog having lodged itself determinedly in my trachea. Outside, the afternoon eventually darkened, and then the lights of Sedlčany went off, one by one. It was freezing so I layered up with all the warm clothes I had, topped off by my parka. I also decided to try the lukewarm tea again, which this time I drank to warm up, even though the taste hadn't improved overnight. What I really craved was hot food. But, like home, that was a distant dream, so I pulled out the bread and cheese and apples and set them on my table. I found a knife and fork, which were made of cheap aluminium (a Czech speciality, I soon discovered), then cut everything into slices and ate quickly, without tasting it. Then I looked down at the empty plate and fantasised about running away.

I started to rehearse the words I would utter tomorrow morning: 'I'm so very sorry, Zdeněk, it was a mistake. I have to leave.'

That was the only thing to do. I could not stay here. I would go mad.

I lay down on my couch and stared up at the ceiling of my cell.

But as I did I knew, with a sinking heart, that I'd never speak those words out loud, to Zdeněk or anyone else. Peter Barr would be appalled and I'd never live down the shame. Moreover, bush kids never gave up. Responsibility was drilled into us. Whatever our job, we'd never leave until it was done. Our over-riding duty was to bring home the mob, no matter what the cost to ourselves. 'Keep going, you're nearly there,' Dad would say, sternly. Besides, I was an eldest child and eldest children didn't give up either.

I lay there in the darkness and thought of another time, long ago, when there was something awful I couldn't escape.

It was a year before I left for boarding school. I was galloping after cattle through thick mulga on the western side of the station. The cattle were wild and 'stirry', the air filled with people shouting, beasts bellowing, horses and cattle panicking. In the confusion and chaos, I smashed into a tree and staked my leg. All bush kids know that a mulga stake requires immediate treatment—antibiotics—to prevent infection. The stick pierced my jeans and went in deep, shooting pain into my leg. But no one heard my screams. M'Lis and Brett and the other stockmen were galloping as madly as I'd just been. Dad was miles ahead preparing the stockyards we were to reach by nightfall.

It was a day of blistering heat and there was nothing to do but to push on and try to keep the mob together and moving. No point getting off my horse and collapsing under a tree; I'd more likely perish from thirst than pain and poison, and we all knew the rules about that.

Besides, my fear at losing the cattle and not getting them safely back to the yards was greater than any pain in my leg. Dad was relying on us; none of us would dare let him down. The cattle were to be drafted and trucked to market. That was how we made a living in the bush. No cattle, no income. We kids contributed to the station work like any of the men. That was our job. So I pushed on through the blinding white heat, my leg swelling and throbbing under my ripped jeans. I vomited several times over the side of my horse. By the time I finally got to the yards the sky was dark. I fell off Sandy, hallucinating. But I'd made it with the cattle, and that was all that mattered.

Pressed into my memory was a pat on the back from Dad as he lifted me into the Land Rover, along with two words: 'Good job.' One of the stockmen drove me home for help, and I remembered lying in the filth of the vehicle as we bumped for miles over the corrugated dirt roads, my eyes closing, joy in my heart at Dad's praise overwhelming the agony.

Memories of that day sent me a clear message: 'Tanya, you are not going anywhere. You will stay here and stick this out until it is time to leave. It was what you were brought up to do. If you give up, the people here will think you are ungrateful, weak and spoilt by the ease of life in the West, and you'll only reinforce prejudices. Worse, you will have achieved nothing, either for the people of Sedlčany or yourself. You wanted an adventure and now you have one!'

And I was reminded of one of the English teachers I had met. 'Our last native teacher was from England,' she had said. 'She was very homesick. She did not stay more than one week.'

The teacher had looked at me searchingly, hopefully. 'We hope you will stay, Tanya.'

My insides had curled.

I knew I could no sooner let down the school, Peter Barr or myself than desert the mob of cattle halfway back to the dam.

7

Lessons in life

I woke, ravenous and feverish, to a sickly dawn. Hot and cold chills drove me out of bed and down to the streets. Outside, the stench of Sedlčany smothered the air and I shivered violently. People continued to ignore me as I hurried along. I arrived at the school spluttering and coughing, looking like a mess. I so wanted a hug, or any sort of touch to feel connected to life, but the hugs I ached for belonged in another country in another hemisphere. When I saw Jindra, she took one look at me and pronounced me ill, and I nearly burst into tears.

But Jindra had no time for my descent into weak-kneed Western self-pity.

'It is normal you are ill,' she said, briskly. 'New people always get ill in Sedlčany.'

That should have made me feel better, but as I was stuck here and couldn't go somewhere else to get better, it did not. I wanted to ask if this had been true for Peter Barr (I doubted it—he seemed beyond such tiresome forms of human frailty), but Jindra was busy giving me her diagnosis. It so shocked me that I forgot my question altogether.

'Your spirit is crushed because of homesickness and this has made your body weak,' she pronounced. 'Your throat is constricted by nerves and the pollution, which your body does not know how to manage. You must now heal your body and mind.'

I felt my face aflame through the chills.

'Do you wish to return to your flat?'

I shook my head maniacally.

'*Tak*! If you remain sick,' she said, with emphasis, 'I will take you to the hospital where we will give you special pills. Then you will stay in your flat until doctor says it is possible for you to leave. In the past you would even be watched while you were there.'

Images of faceless men in trench coats circling my flat with silencer guns and needles poised to inject rose before me. The sheer horror of this prospect forced the cough back down my throat. Jindra then told me that Nad'a would be along shortly to take me to my first lesson. If I wasn't better by the end of the day I had to report back to Jindra.

Fortunately, Nad'a appeared just in time, all brightness and cheer, and within moments I felt better. Being close to her energy was almost as good as having a hug. She gave me a banana ('This is exotic new fruit for us, Tanya—would you like to try for your health?') and I was stunned when I heard they cost A$2 each. 'They're only thirty cents back home,' I said, doubly grateful for her kindness as I demolished the small yellow fruit, its sweet deliciousness giving me a second boost.

'Next, we take the *Turecká káva*,' she said, taking the staff saucepan and pouring me a steaming glass that made my hair stand on end and helped me forget how sick I was. I wanted to ask her whether the Czechs had ever heard of the coffee plunger, then thought better of it. Probably the communists had banned plungers as an example of Western decadence. Why not learn to use your teeth and mouth to sift coffee grains rather than let coffee drinking become slothfully easy?

'Now you learn to be a teacher,' said Naďa comfortingly, leading me down a long corridor swarming with teachers and students between lessons. 'This class is Advanced English. Students are not so used to speaking but they can understand quite well. There is one boy in the class, Pavel, who I think is the best boy speaker in the school at English. He will be able to help you.'

I followed her, high and happy, sickness and hunger temporarily forgotten.

'Tanya, may I present class 3A!'

Naďa led me into a big airy room with high windows. A large group of sixteen-year-old students sprawled across desks, filling the room with chatter and noise. I took a deep breath. Finally, I was here doing what I was meant to do. I would be the Sedlčany version of Mrs Hodder. This would work. I would rise to the occasion and spread inspiration and encouragement, and I would make my time here mean something.

'Welcome, Taaanya!' A lanky boy in the first row stood up, speaking perfect English. He had a shock of blond hair and bright blue eyes. 'I am Pavel. On behalf of class, we wish today to teach you Czech expression.'

I was immediately charmed. So *this* was Pavel. Was he offering me a cultural welcome? Not knowing what to do, I nodded my head and smiled graciously.

Pavel spoke slowly. '*Kde je nejbližší hospoda, prosím*? Please, Taaanya, repeat after me.'

Pardon? I had no idea how to repeat that collection of consonants and the students were sniggering. I turned to Naďa for help but she was looking down at her desk.

'Please,' Pavel said once more. 'You must try. It is necessary expression for life in Czech Republic.'

Clearly my credibility here turned on attempting to engage with local cultural traditions. I opened my mouth and tried. '*G'day yer neigh-ble-shee hos-pod-ah, proh-seeem*'.

The class burst into hysterics and I wanted the floor to swallow me up. Was it my accent? My lack of ability to speak this ridiculous language? I looked despairingly at Naďa but couldn't see her face—she still seemed to be sorting out some papers on the desk.

'*Tak*!' I mumbled to Pavel, using the expression I'd now heard Czechs use to start a sentence. (It means 'so'.) '*Tak*! Pavel, what does it mean?'

'Where is the nearest pub, please?' said Pavel.

It took a while before Naďa resumed control. The class were falling about, no doubt unable to believe their luck. The new teacher had stumbled right into their trap. I tried to respond with some gravitas.

'Thank you, Pavel, I trust that will be helpful during my stay in Sedlčany.'

Pavel threw his head back and laughed. His shining blue eyes met mine and I laughed too. Yes, I would definitely rely on him to help me with this class.

'Now, it is your turn, Tanya,' said Naďa. 'Please, teach the class some special Australian expression, and they can follow you.'

Numerous profane expressions I'd learnt from stockmen over the years sprang to mind. But they were designed for the cattle and the heat and the problems of the bush—far too many swear words, and far too difficult to explain anyway.

'I could tell you how I did school growing up,' I offered and they all nodded, looking interested. An interested class was a good start. I tried to speak slowly but the words rushed out.

'I grew up in a cattle station in the middle of Australia. My sister and brother and I had a little schoolroom that was next to the house. It was made of stone and had one window, and it could just squeeze in three little desks and a bigger desk for a governess. It was freezing in winter and boiling in summer. We started at 7.30 in the morning and finished at 1 p.m. That was because it was too hot to work any later. And when our father wanted us to help him with cattle work, he would stomp across the gravel to our schoolroom in his big boots and order us to come with him. My sister and brother were always excited when they heard his boots coming. I wasn't. I loved school and wanted to stay there with my books. And I knew we would have to make up our school time on the weekends.'

There was much noise and discussion, and many questions. Nad'a translated that the students thought my school life was completely exotic. She added, 'Can you explain a governess?'

'Okay—on cattle stations, there would usually be a young girl who came up from one of the capital cities down south to take charge of the schooling,' I told them. 'The girls were between eighteen and twenty years old. They were not teachers but were interested in looking after kids and teaching and spending time in the outback. Mothers on cattle stations were usually too busy to teach the kids and it was much better to have somebody independent to supervise the lessons.'

All the students were frowning now and there was much discussion as they tried to understand.

'If they were not teachers, how could they teach?' Nad'a persisted.

The irony of her question was not lost on me but I tried to focus on the answer. 'We had booklets that taught us. They were called "sets" and they came to us in the mailbox every fortnight from a thousand miles away, from the Correspondence School in Adelaide. All the teachings and questions and tests were in those booklets and we had to complete one "set" each fortnight. The governess supervised us doing this work.'

The questions came thick and fast. What subjects did I actually study?

'English, history, geography and maths. We had no art or music or sport in school, but we created our own fun outside of school with guitars and games that we made up.'

Spying some guitars in the corner of the room, I had an idea.

'Like you, we sang music and stories about the kind of life we lived. There is a very famous Australian song about the early days. Can I sing it to you?'

I'd been longing to sing since the day before. Now I had my opportunity. The students gathered around. I'd already figured out that music was part of the glue that held this school together. I hoped the students wouldn't mind that my guitar playing was not impressive. I was no more than a three-chord-wonder girl, but three chords were all I'd ever needed for singing around the campfire, sitting on swags in dry creek beds.

Most of the lyrics of those songs were about life in the bush. There were the inevitable sad songs about people, cattle, dogs and horses dying, but also fun songs about bush people living it up at race meetings. Then there were the hard stories about the life we knew. 'It's a hard, hard country,' Slim Dusty sang, along with 'Rusty, It's Goodbye', 'Saddle Boy' and 'Cunnamulla Fella'. We sang Charley Pride songs too; he added a dimension of happiness with 'Kiss an Angel Good Morning' and aching hearts with 'Crystal Chandeliers'. We loved every single one of these songs. When Benny grew up he banged on a stool with a wooden spoon, adding drums to our performances. Benny was a natural and in fact went on to study drumming. He was, however, the only one of us who didn't really love Slim Dusty and Charley Pride; he wrote his own songs for the outback.

So now, in a rush of nostalgia for a country that seemed a lifetime away, I decided to try 'Waltzing Matilda'.

Pavel brought me a guitar and I took it into my hands. As I touched the strings, a sense of comfort blanketed me. This guitar was the closest link I'd felt to home since I'd arrived. I picked out few chords and away we went. Even with a croaky voice, I found that 'Waltzing Matilda' provided a remarkable outlet for my pent-up emotions. I sang my heart out and when I finished I saw shining eyes and smiling faces.

Pavel got up and went to talk to Naďa. After a short exchange Naďa asked me to sing once more and to my astonishment the class joined in for the chorus, singing in Czech. I couldn't believe it—they knew the tune! We finished the song, singing in our respective languages, our different words all held together by the same melody. I'd found the moment I had longed for yesterday.

When I finished, joy radiated from one end of the room to the other and bounced back again. The class clapped and cheered, calling out, '*Ještě jednou, prosím!*'

'They want it again, please,' Naďa translated.

'But how do they know this Australian song?' I was breathless.

There was an extraordinary but simple answer. 'Czech folk singers heard this song from Australia after Velvet Revolution and put Czech words to it.'

So it wasn't just luck—we really did have a song in common! While we might not sing in the same language, we shared the music. I was ecstatic. How powerfully music really could transcend boundaries and borders and language and politics!

As I put the guitar down, I had a thought—why not focus my teaching here around songs? That would make grammar and spelling fun and surely the students would want to learn English more if it involved music. When I told Nad'a, she was enthusiastic. 'Yes, yes, that will give the students some nice way to think about words!'

My parting words to the class were, 'Next time I will tell you about School of the Air. Each school day I spent half an hour on my two-way radio and spoke to my teacher, Mrs Hodder, who was in a broadcasting room in Alice Springs. I was joined by students from hundreds of miles away. I think you will find it interesting.'

A stunned silence followed. The class stared at me as though I'd come from another planet, which in effect I had. They farewelled me with 'Na shledanou, Taaanya!'

Pavel, all blue eyes and charm, came up to the front, shook my hand and murmured, 'Thank you, that was wonderful, Taaanya. Next time, we teach you even better expression.'

'I can't wait!' I couldn't stop smiling, inside and out.

⸻

Outside the classroom, a tall slender girl waited. Long blonde hair fell down either side of a petite face and her words spilt out in breathless fits and starts.

'Hello, Taaaarnya, so please, Taaaarnya, I am Kamila, from 3B, and I wish to welcome you to our school. Also, I would like to invite you on bicycle to visit my grandmother in nearby village for wild strawberry picking in forest when the spring is here.'

Her eyes shining and delicate nose crinkling, she rushed on.

'And please, Taaaarnya, I want to learn all I can with you, I must practise the English speaking *a lot*. I am verrrry happy you are now here with us. I want to be excellent English speaker and I hope you will help me because I want to travel the world and become au pair and study languages and perhaps start my own business. Goodbye! I must go now to next lesson. See you soon, I very much so hope!'

She raced off, all willowy frame and flowing blonde hair and giggles.

I leant against the wall, dazed and disbelieving.

Who would have thought I'd spend a morning with sixteen-year-olds who considered my life exotic? Their beautiful, fresh energy and interest had rejuvenated me and I now felt much better. Pavel and Kamila had given me something additional too: the promise of open doors, a way into their community, an unexpected heart connection with them both. Such a rare gift of trust. It felt precious and I hugged it to myself.

Back in the staffroom, I told Naďa about Kamila and she beamed. 'Kamila is one of the best girl English speakers in the school. You can ask Pavel and Kamila to help you, anytime.'

She offered me another coffee and added, 'Me as well, of course!'

I wanted to hug her too but said no to the coffee.

One *Turecká káva* in one day was more than enough for this Australian girl.

What I really wanted was more food.

'I will take you to the "nearest pub" so you can tell your class tomorrow!' said Nad'a, and I excitedly followed her out of the school. We passed a butcher's shop with beer and spirit bottles stacked in the window and Nad'a told me I could conveniently buy a drink while waiting in the queue, or along with my meat purchase. Next was a tiny store with potatoes and pitchforks in the window: hardware or grocery? But before I had time to ask, Nad'a opened the door to a tiny bar filled with people.

Everyone stared as we walked in, but with Nad'a I felt brave and happy again, like I belonged. We sipped Cinzano in little glasses and I hoovered up a huge *řízek*. Then I bombarded Nad'a with questions about Czech life. Her mother was Russian and she had already travelled a great deal, including to visit her sister who lived in America. No wonder her English was so good! She was passionate about teaching English to enable students to broaden their horizons and travel. 'You and I will work together to help them achieve this,' she enthused.

Buoyed by my connection with Nad'a, I could have talked with her all afternoon, but like every woman here she was busy at work and home and had to leave for her next commitment.

'This weekend, please let me prepare the dinner for you with my family,' she offered.

I threw my arms around her.

'You have no idea how much that means,' I said, overwhelmed with happiness.

Moreover, I could proudly report back to Pavel's class tomorrow that I'd found the nearest pub.

8

Foreign correspondent

It was dark and bitterly cold. I moved slowly and nervously, coughing, trying to orientate myself with Maruška's instructions among the strange street signs. My internal navigation guide wasn't doing so well without a known horizon to guide me. But Maruška had also invited me to dinner at her home, and I was both thrilled and determined to find my way there. She and her computer teacher husband, Franta, spoke good English and had been great friends of Peter Barr, so tonight I hoped to learn more from them about the history of their country.

Finally I found the right place, just after 6 p.m., noting that Maruška lived in a different area of town to me—on a hill lined with older and smaller apartment blocks that looked friendly in comparison to *Panelák* Block Four. The door swung open and I looked up into the smiling eyes of Franta. He shook my hand warmly. Filip, aged two, clung to his mother's hip; his eyes took me in warily as she welcomed me inside.

'Please, take off your shoes. Here are slippers.'

Maruška handed me something faded and furry. 'We need to protect our floors from the snow and mud and dirt. Peter Barr did think it was funny too,' she added helpfully.

'Please.' Franta ushered me into a tiny, spotless living room and I stepped back in time. It was decorated with the furniture I remembered from my childhood—lots of light-brown wood and cabinets with sliding glass doors showcasing glassware, crockery and knick-knacks. It reminded me of Mum and Dad's wedding furniture, which had been considered very fashionable in the 1960s and '70s. The moment moved and swirled; I felt as though little M'Lis, Brett, Benny and I might jump out any minute, in pyjamas, ready to say goodnight.

Franta beckoned me to a low table in the middle of the room where we sat. He opened a bottle of Moravian red wine. Maruška brought egg-topped finger sandwiches to the table. The room was warm and cosy and I felt very happy. I wasn't alone, I'd stopped coughing and I was with people who spoke very good English.

After my first glass of wine, I felt emboldened to ask the questions that had been on my lips since I'd arrived. What was life like for them now that communism had gone? Were things improved? Did they relish their freedom? I didn't dare express my own view—that it was difficult to see that anything much had changed for them in Sedlčany—although of course I didn't know what it had been like before 1989.

Franta listened thoughtfully to my questions. He paused, then spoke slowly. 'It is not so easy question to answer. The life is complex. Nothing is simple or black-and-white. In some ways life is better, in other ways it is not.'

'Communism was very bad for many years—yes, of course,' Maruška added, 'but not so much by the very late 1980s. People were flexible. Most people here were not political. If you did not join Party, you got less pay, but that was okay. We had culture and music, books and art—we had a rich life in different ways.'

I must have looked confused. Franta shrugged. 'We have here the most beautiful nature you can imagine and the nature is a big part of our life. It is not so nice in late winter now, that is true, but in spring and summer and autumn, we can cycle and swim and take canoes in the rivers and pick mushrooms and go camping in the forests. That is the kind of life we love. Sport, being outside, music, family fun. That is how we survived under communism. We made a life for ourselves back then that is not so easy to enjoy now.'

'And why is that?' I was struggling to keep up.

'People are now scared about money and how to make a life. Since Velvet Revolution, people think more of money than the important things. They worry about how to pay the rent, buy the bread. We do not understand this so-called democracy world. We grew up with government paying us to live.' He leant forward, fingertips pressed together. 'This new world is already causing family breakdowns and loss of culture and worries.'

In my head paradigms shifted, collided, slipping with the wine into a form of internal chaos. Could a Western-style free market economy really be that oppressive? Could it cause the Czechs to dangle in transition—not knowing anything but the old and not knowing how to embrace the new? My Western foundations wobbled, as did my now empty glass and I.

'I saw the Berlin Wall fall,' I said. 'I thought it would be the start of something much better.'

Franta considered me thoughtfully, no doubt thinking: *This Australian girl is so naive—did she think we could jump overnight from a totalitarian regime into a market economy?*

Or Czech words to that effect.

'Transition is always difficult,' he said at last. 'We had been occupied for so long. We do not have the skills, the experience, the knowledge to know how to get through transition. Many people cannot and will not change at all.'

'I have prepared our dinner,' Maruška interrupted, and I was thankful for a break in the tension. I needed to get my head around these different ways of thinking. I was also ravenous and thrilled at the prospect of hot home-cooked food.

Maruška laid out plates overflowing with *řízek* (the now-ubiquitous pork schnitzel), warm potatoes laced with caraway, and gherkins. The delicious food bolstered me, and after another glass of Moravian red, I dared to pose one last question.

'Does this new world not offer new opportunities, though? You are free to travel abroad and live as you wish. You can make money if you wish. And you don't have to live in fear of government—or of being sent to Siberia. Isn't that kind of freedom worthwhile?'

Franta looked weary. 'Yes and no. As a teacher, it is hard to have enough money to travel abroad or change our lifestyle. It is true some people will be pleased and will have the money to make much out of these changes. But we Czechs don't move much anyway. It's not part of our lives.'

'Already we see moves in Poland and Hungary to bring back socialist governments,' Maruška added.

I was incredulous. 'Will it happen here?'

'I don't think so.' Both my hosts shook their heads. 'The Czechs are likely to focus on democracy and reform because our big government wants to become part of European Union. But it's not easy. When we have elections in a few years, we'll see then.'

I stumbled back to my tiny bedsit that night, head reeling. Never had I considered the benefits of centralised socialist rule. Or the principles of equal distribution of wealth. Or freedom from worry about making enough money to pay the bills, which in turn gave people the time and opportunity to pursue community and cultural matters. It never appeared on Dad or Mrs Howe's respective Modern European History radars.

Of course, in exchange, these people had to do the work of the government on its terms, but was giving up the 'freedom' they had once enjoyed a small price to pay for that security and lifestyle? For the capacity to 'care for family' and their community as a whole? And for the ability to maintain the extensive, rich culture I was now hearing about?

Frankly, I still wasn't convinced.

I found it hard to see Soviet glories beyond the hunched shoulders under coats fraying at the edges, the vacant eyes, the worn bodies and the grey, polluted streets of Sedlčany. Not to mention the architecturally monstrous *paneláky* that dominated the skyline.

But Naďa had tut-tutted when I told her I was distressed by the *paneláky*. She explained that not everyone thought they were bad. 'Many people were happy to go into *paneláky* when they were built. Many people in the country were living like peasants back then, in terrible places—no running water, no proper electricity, much poverty. The former regime gave them proper home for the first time.'

As I curled up in my *panelák* that night, I tried really hard to be grateful for mine, and kept seeing those paradigms shifting, colliding and reworking themselves.

———⟫●⟪———

The next day I received a real-life example of Maruška's and Franta's concerns.

I'd woken to a blinding hangover (note to self—beware too many glasses of Moravian wine) and headed to school, with a hacking cough and aches all over once more. Several cups of *Turecká káva* bolstered me for the day but by late afternoon I was flagging again. As I headed towards the staffroom for more coffee, my gorgeous sixteen-year-old student Kamila intercepted me. She waved her arms wildly.

'Hello, Tanya, it is so nice to see you, I am so happy you are here. Please, after school I have to take some things to my mother who works at the Sedlčany flour mill. Will you come with me?'

Kamila's energy was so light I felt intoxicated all over again just being with her; she was the equivalent of several bottles of champagne. As we hurried through the afternoon's chill an hour later, she giggled a lot and kept telling me how much she wanted to learn English so she could run away and see the world. 'France, I want to go to France, to learn the language, meet some nice French boy!' She giggled some more.

The factory was situated on the outskirts of town. We entered to a blast of noise. Rows and rows of sweating women worked on production lines that stretched the length of the building and up several floors. They carried heavy bags of flour in and out while the men worked on heavy machinery. Despite the noise, the women wore no ear protection, or any protection for that matter. The building and equipment looked rundown, reminding me of a wartime labour camp. Kamila told me that the women packed bags of flour for eight hours a day. There were three different positions on the production line and the women were rotated into those positions every two hours.

It was hard, mindless, back-breaking work, yet most had worked there for years.

Kamila's mother came over to meet us at the door, a kindly, round soul wrapped in an apron. Her eyes were tired although they lit up as we shook hands.

Kamila's mother couldn't speak English, but Kamila yelled over the noise. 'My mother wishes to invite you for our famous Czech dishes in our *panelák* very soon.'

I was so touched and my thanks felt inadequate. I felt ashamed of my own petty worries in light of the difficult life Kamila's mother appeared to be living—and her generosity despite it. I thought of my own mother, who had never worked in a factory. Mum worked hard on the land and had spent years cooking and cleaning and looking after many people. She was never able to stop working. But she had worked in her own place, in her own space, in freedom. She'd stood under wide blue skies every day, ruling the roost on her own terms. She'd never been forced to work in a place like this, a place that to my eyes seemed so soul-destroying.

Kamila and her mother spoke rapidly in Czech for a few more moments, and her mother's face tightened as she blinked back tears. As we hurried away, Kamila explained. 'With regime change, my mother and her comrades here now have big worry. They could lose their jobs. It may be very soon.'

This seemed like the kind of problem Maruška and Franta had mentioned, and Kamila confirmed it. 'There are problems about costs because mill has to buy new equipment. Before, the government would make the buying. Now it must be the owners. When that happens, there will not be enough money to pay all the people.' For the first time, Kamila's face creased, like she might cry too. 'This has never before happened in Sedlčany.'

As we headed away, she added, 'My mother is not trained in anything else. The wages there are bad but at least it is her job. Her friends are here. What will she do?'

I would have thought escaping that hellhole would be a bonus. But as Kamila talked, it was clear that having something to hold onto, something that you had always known—even working in a sweatshop for terrible pay—was better than the gaping void that lay in this brave new world the Czechs were facing.

Something else was very clear too. My Western loneliness and homesickness didn't begin to compare to these real-life difficulties, and my uninformed Westerner's attempt to understand what these people really were struggling with was unequal to the task.

As Kamila farewelled me back at the school I felt deeply uncomfortable. But even though I didn't really understand what it all meant, and as strange and confronting as I was finding everything, I knew I had a lot to learn here from these courageous Sedlčany people.

9

You will not die on my watch!

Zorka, Ivana, Štěpánka, Luboš, Milan, Jan, Radim, Marek, Lenka, Radovan—oh dear. Who was who? And who was a girl and who was a boy? And assuming I worked that out, how did I pronounce their names, much less spell them? And then remember them?

I spent the first week or so getting on top of the names of my students. Some names were clear, like Petr and Michael. Others were less so, like Jan and André (boys' names, not girls', apparently). Štěpánka and Lenka were girls. Zorka? I had no idea until told (also a girl): this one was gorgeous, with waves of brown curls, and she spoke English beautifully. Things became more complicated when the students talked to each other, or about each other, because when they did they changed the endings and the pronunciation of their names. (The reason? Latin-style case declensions, apparently.)

If the students thought my upbringing was like something from another planet, I was amazed at theirs. They largely knew nothing of the West and had lived most of their lives without communication with the outside world; ironically, this reminded me a great deal of the way we grew up in the bush. They made music together, played games together, created all sorts of activities out of nothing, just like we had. I loved being part of their energy, and sharing music and stories.

However, despite my best attempts to be a useful teacher during the first few weeks, I continued to struggle with my own demons. Every day was grey, freezing cold and smoggy with sulphur. Cold, grey days had always been my nemesis. At boarding school they crushed my being into bronchitis, over and over again, and when I left school I declared I would never, ever again live in a cold, grey place. Now I was dealing with not only more of it but the sulphur pollution as well. Blue skies and sunshine seemed a lifetime away.

And despite the kindness of so many people, I was gut-achingly lonely much of the time. The teachers were busy, my time with them was invariably limited, and the lack of shared language was deeply isolating. Out of school I spent many long, empty hours in my *panelák*.

Oh God, I hated the loneliness. It ate me alive. I realised for the first time how much I was sustained by family, and by a familiar community and language. In the absence of them I was lost, freefalling. But I couldn't tell anyone. That would be shameful, an admission of failure. So I kept fronting up to school with my best cheery face on—*fake it till you make it*—and spent as much time inside those comforting walls as I could.

My fever and coughing also continued to intensify. Eventually, I lost my voice altogether and arrived at school in a state of collapse. Jindra took one look at me and marched me to the

Sedlčany hospital. There she told me the doctor would decide what to do next.

We waited in a big, white cement room lined with long benches, like something straight out of a Cold War sanatorium. I curled up on a bench in the corner, while Jindra sat upright, focused. There was no reservation desk or appointment times, and the wait seemed endless. When I finally got called in, it was into an identical large room with more benches where a doctor was moving between patients. He wore a white coat and did not speak English. According to Jindra, his prognosis—when it came—was pretty much the same as hers. My system couldn't cope with the change and not only was I not going anywhere, I was sentenced to bed indefinitely. But as Jindra looked into my horror-stricken eyes, she said comfortingly, 'I will take you to my apartment.'

Dearest Jindra. She saved me from the fate I'd been dreading most of all: being stuck in my *panelák* with circling spies ready to pounce. I wanted to cry with gratitude.

Jindra was, I decided, an angel. Despite teaching full-time, walking several miles to and from school every day (carrying shopping and books), and caring for two daughters and a husband, she tucked me into spotless white sheets on a couch in her spotless living room and let me sleep for a week. For the first few days I was delirious with fever and fantasised about sunshine and blue skies and red earth, dreaming of the touch of Mum's hands. But Jindra was not going to let me die on her watch.

She had a special regime that involved waking me at regular hours throughout the night to give me 'special pills' and pouring me liberal doses of Becherovka, a savage herbal liqueur that the Czechs swore by for 'health benefits'. It tasted disgusting but Jindra had bought it on the way back from school for me and I was to drink it whether I liked it or not.

During the day, when Jindra and her family were out, I had a lot of time on my own to think about how I could manage things once I got better. I had constant flashbacks to home. One particular memory kept sliding through my befuddled brain.

It involved my sister M'Lis. One day, when she was six, we went out with Dad and our Head Stockman at the time, Charlie, to get the monthly 'killer'. That was a big event in the life of the station. It was how we got our monthly supply of meat to feed the many mouths Mum catered for. There could be up to thirty people to feed every day and she often held two sittings per meal. Beef—fresh, grilled, roasted, salted, brined, curried— was the mainstay of our diet. You couldn't run a cattle station, and keep the stockmen working, without meat—and lots of it.

Getting a killer was a hugely exciting experience for us kids. On that day, as with every other time we went for a killer, M'Lis, Brett and I climbed up on the back of the Land Rover, with Dad and Charlie in the front. Nestled in pouches next to the two men were their precious carving knives, and on the front of the Land Rover lay Dad's long .22 rifle. Normally we left in the mid-afternoon to ensure plenty of daylight but it was already late afternoon when we headed off that day. Dad was in a hurry to get the killer before sunset. It took nearly three quarters of an hour of bouncing over narrow, corrugated dirt roads until Dad found the right mob of cattle.

I watched the sun dipping towards the horizon, feeling Dad's anxiety. Choosing the beast was always a difficult decision. It had to be big enough to provide sufficient meat for a month but not so old that the flesh would be tough or stringy.

Finally, Dad chose his target and pulled up a sufficient distance away so as not to frighten the mob to flight. We huddled in the back, our giggling and carry-on silenced by his hissed 'Quiet!' He then pulled out his .22, leant out of the driver's window, took aim and fired.

The explosive noise of the gun reverberated across the landscape and we crouched, trembling, our hands firmly clamped over our ears until the ringing stopped. Dad then put away the gun and drove straight to the dead beast. Dad was a good shot and never believed in cruelty to animals. He almost always got the beast on the first shot, right in the forehead, to ensure there was no suffering.

'Righto!' he yelled when satisfied the beast was dead, and we three kids jumped off the back of the Land Rover and rushed straight to the closest mulga trees, pulling off branches and leaves to lay out a carpet of about three square metres. The carpet was designed to keep dirt and ants off the meat during the butchering process. We helped to drag the beast onto it, and Dad and Charlie pulled out their razor-sharp carving knives. Sharpening the knives was labour- and time-intensive, and had taken place before we headed out; Dad and Charlie had sharpened each knife on an old turning wheel down at the shed, water dripping down, in a slow and precise process. It was a tough job for two men to carve up a big bullock and they needed their knives to be in prime condition.

We kids moved into position for our next job: holding down the legs to keep the beast stable while Dad and Charlie skinned it, taking off the hide and slipping the knife between the skin and the ribs. This was a difficult and delicate task. You don't want the dead beast to wobble or roll as you are carving. On this occasion M'Lis was on the ground, struggling to hold the foreleg into which Charlie was about to slip his knife, when we saw a flash of silver and heard M'Lis scream. Charlie's super-sharp weapon had nicked her arm, just above the wrist, barely a milli-metre from her main vein. Blood gushed from it like a tap had been turned on. For a moment it was difficult to distinguish the blood of the bullock from the blood of M'Lis. Brett and I stared in horror, expecting her to die there and then.

Dad dropped his knife, ran to the front of the Land Rover, pulled out an old bottle of kerosene and a rag covered in oil and dirt. He grabbed M'Lis's wrist, splashed it with kero-sene and wound the rag tight around the bleeding gash. M'Lis sat still through the process, white-faced, biting back a cry as the kero' stung.

Dad then returned to the task at hand with a terse, 'That should do it. You'll be right, Lis. Hold on.' Dad and Charlie had work to do, the beast was precious, it was already late, there were many mouths waiting to be fed, and we had to get the meat home before dark.

Brett and I thought there was every chance M'Lis might die before we got home. The butchering process took a long time, about an hour, and she did not look well. But we still had more work to do, so we got on with it, gathering more clean branches and leaves to put on the floor at the back of the Land Rover. Once the beast was quartered, the large pieces would be heaved onto the floor, along with the various entrails, and we kids would have to sit on the bloodied quarters to keep them safe until we got home. We would be covered in red of all shades by the time we tumbled out the back of the vehicle, along with the rib bones and 'curly gut' that would go on the barbecue for dinner.

M'Lis sat on the ground in deepening shock. We tried to dis-tract her with our usual game of pulling out the bullock's lungs and blowing them up, which left huge blood circles around our mouths and made us fall about laughing. This was our favourite adventure every month. We made different faces at each other as we tried to make the lungs inflate and collapse. The one who blew up the lungs the most was the winner. Like all our games, they were based on the only world we knew—one that was rough and raw, with loads of space and opportunity for invention. But M'Lis didn't laugh that day.

Finally, the beast was quartered and laid out carefully in the back of the Land Rover. We pushed M'Lis up onto the back, where she clung onto the forequarter and some branches as we thumped our way over the dirt roads again. Brett and I held onto her the whole way, telling her to stay alive. It took nearly another hour and was dark by the time we drove into the station yard. Mum took over, washing off dirt and kero' from the wound, putting Dettol on it, wrapping it in a clean bandage, then putting M'Lis to bed. There was not much else that could be done in the bush.

M'Lis was incredibly lucky—just one millimetre more and Charlie would have taken out her vein. That really would have been the end of M'Lis. She still bears the scar today.

But she was still here.

Now, through my anxious and fearful dreams, I knew I needed to become strong again too, like M'Lis had been that day. I also felt ashamed of the letters I'd been sending back home through the school's fax machine. In them I'd poured out stories of my homesickness and loneliness, and of course they had been read (well, what else had I expected?). Now not only were the teachers dismayed and disappointed to learn my innermost thoughts (which cost me A$6 a page), but Headmaster Zdeněk was furious that I had been clogging up his fax machine.

On my last day in Jindra's lovely, clean apartment, it snowed outside. Cars slid all over the roads and there were accidents across Sedlčany. Snow wasn't expected this late in the year and, unhelpfully, all the snow sweepers had been put away. While the town struggled to deal with injuries and the logistical difficulties caused by this environmental upset, I watched the soft white waves float down outside Jindra's window and made a pact with myself.

When I got better, when I got back to the school, I would give my all, and I would make this the best adventure ever. I'd wasted long enough in my own transition. It was time to adjust and get on with it.

10

Sex and free will!

To my joy, the students and teachers greeted me back at school as their long-lost friend, as someone they'd missed. I was incredibly touched by their cards and flowers, and realised how lucky I was. Then I threw myself into teaching.

Well, to be more truthful, I played a lot of music to the students, got them to sing along, and set grammatical and language exercises from *English for Beginners* to music. We worked initially on 'Waltzing Matilda' and then progressed to a video made by my brother, Brett, called *This is the Life*. I'd brought it with me on a whim and it became my number one teaching tool. The video featured Brett and his friends mustering cattle on horseback under the wide blue Centralian skies, set to a catchy country-rock tune Brett had written and performed with his friends. Bookending the video was footage of Brett and his friend Troy swooping in a helicopter and a Cessna 182 over breakaway bullocks at sunrise and sunset.

'This video is like the true John Wayne Western, but better,' Pavel enthused.

'You have such handsome brother,' Kamila cooed.

The video gave me unexpected credibility with these teenagers, who enthusiastically chanted, 'This is the life!' back to me.

The teachers let me get away with this strange teaching approach, which was lucky, as it meant every class was full of fun and cheek and more than a hint of Australian sex appeal. I had to admit my brother and his friends did look better than movie cowboys as they galloped wildly after cattle, horses gleaming, hooves and dust flying, helicopter blades whirring, the muster culminating in a riotous dance of guys and gals in boots and hats.

The games of my brother and his friends arose out of working like 'little men' all our childhoods. But in Sedlčany, students of all ages carried a different but no less important obligation— they had to care for each other during the day like little adults.

I was shocked to learn that, when they were not in lessons, students wandered around the town or spent time at friends' houses because there was nowhere else for them to go. There were not enough teachers during ordinary school hours to run lessons for the students at once, nor enough classrooms to accommodate them, nor any sports grounds at the school.

Parents weren't usually available because under the former regime they'd been forced to work, so the older students also carried the additional responsibilities of caring for the younger ones. They walked or cycled everywhere, riding bikes to and from school—up to fifty kilometres a day—without complaint.

I couldn't imagine teenage students being so responsible and self-sufficient back in Australia. Perhaps that was because, in my experience at least, Australian schools deemed students irresponsible and incapable of self-regulation unless proved otherwise. With draconian rules imposed upon them, Australian students were always looking to break those rules. In the absence of those kind of rules, the students of Sedlčany stepped up and enjoyed other privileges.

Sex among teenagers, for example, was *normální* here, as was staying at each other's homes in order to have sex— according to Pavel, who one afternoon decided to educate me on the finer points of teenage activities. There was no accommodation in Sedlčany: 'So, Tanya, where else would we go, if not our own bed?'

He was surprised at my surprise.

His easy revelations and the relaxed way students here talked about relationships stood in stark contrast to my own strict Protestant upbringing. In the 1960s and '70s, sex before marriage was considered taboo. Illicit liaisons, if they occurred at all, were fumbling and awkward and usually in the back seat of someone's borrowed car, certainly not in the comfort of one's own bed. The 'fire and brimstone' shame associated with teenage sex, and the risk of an unwanted pregnancy, still made me feel slightly sick at age thirty-one.

But here, teenage pregnancy was rare.

Students talked about nights entwined with their fellow students in the same casual way they talked about the pleasure of singing a song, cycling through the woods, sailing a canoe down the river or quoting poetry (which they apparently did, quite often, even the boys; many even wrote poetry).

Pavel went on to tell me, with all the confidence of a blond, handsome seventeen-year-old, that sex was better with love, but that Czech friendship, in a special way, was the 'highest form of love'.

'We even have special words for Czech friendship in our language—*přítel* or *přátelství*.'

Kamila confirmed this was true. She also told me that the first of May was called the Day of Love when the Czechs carried out their special tradition of Guarding the Maypole.

'Under former regime we had to dress up in special uniform and march in May Day parades. Now we just have fun. Our boys build the maypole from some tree in the forest and take care of it all night so that boys from the other village cannot come and cut it down. There can be ribbons, flowers and dancing—and drinking!'

She paused. 'In earlier times, tradition was the boy would build a maypole in front of the garden of the girl he wished to marry. She would wear circle of ribbons on her hair if she liked him!' To explain the significance of the ritual, Kamila put two fingers together to make a circle, then put her finger from the other hand deep inside the circle and wiggled it. I must have looked startled as she giggled some more. The maypole and the head wreath were sexual symbols? 'In this case there would usually be a wedding within one year.'

Fertility, spring, pagan rituals. Magic!

She twirled a long blonde strand of hair. 'And on this day, first of May, a boy can take a girl under a blooming tree and kiss her.'

A blooming tree! I loved it.

We might have had political freedom in the West over the decades but did we have personal and sexual freedoms? Not like this, at least not at my all-girl Methodist boarding school. And while the East suffered from stifling political control, perhaps in other ways its people enjoyed a form of personal freedom—a sort of individual, sexual free will.

I was learning a lot more from my students than they were learning from me.

————>•<————

What the Czechs did *not* have was free will in their supermarkets.

When I received my first packet of Czech koruna as 'advance wages', I rushed to the supermarket on the main square. It might have been uninspiring to look at but I was determined to buy some food to get my system back in order—some fruit, some vegetables, something healthy. Surely fruit and vegetables looked the same the world over? I thought I'd be alright without an escort.

I entered through the sliding door and came face to face with three aisles stacked to the ceiling with Czech beer, spirits and wine. I'd never seen alcohol in a supermarket before. I could hardly believe half the supermarket space was dedicated to it. Perhaps it was a form of self-medication under communism that had lived on. On the last shelf, bottles of the dreaded Becherovka herbal tonic loomed before me, so I hurried off to find food.

I found it at the back of the supermarket. The fresh fruit and vegetable options were limited—expensive bananas and some wilted apples, potatoes and cabbage, and not much else. There were piles of pumpkin, but it was only used as food for pigs. I was the only foreigner in town and everyone knew where I lived, so I couldn't even pretend I had a pig in my *panelák*.

To my dismay there were shelves of tins and packets filled with things and named with words that made no sense to me. There was also a large dairy and pork section, with many attendants assisting, but as I didn't know what anything was, and people were staring at me, I lost my nerve. Instead, I decided to just grab some essentials and come back later with a student or teacher to help me. Collecting two bananas, two apples, a loaf of dark bread and cheese, I headed for the cashier. I really wanted milk but I'd only seen it in UHT cartons. Apparently fresh milk was sold in 'large sacks' but that was beyond my skill set to find today. I wondered if I'd ever learn enough language to shop here properly.

'*Zastavte!*'

I jumped, shrieked in fright.

A large female supermarket guard with thick, unwieldy eyebrows leapt from the closest aisle, arms raised, tone ferocious.

I stared at her with my mouth open, paralysed.

'*Nákupní vozík!*' she bellowed, pointing to something I couldn't see.

I clutched my items even more closely, terrified now.

People gathered and stared at me, their lips pursed.

'*Dejte si nákup do tohoto vozíku!*'

As I mumbled panicked nothings, she thrust an enormous trolley at me, wrestled the small number of items from my arms and threw everything into the bottom of the trolley. Confused, I stared down at my precious purchases rolling loose and lonely in the cavernous space surrounding them.

'*Pojd'te tudy!*'

The woman gesticulated towards the counter. Her face had turned purple by now, eyebrows vertical with indignation.

I attempted to shuffle forward, pushing the trolley to the left, to the right, one step backwards, one step forwards, head bowed, praying the whole thing would soon be over. When I finally got to the counter, perspiration running down my back, I handed my items to the girl at the checkout and gazed at her for help. She was young; perhaps she would understand. But no. Like checkout girls the world over, she was bored and prone to eye-rolling. She took my money, threw me a handful of change and went back to gossiping with her neighbour.

I tottered out of the supermarket, traumatised.

'You must put your things to buy in a trolley so they do not think you are shoplifting,' Naďa explained after I'd staggered into school. Shoplifting? I looked around wildly, expecting the secret police to arrive any minute.

'But I only had a few things! Besides, the trolleys are huge! And they don't even work! They go to the side, backwards—but not where you want them to go. It's ridiculous!'

Naďa shrugged. '*To je normální,*' she offered, repeating the oft-used Czech expression that seem to represent circumstances that were anything but normal.

Then she kindly invited me (yet again) home for dinner with her family and recommended in the meantime that I buy food from the little road stalls presided over by old ladies—the *babičky* (grandmothers). The options weren't plentiful there—mainly bread rolls, fruit, milk and nuts—but it would save me from the supermarket and any more troubles.

I took up her suggestion and became an overnight road-stall convert. Almonds were available in this country and I bought bags of them from the little stalls. There were also fresh crusty rolls, plus a delicious yoghurt and a form of cream cheese, both of which were popular and available at the stalls. And with the help of the tough old ladies wrapped in aprons behind the tables, I bought whatever fruit and vegetables were available. They would sombrely write the cost of my purchases on the brown paper bags, take my proffered money, wave their finger sternly and hold out their palm if I needed to provide more, or hand back coins and notes if I'd given them too much. I never had any idea what it all meant. At night I scribbled the Czech names of my purchases into my diary and tried to memorise the words and the sounds. Then I would go back the next day and try them out on the old ladies. Every day I smiled at them hopefully but they never smiled back. No matter—I was grateful.

My diet was strange and lacking in variety, but without access to regular meals I started to lose weight. *Not bad as holiday strategies go*, I thought.

11

Words and music

Peter Barr's presence remained a constant in my life in Sedlčany—a bit like the ghost of Banquo, just without the bloody bits. The fact he'd got on top of the language and I hadn't was an ongoing sore. Moreover, how much of what I said did the students and teachers really understand? Not a lot, I suspected.

It was for that reason my video *This is the Life* spoke a thousand or more words. We might not share the language but the images and music joined us at a deeper, more visceral level. And I didn't understand anyone unless they spoke in English, and even then there were very few who had a sufficient grasp of English to hold a comprehensive conversation. Hand movements, pointing and facial expressions got me by but if I was really to make the most of this adventure, I had to reconsider Peter Barr's advice to try and learn Czech.

So I spoke to Naďa about it.

Naďa looked doubtful. 'Czech is very difficult. Even our students have many problems. It is much more difficult to write than to speak. Also, we have high Czech and lower Czech. Better in your short time with us that you focus on English, which is what the students want.'

But Peter Barr had learnt it—shouldn't I at least try?

So I tried, and Naďa was right; it was unbelievably difficult.

High Czech was an ancient, formal style of speaking and writing, relied upon in special disciplines such as medicine and law and even some parts of teaching. Lower Czech was spoken and written in day-to-day life. There were endless consonants and six additional letters in the alphabet to create words like *čtyřikrát* ('four times'), *zmrzlina* ('ice cream') and *přijďte* ('come')—and they were some of the easy ones. Most challenging was the structure of the language. Czech was based on a thing called class declension and boasted a structure similar to Latin.

I had no understanding of class declensions or Latin (unlike Peter Barr who had knowledge of both).

So the next best thing to do was to listen closely to people and ask questions. Although this did not always help. For example, *no* meant 'yes', and *ne* meant 'no', and I was constantly confused.

Just imagine this scenario: someone asks a question. In response, the other person shakes his or her head dismissively and says, often quickly and with some force, what sounds to my ears like, '*No no no no no.*' But what they've just said is 'Yes yes yes yes yes'. Time and time again I heard what sounded like a long, almost irritable rejection, and then someone would turn to me and say, in English, 'So. Okay. We go—we do.'

Then there was *ř*, one of the six additional letters in Czech. It was pronounced with a roll and a special use of the tongue.

When I tried to pronounce it, the students fell about laughing, telling me I pronounced my ř like little children did. Naďa kindly told me not to worry as the Czech President, Václav Havel, couldn't pronounce his ř properly either. I guessed it was like a lisp in English, although more embarrassing.

'*English* is what we want you to speak to us' was a common refrain, so I almost gave up before I started.

———————

Then there were the Czech composers Maruška had mentioned on my first day. I still knew nothing about them but suspected that I should. While I was unlikely to master the language, despite Peter Barr's urging, I knew I had a better chance with music. And I knew that it was important to try.

One morning at recess I approached Maruška. 'I'm learning some folk tunes with the students but I'd also like to learn about your historic Czech music too. Is there anything you could suggest?'

Maruška looked surprised, as well she might, but introduced me to *gymnázium* maths and music teacher, Helena, who she said could teach me everything there was to know. This would be a big step up in my Czech education and I was both nervous and excited.

Helena invited me to her little apartment the following week. I went after school and found a snug den artistically furnished with rugs and colourful prints. A yoga mat was in the corner, and herbal tea was brewing. In that den Helena often listened to guided Indian meditations on cassettes and practised tai chi. I could hardly believe that a true bohemian like Helena existed, nor that an apartment like hers had survived the communists.

Helena was, however, a teacher at heart and kicked off our tuition with a strict Czech history lesson.

'Our composers are, how you say, foundation of Czech life,' she said. 'We start, always, with Bedřich Smetana and his famous work *Má Vlast*.'

I quickly pulled out my notebook and started scribbling.

'In English, that means "My Fatherland" or "My Country". My two favourite poems from the work are "Vyšehrad" and "Vltava".'

She raised her arms as if to start conducting an orchestra.

'Vyšehrad was a castle on a big rock that stands high over the River Vltava. Czech legend says that in the seventh century, the wise and beautiful Princess Libuše stood on that rock and had a prophecy of Prague. In her vision, she saw "a great city whose glory will touch the stars". It is said that Prague is built on the foundations of her feminine vision.'

I was awestruck. How many countries had birthrights bestowed by a long-ago princess envisaging a city of beauty from within a trance?

'Next is Vltava—our big river in Prague. In the piece, you will hear in the violins the baby river trickling small in the mountains until it grows in power and roars to Prague with whole orchestra.'

As Helena spoke, she pulled out a cassette tape and clicked it into a tiny cassette player. Violins soared and danced until the orchestra swept to its majestic finale, the grandeur and splendour of the music bouncing off the walls.

'Next in time, after Smetana, came Antonín Dvořák.'

Dvořák was a violist, violinist and composer of romantic music who incorporated folk music into his works, such as the 'Song to the Moon' from his opera *Rusalka*, and the fast and furious Slavonic Dances. He was invited to New York during the 1890s where, consumed with homesickness, he poured his longing into his most famous work: Symphony No. 9 in E Minor, *From the New World*.

Helena clicked 'play' again and soon the room was filled with the haunting intensity of one man's homesickness. I knew homesickness only too well. As though a plug had been pulled away from my heart, my pent-up emotions poured out like the River Vltava heading to Prague.

'*Tak*!' Helena's face was a study of rapture as I wept. 'Dvořák had a pupil called Josef Suk. He became famous violinist and composer and fell in love with Dvořák's daughter.'

She smiled mysteriously.

'Suk wrote famous pieces such as *Serenade for Strings* and *A Summer's Tale*. We say that you can hear the countryside in Suk's music—the freshness of the dawn and the sound of the lark and the feel of the wind and the splash of the river and the beauty of the spring in each note.'

Her eyes were wide, dark.

'*Tak*!' She leant towards me. 'Even our most sophisticated Czech classical music is based on life in the country, the folklore, the famous fairytales and legends, the peasant music from former times.'

'Just like our Australian country music is based on our life in the bush,' I burst out, unable to help myself. I'd made another link between Central Australia and Central Europe—something about the isolation we shared and what it produced—and it was both intriguing and thrilling.

Bundling up the tapes for me to take away, Helena finished triumphantly. 'We Czechs are bound to our history and our present—to stories of our princes and princesses with magical powers, to our wise witches and fantasy beings, to our woods and our streams and our mountains and our valleys—as though they are all the one thing.'

I felt transported. Parallel universes slid before me. Memories of my childhood fantasies were returning in whispers and images. I couldn't find my own words but my body connected—surreally, magically—to Helena's words.

Helena took me to her door and added, almost as an afterthought, 'Do you know that the positive energy of the students affects us? Do you realise how much you come alive and shine in their company? Especially when you sing with your guitar with them?'

I stared into her eyes.

She nodded sagely. 'It is no accident you are here with us. Six months ago, did you have any idea you would be in classrooms filled with Czech students? Maybe you were here in a former life.'

Maybe Helena was a wise witch. I threw my arms around her in gratitude.

As I headed back towards my *panelák*, I noticed that the smog wasn't quite as bad. The freezing grey days and bone-wracking chill were starting to relent. The six layers of clothes I usually wore were reduced to three. Sedlčany was thawing and so was I.

On the corner of a road I stopped. There stood a tree in blossom. As the sweetness of its tiny white scented flowers curled up towards me, I gulped in breaths of relief and joy. Through the thin, pale light, I saw fields of green rolling away into misty blue hills in the distance, and those fragrant buds and the promise of spring felt like my own personal miracle.

12

Benešov

When I'd been at Sedlčany for nearly two months, Head English teacher Jindra kindly arranged a weekend away for me. I was to go and stay with another teacher, Jarka, in a nearby village.

I was filled with the same thrill I had felt at boarding school when an exeat—a weekend escape—from boarding school approached. This would be my first time away, solo, in the Czech Republic, and it felt like I had grown up and was now enjoying a prefect's privilege.

On the Friday afternoon, I walked to the railway station with my gorgeous Kamila, who came to help me buy a ticket. After hugging her goodbye, I boarded a one-carriage steam train that looked like it was straight out of *Noddy*. We headed to a town called Olbramovice, which sounded charming, and as the train choofed (literally) out of the station I sat back, taking in the mass of bare tree trunks flashing past, spindly and dark in the evening light. The light greens on the woodlands were translucent, magical, and hinted that the much-heralded Czech springtime was on its way. I couldn't wait for it to really be here.

I remembered the drive to Sedlčany on my first day and the glimpse of Prague, which had felt so close for those few glorious seconds as we drove past it. Prague now seemed a long way away, out of reach, from another land. Moreover, the challenges I'd faced in my early days in Sedlčany meant I'd not had the courage or energy so far to look beyond the town borders.

I wondered when Peter Barr had first gone to Prague. Had he gone alone? How did he find his way there? I knew he had browsed through bookshops and attended Havel's plays in underground theatres. He'd gone to classical concerts and met friends there. He'd also encouraged me to go as soon as possible. However heading to Prague on my own meant I might end up in Poland rather than Prague. I struggled to understand signs and directions without help and certainly couldn't hold a conversation with a bus driver or train conductor.

The train tooted as we arrived into Olbramovice and I leapt off the train, anxious not to miss the station.

Jarka and her husband were waiting in their little car and welcomed me warmly. They told me we were heading to a restaurant in the next town, Benešov, to meet friends for dinner. Well, at least I think that's what they said, on the basis of much finger pointing, sign language and dictionary examination. My hosts could not speak English so it was all a bit of a guess, really. They smiled at me and I hoped my eager smile in response properly conveyed the degree of my gratitude at being here with them.

We drove to the restaurant and they led me into a long, low-roofed building. It was dark-panelled and smoky, filled with people chatting and dining and enjoying their pork and beer.

People stared as I followed my hosts. Yet again my appearance, my clothes, everything about me shrieked, 'She's not one of us.' Most Czech women I'd met so far were beautiful and tall, with those famously high cheekbones.

Mostly I accepted our differences but tonight I just wanted to feel normal, like everyone else. I suddenly wished I was wearing a gorgeous dress and high heels and having an ordinary old Friday evening with friends, like someone who belonged—guzzling wine, gossiping, laughing, as the locals here were doing. I wanted to feel pretty, not the 'strangely dressed foreigner' who was always out in jeans, sandshoes and a thick pink parka to avoid freezing.

My hosts fortunately had no idea of my manic internal dialogue and they ushered me towards another couple at a table. Everyone shook hands cheerfully and the four Czechs began chatting among themselves. I sat alone, determinedly running through the list of benefits of the evening in my head: this was a time to embrace the opportunity, enjoy the moment; to be glad I was finally out of Sedlčany; to make new friends and have new experiences I could write about afterwards. *Don't worry about your clothes and what you look like*, I said to myself. *Be grateful for tonight. Make the most of it.*

But I had finally escaped Sedlčany, and my tightly bottled emotions decided they were free to do likewise. They started leaping out of every pore with the energy of a suppressed Jack in the Box. When the waiter handed around menus and everyone perused them and exchanged ideas, my feelings shouted, 'I can't read this, I'm like a child no more than three years old, I'm utterly dependent, I can't talk to anyone about this. I am a *nobody*!'

A loud noise at the door distracted me from this onset of despair.

Two men entered the restaurant, one a round, cheerful-looking fellow, the other very tall and thin. Two other men walked towards them and there was animated handshaking, laughter and backslapping, and fast conversation in Czech. As I watched them, I had another realisation. I'd flown away from Australia because I didn't feel I belonged there, yet my sense of not belonging was only magnified here. The truth was out. I didn't belong *anywhere*.

I stared down at the meaningless words of the menu under the cheap plastic. Emotions continued to taunt me: 'What's the point? There will only be ten different versions of pork, cabbage, dumplings and potatoes. Why even bother looking? They are all the same everywhere. They don't change!'

The waiter arrived to take our orders. I wanted to say 'Anything but *řízek*, please', but I didn't even know how to say that. What I really craved was a big, juicy steak, cooked rare on the barbecue, accompanied by a fresh salad topped with a piquant French dressing. But I couldn't have what I wanted and I couldn't say what I didn't want so I was stuck with Jarka's decision, as if I was a child. My powerlessness in that moment was so all-consuming it seemed to cover the entire restaurant like a black shroud. Jarka must have felt it, because she whispered hopefully to the waiter; I heard *anglicky* and *Australanka*, but I didn't feel hopeful. I wanted to dissolve into the table, into the floor, and back to *Austrálie*.

Then something very strange happened.

The waiter's eyes lit up and he spoke rapidly to me, gesturing for me to stand up and follow him. Glancing anxiously at my hostess, I took her nod as an assurance I wouldn't end up in a gulag and warily followed the waiter towards the back of the restaurant, wondering what awaited me. An English menu?

We walked through a haze of smoke and the waiter stopped in front of the group of the men who'd greeted each other earlier. They looked at me and looked at the waiter. There was lots more hand-waving and gesticulating and then raised eyebrows. Panic trickled through me. Who were these guys? Did they have a menu? No. Were they secret police?

Just as I was turning to run, the man nearest to me grinned and extended a big furry paw.

'G'day. How are ya, mate? I am Míša.'

My whole body rooted itself to the floor. I stared blankly at this man's laughing eyes, his short and stout physique, his dark hair and dark beard. My mouth opened but no words came out.

Míša pointed to the tall, bearded man he'd walked in with. 'This is Jarda.' Speaking English in a strong Czech accent, he went on. 'Welcome! Jarda and me—we are Czech-Australians. Would you like to join us?'

My tongue still would not work. Neither would my legs.

The tall man also spoke with a strong Czech accent. 'And so, please, what is your name?'

'Tanya,' I finally managed but my brain and body could not compute what was happening. Finally, I managed to blurt out, inanely, 'Who *are* you?'

Míša answered, his eyes deep dark pools of amusement.

'We are Czechs, born here, now live in Australia. We are here to do some business with our colleagues, Pavel and Honza,' he pointed to the other two men. 'When Jarda and I walked in, Pavel and Honza were already here, and Pavel stood up and called out very loudly, "The Australian kangaroo arrives!" The waiter heard this.'

They all laughed some more as I continued to stare, bemused.

'*Tak*! Tanya,' Míša said cheerfully, pulling out a chair and helping me into it. 'Why are you here yourself—and so far out in the countryside? This is a place where only Czechs come, not foreigners. Four years ago, you'd be shot for being here, or arrested at least. It is lucky the waiter brought you to us!'

Both Czech-Australians laughed and I started talking. Then I couldn't stop.

'You need a drink!' Jarda decided. He called the waiter over and ordered me a small beer. 'Please, if you like, we will arrange with your friends for you to have dinner with us tonight.'

With undoubted relief, Jarka handed me over to the custody of my Czech-Australian saviours for the evening.

'So now we can explain the menu for you. What would you like to eat?'

'Anything but *řízek*! Please, no *řízek*!'

They laughed. They thought it hilarious that I was desperate to avoid their beloved pork schnitzel. Instead they ordered me trout with almonds (which I said I would only believe existed when I saw it with my own eyes), and they further explained that the reason I'd been served *řízek* everywhere I went was that the dish represented Czech hospitality. 'People have done it to be kind to you, Tanya,' said Jarda. A stab of shame hit me, but not hard enough to override my relief at finding something non-pork-based on the menu. If I couldn't have a steak, trout would be sensational.

'Please,' I pressed, still confused about the scenario in which I'd found myself, and grappling with cultural niceties that were clearly beyond me. 'What is your connection to Australia? Why did you go there?'

Míša and Jarda told me their story and a strange sense of serendipity flooded through me as they talked.

They had grown up in Prague under communism but fled the Russian tanks after the Prague Spring of 1968, that dark stain on the already very dark stain of Czechoslovakia's decades of occupation. I remembered it from *The Unbearable Lightness of Being*.

They gave me a potted history. The Prague Spring infamously represented the Soviet crushing of a short period of 'socialism with a human face', a liberal approach to life developed under the Prime Minister at the time, Alexander Dubček. It was the 1960s, and intellectuals and artists flourished; free speech was allowed. Václav Havel was in his element at the time, writing plays and criticising communism. But the Moscow masters took a dim view of such human-like behaviour.

They invaded the country in August 1968, abducted Dubček and, high in the Ukrainian mountains, told him he would be executed. Russian tanks rumbled through Wenceslas Square, the country sat frozen with fear, Dubček was subsequently spared (but publicly humiliated; he would never speak in public again) and his 'confession at the Kremlin' led to a long period of Soviet 'normalisation' and harsh controls throughout the 1970s.

The waiter interrupted. He put in front of me a plate of what was undeniably trout. The fish was large and whole with bones intact; it had been steamed in butter, sprinkled with parsley and scattered with slivered almonds. My eyes goggled, mouth watered, salivary glands jumped. I hadn't known what to expect but this far exceeded my expectations. Fingers trembling, I picked up my knife and fork, took a small mouthful, avoiding the bones, and murmured, 'Oh my God, this is delicious'.

Jarda and Míša continued to talk, happily eating řízek themselves, while I devoured the fish and their story.

Following the Prague Spring, most Czechs were fearful of wide-ranging executions and being shipped off to Siberia, a repeat of the Soviet's tactics when they took over Czechoslovakia following the end of World War II. Back then, in the late 1940s and early '50s, there were fake trials, and thousands of people 'disappeared'. It was a time of tyranny and terror. Jarda and Míša had decided not to take the risk of history repeating itself. They fled one night in 1968, under cover of darkness, before the borders were closed, taking their wives and some friends, but otherwise leaving everything they knew and loved behind.

They became immigrants, moving from camp to camp through Europe. Finally they washed up on Australia's shores, where they lived for some years in migrant camps in Melbourne. The Nissen huts they lived in were primitive—freezing in winter, boiling in summer—but having reached the other side of the world, they knew there was no going back.

'That sounds terrible,' I said, feeling ashamed we'd put such lovely men into those kinds of camps.

'It was okay. We were young, we survived,' Jarda said, philosophically. The greatest problem was their homesickness for Czechoslovakia, exacerbated by the knowledge that they could not return to their home country again for fear of imprisonment—or worse. Imagine their joy following the fall of the Berlin Wall, which then triggered the Velvet Revolution and the opening of the Czech borders once more.

I remembered the Velvet Revolution was a Havel term, given to describe the essentially bloodless coup he and his party, Občanské fórum ('Civic Forum'), led to overthrow the communist regime in late 1989. Given nearly 200 students were beaten savagely and hospitalised as a precursor to the collapse, 'Velvet' was clearly a relative term. But this was a country that had known real savagery.

'There are many of us visiting here in the Prague just now,' Jarda went on. 'Do you know of "restitution"?'

I shook my head, so they told me about the current legal process of returning property unlawfully taken by the communists back to its original owners. Jarda and his brother had been handed back their family's apartment block in Prague. In partnership with Míša, they were reconstructing this building. They had driven to meet Míša's solicitor and colleague, who lived in Benešov, to finalise business over dinner. 'So that is our story!' they finished.

'I can't believe this coincidence,' I kept repeating in disbelief. Pavel and Honza, who did not speak English, ordered more beer and spoke among themselves, resigned to the fact that business was over for the evening.

Míša looked down at my feet.

'I can guess you are from the Northern Territory, yes?'

My world—my heart—stopped.

'I can see some red dust on your shoelaces. I know the Tropic of Capricorn that runs through that area. I have camped there.'

I glanced down at the ochre red of Central Australia stained into the white shoelaces on my sandshoes and looked back at him dazedly. Despite my best efforts, I'd not been able to scrub the colour out.

'You've been there? To Alice? To my *home*? No!'

'Yes!' He laughed wickedly, pleased at the connection himself.

I didn't believe him. It was a ridiculous, incomprehensible coincidence.

'It is true,' Míša nodded. 'I have loved your outback ever since I came to Australia. I have travelled to Central Australia and all over Australia. When I saw the red dust, I knew you were from there.'

This man was psychic too?

The connection was overwhelming. Not only did Míša know Australia, he knew the outback, *my* country. He had probably slept on the hard earth under the enormous black sky of dazzling stars. Felt the red dirt under his feet, held it in his hands. Smelt the heat, heard the crackling of dried leaves under the midday sun, tasted the burnt air, listened to the explosion of bird sounds at dawn. I clenched my knuckles furiously under the table. Tears stung for the second time that night. Then I laughed at the impossibility and improbability and sheer serendipity of everything that had happened that evening.

'Come and visit us in Prague,' Míša suggested.

'Prague!' My knees felt weak.

'Prague is such beautiful city. Have you not been there yet? We will be there next weekend.' He added, as an incentive: 'You can talk English for a whole day—and no *řízek*!'

Jarda nodded slowly. 'You can meet my friend from boyhood days, Karel. He still lives in Prague and speaks English. I am sure he will be able to help you. He is an engineer and reconstructs buildings all over Prague. He has many contacts if you would want to try for work in Prague when you finish at Sedlčany.'

I hesitated. I was two-thirds through my time in Sedlčany and didn't want to be disloyal. I hadn't even thought about what I'd do when I got to the end of my time there. There was something else niggling at me too. These men were strangers. Lovely men, yes, but still strangers. It was one thing to meet them here, with the protection of my host family barely five tables away, but in a foreign city? Were they really trustworthy? And how would I find them? What if I got on the wrong train and really did end up in Poland?

But Míša persisted.

'There is so much beauty and history in Prague that was not destroyed by our former occupiers. We will meet our friends on an island in the famous River Vltava—next to the Žofín Palace where there are winter balls. You cannot miss this!'

Images of Viennese balls and violins and swirling men in black tie and women in gowns danced in my head and I could hold out no longer. 'But how will I find you?'

'It is easy. We will draw you map. We will meet you in the Old Town Square in Prague under the clock.'

Under a clock? I stared at them in disbelief.

'It is big clock,' said Jarda, scribbling on a beer mat, adding times and names. 'Astronomical clock.'

'I wish to tell you something before I go, Tanya,' Jarda said, as we all shook hands. 'I hope it will help you with your struggles. Míša and me, and our families, we went to Australia with nothing. We had no English and it was unbelievably hard. But we managed. Just accept where you are right now. Make the most of it. Nothing lasts forever. You have only two months before you can leave again, if you so wish. We had to wait twenty years for that luck. And we didn't even know it would happen. We just got lucky.'

In that moment I wanted to dissolve. Jarda had guessed what I hadn't wanted to put in words. They understood. They had been there too—only for them it had been much, much worse.

Míša touched my cheek gently, as if I was a child. 'Your face is open book.'

'Karel will help you, I know it,' Jarda repeated, thoughtfully.

13

Fairytale Prague

'Pardon, *prosím vás* ... excuse me, please ... *promiňte* ... pardon ..'

The alleyway was narrow and my attempts at Czech were lost in the babble of teenagers crowding around a woman with an umbrella above her head. The group filled the stone passage and blocked my access to the far end.

No one took any notice of my attempts to get past them. The anxiety in my stomach rose and fell with each breath. How would I get out of there? I was running out of time.

It had been a long morning already. I'd headed out from Sedlčany on the 6.30 a.m. bus, clutching Kamila's written instructions on what to pay, when to get off and how to get into the Old Town. En route we stopped at a village. There we were delayed fifteen minutes as the bus driver shared a beer and chat with some locals. (A beer? At 7.30 a.m.?) Once we did finally reach the Prague terminal, I had to find my way through the complex metro system. Now I was stuck in an alley—and possibly lost.

As I turned back, a shaft of soft spring sunshine hit my face. Following the light, I found myself unexpectedly in a side street. It was lined with high houses that went straight up into the sky, their narrow windows looking down onto curving cobbles. Red flowers spilled out of baskets along the windows and the air was fragrant with blossom.

I stopped, breathed in and out, steadied myself.

I was here. I was really here.

In Prague. Exactly two months to the day since I'd arrived in Sedlčany.

Now all I had to do was find my Czech-Australian friends.

In a square with a clock.

———

When I did find the Old Town Square—Staroměstské náměstí—it felt like time had stopped. For a moment I was Alice, falling into my own wonderland, stretching out my arms to fantasy, then landing on tiptoes and gazing around at an enchanted world as far from my idea of reality as could be imagined. Yet in the same instant I knew this scene was magically close to my childhood imaginings. In that split second of glorious realisation, I wanted to fall on my knees in wonder and gratitude. I'd found the home of fairytales! And I'd not only found it, I was *in* it, with worn cobblestones underfoot and a glittering castle presiding grandly over me.

I leant against a corner wall, Kamila's crushed piece of paper hanging limp from my fingers.

Let's Go Europe told me this square—surrounded by palaces and churches, shining silver and gold in the morning light— had been around since the eleventh century. Tiny shops were painted in different shades of soft pastel yellows, pinks and blues. They looked like dolls' houses, yet my guidebook told me Kafka had lived in one of them and had also written there. There was the clip-clop of hooves on the cobblestones and two beautiful black horses trotted past, pulling a carriage presided over by a master adorned in red-and-gold braid and a top hat. There was no royalty inside, but two glamorous girls with their hair shining in the sun. They waved as they passed by, princesses for the day.

I tried to breathe.

I was standing in a place I instantly felt I belonged, had *always* belonged. It was utterly familiar. Old patterns and lines traced their way through my heart, brain and soul, emerging into the light as though surprised but glad to be back where they belonged—in a city that was as familiar to me as every vision and tale of my childhood.

I was seized with the desire to dance wildly, twirling around and around, singing and laughing. I had waited my whole life for this moment, and now it had arrived it was smiling and saying, 'Welcome, old friend.'

'*Ahoj*, Táničko!'

Míša's cheery face came into view. He wrapped me in a huge bear hug and I crumpled at being in the warmth of someone's arms. I also noticed, with a happy shock, that he had used the diminutive of my name. Czechs did that for their lovers, children, relatives or people they cared for. It was like calling me something like 'Tanyikens-cootsy-coo'. Happiness flooded me from top to toe. I was one of them, now.

'Your timing is perfect,' he grinned. 'Now you can see our famous Astronomical Clock in operation.'

We stood back, me somewhat unsteadily. Míša pointed to an enormous, ornate clock on the edge of the square. The clock boomed the hour. Wait—there were two clock faces, and a procession of miniature and vividly painted sculptures moved above them both. The air was filled with a frenzy of shrieks and snapping cameras. Through the din, Míša yelled that one clock represented the sun and moon, and the other months of the year, and that the sculptures represented the twelve Apostles. The oldest part of the clock had been created more than 500 years before I was born. Everything felt unreal, surreal; I was now Tanya in Wonderland.

A tall, bearded man emerged from the crowd—Jarda—and the moment of happiness was complete. He hugged me too, and even though I barely came past his knees I felt overwhelming joy at being hugged by a second human being in the space of five minutes.

Jarda introduced me to his wife and a nearby group of friends, all of whom smiled warmly and welcomed me in English. Most of them were also Czech-Australians. I shook lots of hands and trembled with gladness. From the darkness of Sedlčany to the lightness of Prague—it was like coming up from the deep without stopping midway for the decompression process.

'There is one more person to join us,' Jarda told me with a frown. 'Karel. But he is late. He is always late.'

'*Tak! Jak se máš*, Táničko?' Míša asked kindly, and I was so relieved to be asked 'How are you?' that I poured out my bus-and-beer story.

'Seven-thirty a.m. Can you believe the bus driver got out to have a beer at 7.30 a.m.? Is that *normal*? Is it?'

Míša was still chortling when I was interrupted by someone speaking in Czech. But this Czech sounded different to my ear, different to that spoken by the Sedlčany people. It was lilting, with a singsong quality. I turned around, mid-sentence, then stopped completely.

A tall, well-built man was greeting everyone enthusiastically. Wearing faded jeans and a blue denim shirt with sleeves rolled up to three-quarter length, he looked like the main act who had just taken centre stage. On his own terms. For several minutes there was a hearty round of back slaps, handshakes, kisses and conversation—and much laughing. Finally, he turned to me and bent down to take my hand. I stared up into eyes that were blue like the sky, like the sea. Eyes that owned the moment.

'Good morning,' the voice said in heavily accented and quaintly formal English. 'You must be our Australian teacher who has come to our beautiful Prague to visit us today. I am Karel Kolář. Very pleased to make your acquaintance.'

'Er, yes, thank you . . .'

'*Tak*!' he went on breezily, with the relaxed air of an old friend resuming a half-completed conversation, oblivious to my glazed expression. 'I heard you asking for some explanations from Míša about our special culture? I can help. You must know there are two things Czech men cannot refuse: beautiful women and our most excellent beer.'

Pardon?

'It is normal for some driver to want beer when on long drive,' he continued, nodding confidentially. 'Ah yes—that should not be surprise. What was surprise to me'—he let the emphasis linger—'was the bus driver did not ask you to join him at his side.'

I stared back at him in disbelief.

'*Tak*! We are verrrry happy the bus driver did not keep you,' he went on, as though this was the most normal conversation in the world to be having with someone he'd just met. 'It is much better you are by *our* side.' He finished with a flourish. 'Welcome to beautiful Prague and I hope you have happy day with us.'

Jarda rolled his eyes. 'Yes, Karel has special sense of humour. I hope his stories and advice improve as the day goes on.'

Undeterred, Karel said, '*Tak—jdeme na pivo!*'

So, let's go for beer.

I wanted to laugh, to stand a while and let the strangeness of everything sink in. I had two new friends who saw me as a real person because we shared a country—two countries, in fact. Now a third person had suggested he had not just seen me but considered me beautiful. Admittedly, I had worn my best jeans, a blue silk shirt and a little scarf knotted around my neck, and I'd lost several kilos over the previous two months. But I was still squashed inside my pink parka and wearing my sandshoes. Perhaps it was my new haircut. Nad'a had taken me to her local hairdresser and for the princely sum of A$3 I'd had a trim. Whatever the reason was, it didn't matter. Karel had said I was beautiful and my morning was shining all over.

Perhaps Karel was the Mad Hatter in this Wonderland maze.

Jarda led us down a labyrinth of crooked streets, which he explained was called the Royal Way. It was once a processional route trod by newly crowned kings, and it led to the high black towers that bookended the River Vltava.

'And here over the river is our Charles Bridge—in Czech it is called Karlův most. It is for people only, no cars. Built in four-teenth century by our king, Charles IV.'

On my first day in the Czech Republic I'd looked down at the much-lauded River Vltava from Zdeněk's car and that beautiful bridge. Today I walked towards it. It was straddled by the wide and grand bridge of ancient stone, lined with statues and crisscrossed with people. Painters and musicians busily plied their trade on top as ferries cruised underneath. On the other side a spread of palaces and churches and gardens climbed several high hills. Above them sat the jewel in the crown that I'd seen from the Old Town Square—Prague Castle—with more Gothic towers and silver spires piercing the blue. A battlement wall ran under the grand castle, and Míša confirmed that yes, that was Havel's home.

'Can we go there?' I felt like a desperate kid.

'No, unfortunately not just now.' Jarda instead directed us along a path that followed the Old Town side of the river. 'You will remember, we will have beers on a small island up here a little way. It is called Slovanský ostrov. My friend has bar on a pontoon there.'

No matter. I'd already decided I was coming back to Prague, now I knew how to do it. I'd broken through my own fear barrier and a world of possibilities awaited. Even if it took my entire salary, I'd find a way back every weekend. Peter Barr's legacy would live on. Just thinking about that made me feel strong and independent again. I wasn't stuck, I wasn't trapped. I could make my time in this country anything I wanted.

We wandered through the sweetness of the morning. Blossom hung from trees lining the bank. New green leaves sprouted and fragrance filled the crisp freshness of the air.

'They are chestnut trees,' Míša explained. 'Very famous for Prague.'

Jarda turned to me and pointed ahead. 'Here, now, Táničko, is the island, and in the middle, you will see the Žofín ball house!'

Just when I thought it would be impossible to see any-thing more beautiful than what I'd already seen that morning, an imposing yellow, white and gold mansion rose up before us, complete with gilded balconies, etched pillars, sweeping driveway and manicured gardens.

'Ahhh . . .' I breathed out in equal amounts of awe and delight.

'You know about Žofín?' Karel raised his eyebrows. 'And are you okay?'

But I couldn't answer. I was lost inside memories: of a record of Strauss waltzes called *The Blue Danube* that Mum used to play when I was a little girl. She used to pop it on our little record player and dance with me in her kitchen. It was always hot, with several stoves going; Mum was invariably cooking mountains of beef. But, absorbed in the grandeur and joy of the music, we might as well have been two of the princesses depicted on the cover of the record. They wore long blue ball gowns and waltzed proudly, in the arms of men in black tie, around a magnificent ballroom with high sash-windows and glittering chandeliers.

Now I'd arrived at that ball house! I was sure of it!

When I was able to get my voice back, I burst out, 'This is—this is—perfect! Could a—a foreigner like me dance here?'

I gazed around at my new friends, begging them to say 'Yes!' and not laugh. I caught Karel's eye. He held my gaze, as though he understood my question, as though I was not crazy. He nodded casually. 'It is Czech tradition to dance. All Czech people dance—waltz, polka, gypsy and folk dances, and even the American foxtrot and jive. We must see what we can arrange for you while you are still here.'

Then he looked at me slowly, sideways.

My brain synapses fired wildly.

Jarda interrupted by pointing to a little pontoon rocking gently on the water. I followed them down and sat between Jarda and Míša at a long wooden table next to a bar. It was like having two older brothers—just wonderful. The owner came. More back slaps ensued, foaming beers were served, and Jarda raised his glass.

'Here, we all celebrate being back together again after so long. We celebrate because for the last twenty-five years we never thought we could come home.'

Home.

'It is the word that means the most to a refugee,' Jarda said simply.

I knew he was speaking of the depth of anguish felt by people who'd lost their country, who couldn't go back. He'd been one of them once. They all had.

The poignancy of it bit the air, bruised and bitter.

I wanted to say that I was reminded of the Australian Aboriginal concept of connection to country, the basis for the Aboriginal way of life. I now knew, to my core, that connection to country was a primal human need the world over. It gave you a link and a relationship to what came before; it offered nourishment and purpose for the present; it held out hope for the future. Without it you were lost, a speck, a nobody. I'd had a taste of life without it, a stranger in a strange land. But then it didn't feel right to speak. My experience was so limited and they knew there was an endpoint to my time away from home.

Fortunately, Míša broke the melancholy atmosphere by turning to me and raising his glass. 'And we also celebrate the arrival of our little kangaroo into our home. And for her, Czech pizza—no pork *řízek*!'

'Hurrah!' I shouted, cheered and hungry.

Jarda's friend brought out plates of Czech-style pizza and we tucked in. They were adorned with tomato paste and herbs, burnt crisp at the edges, and they tasted fantastic—I'd forgotten how good a pizza could taste. We ate and laughed and watched white swans gather along the tree-lined water's edge. More boats and ferries cruised past. Jarda and Míša did their best to translate the free-flowing Czech conversation and numerous jokes. It didn't even matter that I couldn't understand most of the conversation. The fact that I could talk in English if I wanted to—not to mention that I was surrounded by people who knew both this place and my own—was sheer bliss.

At some point Karel moved down the table to sit opposite me. 'I am most curious to know why you are here with us, Tanya.'

I tucked my hair behind my ear, girlishly glad he wanted to know my story, and I told him.

'You are unusual, Tanya, to come here alone. It is courageous thing to do. Especially to go out to somewhere like Sedlčany where they would have almost no experience with the West.'

'But that is the reason,' I said breathlessly, remembering why I'd come in the first place. 'To learn about places that no one else in Australia knows about. To have those experiences. And—' I paused, took a chance, 'I've also dreamt of finding somewhere like your Prague since I was a little girl, since I saw pictures in fairytale books.'

Karel leant back, put his arms behind his head. 'Ah, so you are a romantic too. Perhaps you are Czech girl at heart—one of us.' He held me in his gaze, his eyes as blue as a Central Australian sky.

I blushed, rushing on. 'Your part of Europe represents one of the last great areas to explore. Not just for romance, but for history, for politics—everything.'

'*Tak*! You could be a spy too, like your James Bond.' His eyes twinkled as he refilled my glass. 'It is big pity you did not come when communism was here. You could have tricked our special Chief Comrades. They would have had no chance against your charm and cleverness.'

I giggled.

'But you are lawyer, yes? In our country, our Dear Comrade Leaders would not let us to try something for the fun. We are given some special role and we stay working there until we are allowed to retire or die—whatever our Leaders let us do first. We must live our lives'—he spread out his hands as though preaching from the pulpit—'for the glorious benefit of the glorious Motherland.'

I couldn't tell if this was another joke or not, but Jarda came to my rescue. 'Karel, it is not unusual for Australian people to leave jobs, to visit Europe. They have not had special experience of life under communism where our Comrades dictated how we live.'

Then it was on: everyone joining in, shouting out stories about the risible requirements of the former regime. It seemed Karel's joke had more than a grain of truth in it (and he assured me that if the Comrades decided it was time for someone to die, they made it happen).

'You should read Kafka,' he said, 'if you want to understand what it was like to live under totalitarian regime. Kafka was ahead of his time.'

There was Kafka again. My eyes locked with his. It was both terrifying and intoxicating to be part of this strange discussion, or at least the cause of it.

'But if you want to really understand the Czech psyche, Tanya, and how we survived under occupation, you must read *The Good Soldier Švejk*.'

I was about to ask him what he meant when the strangest thing happened. The group started wheezing and snickering, shoulders shaking, guffawing and howling, banging the table, roaring, 'Švejk, Švejk, Švejk', as though he was a favourite son or famous football player.

'Ah, Švejk!' repeated Karel, when he managed to recover from his own chortling fit. 'Let me explain. It is our famous novel about how most stupid drunkard soldier could outwit his occupiers by being both stupid and drunk.'

I stared at him. This was the cultured country Peter Barr had talked about? Stupidity meant survival?

Jarda stepped in to assist. 'It is a book from Austro-Hungarian occupation time but is famous as a symbol of our resistance. For we Czechs to endure our many occupiers, we have played a game against them. We pretend they are very brave and important and that we are the fools and buffoons, but really it is the other way round.'

I tried to understand. It appeared the greater the power and cruelty wielded by the authorities, the greater the satire heaped upon them by their subjects. The authorities—of which there was no shortage—would always lose out to the cleverness and wit of their subjects, to the glee and mirth of the subjects.

'*The Good Soldier Švejk* helped us not to go mad, lose our minds,' Karel said. 'We have very good jokes too,' he added, immodestly. '*Tak*, Tanya, still there are these problems. Many of the occupier buffoons remained after Velvet Revolution because they were one of us. They still run our country. And so our jokes must continue!'

My thoughts jumbled about as I tried to make sense of the contradictions before me. We were sitting in a fairytale setting created during the eleventh century, infused with centuries of (mostly) brutal occupation. In this most recent century (at least) the Czechs had learnt to live double lives, pretending and saying one thing while thinking another. No wonder Eastern Europe produced such good spies.

Karel looked at me with his blue eyes. '*Tak*! Tanya, do you have enough stories of the people here for one day?'

I smiled faintly, noting the irony of his comment. There had been more stories today than I could have hoped for.

'And so, it is time for the famous Bohemian Sekt, yes?' He clicked his fingers. 'We need the *šampaňské* to revive after all this difficult talk of our special former regime.'

The owner materialised from the back of the pontoon and popped a bottle. He poured bubbles into tiny breast-shaped glasses. The glasses were 'famous Bohemian crystal', according to Karel, who then gave me a slight bow as he handed me mine. Not only was Karel incredibly interesting, he was ridiculously charming. We might have been at Rick's in *Casablanca*.

Then somebody called out from the back of the pontoon, 'And now we dance!'

Before I knew it, a tape recorder was produced, Czech folk music rang out, and Karel held out his hand.

I was in Karel's arms. He held me in the commanding way of an accomplished dancer and led me in a waltz across the slightly unstable decking. The others joined us, laughing and singing. I was conscious of my stumbling feet and jeans and sand-shoes. I was also aware that Karel had realised I really did want to dance—and that he'd made it happen. My life seemed to be spinning out of control.

'Just relax,' he murmured.

It was not easy to relax. I was also intensely aware of being held so close against his body. He was very tall while I barely reached his shoulder. I breathed in the crispness of his denim shirt and the musky, sweet scent under his collar. Then I tried not to. To do so would be dangerous. I knew the signs; I knew the slippery slope. Yet I couldn't stop myself. I breathed in, shakily, hungrily, like a prisoner starving for air. His hands were strong, with long, graceful fingers like those of a pianist. They curled easily around mine.

It had been so long since I'd been in someone's arms, feeling safe, special, feminine. Dear God, I didn't want the moment to end.

'You know how to dance too,' said Karel, as we ended. He looked down at me. 'Yes, perhaps you *are* Czech girl at heart.'

My cheeks were hot. I didn't want to let go of his hand.

As if he had guessed it, Karel added, 'May I show you something, Tanya?' He led me to the edge of the pontoon, only casually releasing my hand as he pointed up to a line of high dark hills above Prague Castle.

'If you come back to Prague, here is beautiful Petřín Hill to climb. At top is special Eiffel Tower imitation from Paris and most beautiful view of the Prague. Halfway down is monument to our most famous romantic poet, Karel Mácha.' He paused. 'And from there, you will see why they call Prague the "City of a Hundred Spires". In the night-time, they are stars on velvet.'

Stars on velvet?

I thought of the Australian men I knew. Their poetry was football and cricket, the corporate world, the stock exchange, Carlton beer. They shunned emotions and displays of weakness; their pride lay in results, outcomes, legal wins, sporting scores, power.

Yet this Czech man talked about the beauty of 'the nature', the seasons and his city. He talked about bubbles named after Bohemia and could waltz beautifully. He took pride in his country's medieval architecture and nineteenth-century poets.

His blue eyes met mine.

Dangerous sparks flashed deep within. Karel had unlocked something, infiltrated my months of emptiness and starvation for connection. But this wasn't just any kind of connection. It was something different—something I'd hungered for but not been able to find at home, something I couldn't even articulate but had longed for, instinctively, for many years. A man who knew that words of beauty and history and poetry would enchant me.

There and then I wanted Karel to take me back into his arms, to dance with me once more. Perhaps this might be a dance that worked. Could it? I felt like a bird released from captivity: bewildered, vulnerable, open, stretching for the sky.

Warning bells were clanging but I didn't want to hear them.

⸻

The day drew to its inevitable close. As I prepared to leave my new friends, my heart hung heavily. Already Míša and Jarda felt like safe, kind older brothers, and it was a wrench to leave them. As if they were mind-readers, they drew me to one side: there was a plan. In several weeks' time they would all visit another friend, Ludva, at his cottage in the Šumava mountains. Would I care to join them? If so, they said, they could draw me a map and write some instructions on beer coasters, and I would meet them at a town about an hour by train from Sedlčany.

I said yes before they had finished describing their offer. I hoped the beer coasters would work; I had no other way of getting in contact with Míša and Jarda before then. There was a pay telephone at the Sedlčany post office but no guarantee I could get a line to Prague during the day to confirm plans. The phone lines were invariably congested or simply unavailable.

The school had one fax line but none of the gang had access to a fax at their end. The post was slow and unreliable so even writing to each other to organise where and how to meet was risky. The beer coasters were my only hope of finding them.

'Thank you! To all of you, so much. For everything. I can't tell you what this day has meant to me.' *And what hope you have given me*, I added silently.

I stood up to go and catch my bus, unsteady, lightheaded.

Karel quickly held out my coat and stood behind me to help me put it on. As I slipped my arms in the sleeves and pulled the coat around me, he straightened the collar, letting his hands linger on my shoulders. I was intensely aware of him, aware of his fingertips slowly and lightly tracing their way down my arms. He paused, just long enough for me to wonder if he was telling me something but not long enough to know for sure.

I managed to turn around. My breath caught in my throat. 'Thank you.'

Inclining his head, he handed me the corner of a second beer coaster.

'If you have problems, here is my phone number,' he said. 'Unfortunately, there are more people wanting to talk in this country than there are phone lines, but it is for you as . . . how you say . . . a safety rug.'

'Blanket,' I said in a rush, putting both coasters in my pocket.

Míša and Jarda hugged me and everyone shouted farewell. '*Na shledanou!*'

Above me, Prague Castle was ablaze with lights and the city was a glittering fairyland.

Karel turned and fixed his eyes on mine.

Stars on velvet.

14

Do I stay or do I go?

I returned to Sedlčany revived and reinvigorated.

'You seem ten years younger after Prague!' said Naďa.

I excitedly told her about my wonderful new friends Míša and Jarda and then added that I'd met a gorgeous man named Karel. When I mentioned the pending trip to Šumava, she clapped her hands in delight, and prophesied that I'd be staying in her country a lot longer than planned.

But it wasn't only me, and the birds and the bees, who'd been reborn.

Spring had arrived and galvanised Sedlčany. The main square was now filled with teachers and students eating Czech ice cream (a delicacy of which the Czechs were very proud) and, to my surprise, more people were starting to smile. Not necessarily at me, but at each other. The school buzzed with the prospect of excursions near and far: cycling trips to the river, a baroque concert in a nearby castle in which English teacher Blanka lived, student classes in the wider community, and singing with guitars around fires at night. The invitations came thick and fast. I felt like I'd gone to Prague and come back to a different world.

I was particularly excited to hear about the castle. 'There is a castle here in Sedlčany too,' Kamila told me. 'It is very small and beautiful, called Red Castle. I will take you there after school. We can have a picnic.'

I couldn't believe it. To think I'd wasted so long shivering alone in my *panelák* when there was a bona fide castle within walking distance! Did this mean the town Sedlčany might once have been beautiful, in a time before *paneláky*?

'Yes, of course,' Kamila nodded. 'Our town is nearly 700 years old. There will be big celebration in July. Fireworks and parades. You must be here to see it! We can go together and dance all night!'

I leapt back into teaching with my soul restored, eager to embrace all that lay ahead of me. We played lots of music in class, working the nouns, verbs and adverbs around the songs, while the students continued to learn more vocabulary related to the wild outback of Australia. Fortunately the school con-tinued to let me get away with these strange methods because the students seemed to love their lessons.

The skies brightened earlier and evenings lingered. The land-scape emerged from its barren cocoon and stretched out with colour and new life—as did I, enchanted at what was unfolding before me. Winding country lanes overhung with trees of pink apple and white cherry blossom. Delicate primroses and wild strawberry bushes lining the roads. Pretty shades of cream and apricot showering the once bare outline of orchards. Across the hilltops thickets of tall pine trees smelt sweet and musty with the fragrance of fallen cones, and sunlight strands interlaced the woods of oak and beech trees, thick with dense glossy leaves and alive with birds. The unfamiliar cacophony of their songs and calls could be heard from dawn until dusk.

I couldn't believe it. Not only had I just found the fairytale city of my childhood books, I'd found the countryside for which I'd searched in vain throughout England and Western Europe. This was exactly the untouched, fabled countryside I imagined the Famous Five would have cycled through.

Indeed, this countryside was now filled with children cycling up hill and down dale. The students lent me bikes and took me with them on their excursions. I wasn't an adept cyclist, which perplexed them—even three-year-olds were expert cyclists here—but they generously included me in their fun and I revelled in it. If I had had to leave and return to Australia right then, I would have been satisfied, that aching unmet need of 1989 now fulfilled.

I also walked a great deal on my own, after school and on weekends, exploring the woodlands and copses and meadows, safe in my aloneness, singing with my own joy. 'The nature' and I had found one another at last, after a long, frosty beginning, and it was like an overdue meeting of lovers. I couldn't wait to get out into it every spare moment I had, soaking it up, letting its gentle touch heal and caress my arms and legs and face. My soul was restored.

There were trips further afield too. I was invited to go with the final-year students for a week in Moravia, a region in the south. There would be swimming in the lakes and wine tasting in famous cellars buried in the hillsides.

'Do you *really* take students for wine tasting?' I asked Nad'a, to make sure I'd understood correctly.

'Of course—is very cheap.'

That wasn't the point of my question but it raised my curiosity. How much? Approximately twenty cents a carafe. *Marvellous!* I thought, but they were still students.

'Yes,' she shrugged. 'But our students are sixteen, seventeen or nearly eighteen and why not for them to be part of the experience?'

I explained our drinking rules back home. She thought those rules draconian.

'We teachers are happy to have the camaraderie with our senior students. It makes them responsible. Soon they will be in the outside world and it prepares them.'

I was reminded yet again of the difference between our two worlds. Sedlčany was locked in time in so many ways, yet it had both preserved the innocence of childhood for its youngsters *and* treated them with respect as young adults. Every day I scribbled more and more in my diary, increasingly fascinated by this new world.

'Tanya, please come with my cousin and me, and we will cycle to the river this Saturday. I will take you out on my uncle's sailing boat,' said Pavel later that week. 'I want to show you some history and tell you all about how I am going to America as soon as I finish *gymnázium*. Also, you told me you grew up riding horses. Well, my uncle has horses, and we can go there another time too.'

Pavel could always be relied on to come up with great ideas for adventures.

It was bone-chillingly cold on the river that Saturday but exquisitely beautiful as Pavel and his young cousin navigated a little white yacht along the wide, gleaming waterway. We ate sausage and rye bread, followed by apples from Pavel's parents' cellar. On either side of the river, darkly wooded hills towered over the banks, and campfire smoke lazily drifted from the banks where locals were fishing. The water was smooth and reflected the triangular peaks and feathery clouds above us. Canoes and other yachts wound their way up and back along the river and we waved and shouted '*Ahoj!*' as they passed. As the day wore on, we saw their occupants heading back to campsites. Soft reds smudged the tips of the clouds overhead and in the water below, and all around us was absolute stillness.

It was complete bliss.

'Look here, Tanya, you now see this very big house in field in front of us? It is 300 years old. We will stop by side of river and walk to it.'

A large house, almost overgrown with ivy and crumbling with neglect, stood alone in a grassy patch. Yet with its fading frescoes on the walls, a large entrance hall and high windows, it had evidently once been a stately home. We peered into the dust and cobwebs hanging off the cracked chandeliers and Pavel told me the story.

'When the communists took over our country after the war, they sent many people to jail. Like the man who owned this house. They chopped off his finger, let him starve to forty-five kilos.'

'*Why?*'

Pavel explained that the communists intended to make it clear that there was no place anymore for the bourgeoisie. Property, business and money now belonged to the state, for the greater glory of the Soviet Union. Industries and businesses were nationalised, and private properties, like this one, were confiscated. The owners were tortured to 'send the message'.

I tried to imagine what that would be like: a rap on the door in the middle of the night, the secret police descending upon our home to take Dad away as punishment for having spent his whole life working hard to build a business and provide for his family. I shuddered at the thought of him locked away in a solitary cell, starving, minus a finger.

Yet perhaps this man was lucky, Pavel said. In the nearby village lived an eighty-year-old woman whose husband had survived a Nazi concentration camp in Poland only to be executed by the communists on his return home to Czechoslovakia. His crime? Also for being 'too bourgeoisie'—a term, it seemed, designed to catch anyone who did not worship Stalin and his so-called Marxist theories and the Revolution in Russia.

Pavel stared out over the field, his face set.

'That old thinking is still here, everywhere, in my country, even though former regime has gone.'

This was becoming a familiar refrain.

'If you want money or want to build a better life, Tanya, there is still shame about that. People gossip, say bad things. They have been—how you say—indoctrinated so long to think it is wrong. It is why I must learn the good English and get out.'

We walked back to the yacht and he hoisted the sail. 'I want to start somewhere new. Travel to America and make money where it is good to do so.'

Those paradoxes again. The East and the West were back-to-front in so many ways, and not just regarding the location of boots and bonnets in cars. The Czech shame of which Pavel spoke was a reference to all that the West held sacrosanct—free commerce and trade, personal wealth, financial freedom—while shame in the West was all about the personal freedoms that the Czechs considered *normální*.

If one took these differences to their logical conclusions, they were both a farce. What was so-called right and what was so-called wrong were simply determined by which side of the Iron Curtain you were born on, or on which side of the globe, or the equator . . . or who was in power, where and when.

Absurd.

It was also the great thing about travel. You could take the views that you had grown up with and tip them upside down, looking at them in a different way, through a different prism. You could come to realise that life was not black and white—as most of us are brought up to believe—but much more complex than that.

I reflected on Pavel's bravery. He might not find the streets of America paved with gold but he'd have a damn good try.

Pavel told me more stories of the history of his country. It was difficult to get the stories out of older people; mostly they didn't want to talk about it. But Pavel was open and as keen to teach me as I was to learn. Studying Modern European History with Mrs Howe in Year 11 was an entirely different experience to hearing it live, especially from someone whose country had been so affected and traumatised during the twentieth century. Pavel made it clear it wasn't just the communists who had caused great trauma. There had been many occupiers prior to that time.

The Czech Republic's location seemed to be its major problem. Being situated in the geographical centre of Europe without natural borders (like mountains or a sea or a port) and without a large, fierce army, made the region a natural and easy target for aggressive predators. For centuries the Kingdom of Bohemia was controlled by the Holy Roman Empire; then by the seventeenth century it was controlled by the Austro-Hungarian Habsburg empire. After World War I and the collapse of the empire, independent Czechoslovakia was born to much celebration. For twenty precious years, literature, music and political debate flourished.

Nazi Germany, however, changed all that. They marched in with their hobnailed boots and tanks to occupy the country prior to and during World War II and did their best to wipe out all the Czech Jews and anyone else they didn't like.

Pavel mentioned the name of a village close to Sedlčany.

'When the Nazi soldiers arrived into those villages, young boys, much younger than me, were forced to dig graves for their parents. They had to watch as their parents were shot, then put the bodies in the graves. They were loaded into trucks for Polish concentration camp. Most did not return. That village is filled with headstones and sadness that cannot be cured.'

As I was coming to terms with that, he added, 'There is one Czech village called Lidice that the Nazis totally destroyed. They killed everyone and burnt the town and buried it so it did not exist anymore. The Nazis even took the name of the town off the Czechoslovakian map.'

Then he told me about Terezín, a town that the Nazis turned into a concentration camp. 'More than 200,000 people were sent there. Nearly three-quarters died from terrible conditions, hunger, torture. If you visit, you can still see some children's drawings. The children drew of the life around them. It is very'—he paused, tilted his head—'special. Today we can be thankful many of these pictures survived even if the children and their parents did not.'

I wondered how people could grow up with these layers of atrocity without being affected. I supposed the answer was that they grew up anyway, and the atrocities did affect them. The silent, closed faces of the people in Sedlčany reflected lives that had known more oppression, grief, terror and sorrow than someone like me could ever imagine.

It occurred to me that the history of oppression of this country must be one of the reasons the Czechs celebrated their 'nature', as they called it, so intensely and held onto their culture so proudly. When so much else was taken away from them, the essence of their souls was still represented in those lovely things, embodying what it meant to them to be Czech.

I knew I'd soon have to decide what to do once the school term ended. The teachers had kindly invited me to stay on for the next term and I was thrilled at their faith in me. I loved my students and felt there was so much more I could do in my role to help them grow in their knowledge and use of English. There was also a great deal more I could learn from the students; unlike the adults, they were neither closed nor intimidated by speaking out on anything in which they were interested. My hand could barely keep up with my thoughts each night as I recorded all I learnt in my diary.

Yet, like a mythical siren, Prague called through my dreams.

Míša and Jarda had reiterated the greater possibilities that existed in Prague and Karel had gallantly offered to assist. It was an intoxicating thought. Not only would there be the chance to speak more English, but perhaps I could carve out a life in that fairytale city—and, I had to admit, be closer to Karel. While I'd only met him once, I'd seen something in his eyes that I knew I wanted to connect with further.

It was a struggle to decide on the right thing to do.

Sedlčany now held my heart in a way I'd never expected. And I didn't know anyone in Prague apart from Karel, and had nowhere to stay and no job to go to. Even Karel admitted he had no teaching contacts there, nor did he know of any English-language schools.

I decided to wait until the Šumava weekend before making my mind up.

15

Šumava weekend

The roads to Šumava were lined with pastel-coloured statues of saints where one could rest and pray, and wave down a bus if needed. But I was nestled inside Míša's little car with one of his colleagues, Pepík, and spent most of the trip to the mountains gazing, enraptured, at the spring scenery, and the real home of fairytales.

Little roads off to the sides were marked with wooden signposts, their squiggly words seemingly designed for fairy folk and leprechauns. We passed through villages where craggy men in peaked caps presided over clip-clopping horses and carts. Tumbledown stone houses of faded yellow were tucked along narrow, twisting streets, and blue chimney smoke curled high into the sky.

In my excitement I talked to Míša non-stop. It was such a relief to speak quickly in English again, without having to stop to explain words. I suspected Pepík, who did not speak English, found it a much longer trip than I did.

At lunchtime we stopped at a tiny wooden *hospoda* at the foot of the mountains. It was smoky and filled with old men drinking beer. Deer antlers and old paintings of Czech hunts lined the walls. It also smelt a lot like drains. After the obligatory *řízek* and *pivo*, I looked around for the 'Ladies WC'. I couldn't find it so asked Míša for help.

He grinned and pointed to a door with a picture of a man in a cap. 'You go in there.'

That sounded odd but I nodded nonchalantly to show I was an experienced traveller and unafraid of new experiences. I headed off and pushed the door open.

And crashed into another room.

Full of urinals.

And men.

And a stench so bad I thought I would bring up my *řízek*.

Several men were lined up against the wall, spraying urine everywhere and yabbering. They leered drunkenly at me as I walked past. One had no teeth, just red gums, and was leaning against the wall, fumbling with his fly and smoking. At the end of the room was another door that inside offered three cramped cubicles.

Dear God, let this be the Ladies, I prayed, hoping no one would follow me. I rushed into the first filthy cubicle, then as quickly as possible rushed back out, washed my hands and ran past the men smirking openly at me. My heart banged all the way back to the table.

Míša laughed and told me about an old Czech joke: 'You can find a Czech pub in any village by following the stink of WC.'

I was still in a state of disarray when we headed out again. Worse, after another hour my bladder again demanded attention, and I begged Míša to stop.

'You need to go *again*?'

'It's the *pivo*,' I said through gritted teeth, jumping out. What did he expect, anyway? One-litre glasses of beer were way too much for this Australian novice.

Rushing into the nearby forest, I crouched down in relief but almost as quickly I jumped up, screaming. Once Míša stopped chortling, he said I'd most likely planted my bottom onto the country's famous *kopřiva*—stinging nettles—and I spent the rest of the trip to Šumava clutching my rear, whimpering in agony, while Míša and Pepík wiped the tears from their eyes. So much for the impressive reunion I'd imagined with Karel.

By the time we arrived at a small stone cottage nestled in a picturesque valley, I was no longer focused on anything but pain and rage against Czech toilets, *kopřiva*, bladders and beer. Míša had promised me that our host Ludva would have some ointment that would soothe the stinging and I'd begged Míša to take me straight to him. The last thing I wanted was for Karel to see me like this.

But Karel, Jarda and his wife Jitka, and a bubbly Czech-Australian blonde named Naďa were heading towards us, intent on hugs, backslapping and cheek kisses.

'Taaaarnya, how good of you to join our small gathering in the mountains,' Karel said chivalrously as he helped me out of the car. It was the same disarming, halting textbook English I remembered. He shook my hand and kissed my cheek.

For the first time I really noticed that everyone was older than me—not that it made any difference to how we connected. I also noticed that Karel was dressed in the same faded blue jeans, denim jacket and white T-shirt he'd worn on my visit to Prague. As I gazed up at him, I lost all sense of feeling and was reduced to offering only a finger-twisting, breathless 'Thank you!'

Míša quickly explained the predicament of 'Tanya and the WC and the *kopřiva*' and amid much suppressed laughter Karel leapt in.

'Oh dear—our WC in country pubs are special experience. And our famous prickle plants most unfortunate. May I recommend you spend more time with me? I would not let such problem happen. I am expert in the Czech nature.' He shook his finger at Míša. 'My poor friend here has spent too long in Australia and forgotten about our dangerous countryside and its pubs.'

Míša retorted with something unpronounceable, then said to me, 'Now I take you to Ludva for recovery, my little kangaroo.'

Ludva was a tall, charming man with a red beard who we found chopping wood at the back door like he belonged in another century. He and Míša shook hands, with more robust backslapping. On hearing my story, Ludva said, 'Goodness me, come inside with me, please, Tanya. I can help.' He spoke very good English, which was not surprising; when the Czech-Australians had headed Down Under, he had headed to England, where he had lived ever since.

'Let me see . . .' He searched in an overflowing cupboard and pulled out a tube of ointment. 'It is not so new but it will help take away the pain of the stinging nettles. It has magical Czech properties!'

'Thank you,' I gulped, red-faced.

He pointed to a tiny room at the back of the cottage and I ran, ointment clutched between my fingers.

When I emerged I felt much better, largely thanks to the magical properties of Ludva's ointment. But I felt awkward and embarrassed. I hovered nervously in the doorway, not knowing what to do. Everyone was sitting on benches around a large fire outside the front door, layered in jackets and scarves, chatting away in Czech and drinking beer. The Gang, as they called themselves, were in high spirits.

Eventually, I forced myself to move out of the shadows and Karel saw me. He stood up and gestured for me to sit next to him. I smiled shyly, my anxiety subsiding, my bottom completely recovered in that moment.

'*Tak*! I hope you feel better now, Tanya. And how is life in the Sedlčany?'

But before I could answer, he conjured a rolled-up newspaper like a magician.

'I have brought for you this American paper from Prague. *The Prague Post*. It has some work advertisements for English schools in it. It may help if you are still interested.'

My fingers shook as I took the paper, thrilled, and devoured the English words. Karel couldn't have given me a better present. I loved newspapers but hadn't read one for nearly three months. This one was full of stories of life in Prague that I understood: politics, expats, jobs. There was also a world news section, with stories on Britain and the United States and the troubles in Yugoslavia.

I flicked through excitedly for advertisements and sure enough they were there. 'Karel, there are three schools looking for English teachers!' I cried out. Two had unpronounceable names but the other, surprisingly and simply, was called 'English House'.

'*Tak*! This seems, how you say, a promising sign, yes?'

'Yes, yes!' I had an overwhelming desire to hug him, then restrained myself. 'Thank you so much, so very much.'

Prague now felt possible in a way it hadn't before.

—>•<—

Two more couples arrived: Standa and Ivana, and 'Growing Boy' Peter and Vladěna. They were childhood friends of the group, and were charming and welcoming to me.

Standa was great fun and he had a cheeky laugh. He told me Karel was responsible for Peter's nickname 'Growing Boy', which celebrated the stomach Peter was growing as a result of a lifetime drinking beer. Growing Boy rubbed his impressive stomach, his eyes twinkling mischievously. Ivana was blue-eyed and blonde-haired, while Vladěna was petite with huge, beautiful eyes. Both women spoke a little English. I loved them all immediately.

'Time for celebrations,' said Ludva, officially declaring the party had begun. His neighbour had caught a pig in the forest a few hours before our arrival and the Czechs were wild about their game. Large and pink, this hapless pig was now turning and roasting and crackling before us on a spit, giving off succulent aromas. The neighbour had also brought mushrooms, picked in the same forest last autumn and preserved. Hunting and gathering were de rigueur in the mountains.

'This is like being home.' I turned to Karel. 'We used to kill our own meat too. It was normal to live off the land like this.'

My past and that moment in Šumava lurched against one another, careered, bounced.

'This is very interesting,' Karel said. 'Perhaps we have more in common than not, Tanya?'

He held my gaze and I wanted the moment to last forever.

As the stars emerged overhead, we ate and drank our fill, and then it was over to the real business of the evening: music.

Instrument cases were opened. Jarda, Karel and Ludva tuned up their guitars and Míša handed me his.

'Tanya, you tell me you play guitar with the students, so please, we would like you to play "Waltzing Matilda" for us.'

Most of the Gang were serious musicians and had played for decades. Many of them still performed in bands. Yet here they were, together after so long, watching an Australian girl coming off a much lower base. I held the guitar nervously and looked up at them all. Like a teenager, I wanted them to like me, to like my playing, but I was only a three-chord-wonder girl. For a moment I was paralysed. Then I put my head down, took a breath, and after a few strums the music took me with it and I felt the familiar elation that came with being part of something bigger than myself.

'Waltzing Matilda' turned into a huge jam. Everyone joined in with vocals, lead and bass guitar, banjo, mandolin and plenty of harmonies. The cottage and the nearby countryside were rocked with song. By the time I'd finished, I was flying high. I'd passed the test, playing in front of such accomplished musicians, and I saw Karel's eyes upon me. Our eyes locked, held, I laughed out loud with happiness. Perhaps he would want to play music with me again. Perhaps I could learn some Czech folk songs from him.

Later, much later, we crawled into our sleeping bags. I dozed off to the chuckles of Ludva and Karel, who were still telling jokes, and Vladěna's cross '*Sklapni!*' ('Shut up!')

I wished my sleeping bag was closer to Karel's.

Then I told myself to *sklapni* as well.

———————

Over strong black coffee, dark bread, cheese and yoghurt the next morning, Ludva announced, 'Today we make trip to our famous nearby castle.'

Back home, if anyone had said on a Saturday morning they were off to visit a castle, they would have been telling stories— literally. There were no castles in Australia and, furthermore, the Australians I knew considered the weekend a sacred time of relaxation and sport. Gearing up to explore places of culture and history was unheard of. Yet this activity was commonplace for Czechs.

We headed towards Velhartice hrad, a ruined thirteenth-century monolith that once housed the crown jewels. Even from a distance, the tower soared above the countryside. The castle itself had massive stone walls that reached for the sky, like the castle in *Jack and the Beanstalk*. A red turret perched on the pinnacle of the tower like a cherry.

'Special, yes?' Míša grinned.

Yes—extraordinary, in fact. Any minute I expected to see Jack climbing up over the top and a giant stomping past shouting, 'Fee-fi-fo-fum . . .'

Inside the castle walls there was an enormous cobbled entrance, and beyond that a small ticket booth. The place was deserted except for a fierce lady wearing a grey cardigan and pinafore who peered out of the booth She appeared to hold the dual role of castle guard and ticket attendant.

The Gang became increasingly noisy—no doubt excited at seeing a castle after so long—and Jarda shouted 'Shhh!' Perhaps there were rules in castles, so I followed his instructions and did what I was told, excited and a bit nervous myself.

But as Jarda headed for the ticket booth, the Gang became even noisier. Then they started to act like, well, bored school-kids. Growing Boy and Standa wrestled with Míša and Karel until Míša and Standa fell to the ground, legs splayed in the air, crowing with laughter. Pepík stuck out his tongue at Jarda, Ludva stuck his fingers up his nose, and meanwhile Jitka and Naďa, and Ivana and Vladěna held hands, pulled faces and giggled like naughty little girls.

Er—was there something in Jarda's instructions I'd missed?

All the while Jarda and the ticket attendant continued to speak, with much gesturing and pointing towards the group with earnest, solemn faces. Eventually Jarda concluded his conversation. Nodding to the lady in apparent thanks, he rounded up the group and herded us towards the entrance. Everyone shouted and pushed and shoved, ignoring Jarda's stern tones of admonishment. I followed, mystified. It was only once we were inside an ancient and empty hallway that the Gang fell apart in hysterics.

'What is going on?' I begged, the only one left out of the joke.

In between snorts and chuckles, Jarda told me he had persuaded the attendant that he was overseeing a group of inmates from a mental asylum in Prague and, after observing the antics of the Gang, the attendant had accepted the story and let everyone in at half price. This trick proceeded to keep the Gang in stitches for hours.

But why do it? It made no sense to me. The tickets weren't expensive, and the Gang were more than grown-up. Why pretend to be psychiatric patients?

Then I remembered that outwitting those in authority was still a national sport. It was not the principle of saving money that motivated the Gang; it was the sheer pleasure of continuing to outwit those who held rank, right down to a ferocious-looking ticket attendant guarding an old castle.

'As you say in English, old habits die hard,' Jarda said with a wicked grin.

'You are lucky,' said Karel. 'You have now seen the antics of Švejk in the live.'

Back at the cottage that night, I raised the topic of Prague and everyone agreed I should apply to the schools.

The general view was 'Proč ne?' ('Why not?') 'You can always visit Sedlčany if you miss your friends there, but Prague is good for someone young like you.'

I wasn't so young—thirty-one felt almost ancient to me—but I knew they considered me young. Naive, too, and probably foolhardy. As a result of some surreptitious questioning, I'd concluded the Gang were all about fifty, yet they had the energy and humour and joie de vivre of people half my age.

'You are very welcome to stay with me while you find what you want,' Karel added.

My stomach leapt about a bit at this point. It was a tempting offer, and slightly dangerous.

Actually, it was ridiculously dangerous.

'Thank you, but I wouldn't want to impose.' My voice was jerky.

Karel laughed. 'Není problem. We Czechs all like to be together, you can see that. We cannot have you on your own in Prague. That would not be nice for you—or us.'

The pressure slid from my shoulders and I thanked him. Despite Prague's glittering allure, it was a big step to take.

'I can help you learn about Prague, too, if you wish,' he added. 'Every day I crisscross all of the Prague by foot. It is necessary for my work as engineer to know every tiny street and historic building like, how you say in English, the back of all my fingers.'

'Hand,' I automatically corrected him, and then flushed.

He stretched out his fingers languidly.

'This is good. I can tell you are good teacher. In the past I learnt from secret books and newspapers and sometimes could even tune into forbidden frequencies on radio, like BBC. It kept my hope and spirit alive. Now it will be great to have personal lessons!' He beamed, adding, 'I try to make my two daughters to learn as well.'

My jaw dropped and my stomach lurched.

I should have realised he was married.

Karel went on smoothly. 'My eldest daughter Šárka, who is twenty-one, speaks English quite well. I would like her to have chance to speak more. My youngest daughter Radka, who is eighteen, does not speak English. This is despite my encouragement. Perhaps you would also be very good teacher for her.'

'Yes, yes of course, if she would like to learn.' I tried to sound professional. 'And'—I couldn't help myself—'your wife?'

He paused again, a beat. 'There are just my girls and me.'

'Ah.'

'Yes. When Míša and Jarda escaped in 1968, I stayed to be with my wife and family. Simply, I could not leave my country. But my wife and I are divorced many years now. My girls are the most precious thing in my life.'

My head banged with conflicting thoughts. I felt overwhelming thankfulness that Karel wasn't married, yet bewilderment; he was a man of responsibility with daughters. I had not anticipated this. Images of the two Karels collided, crashed.

***

I don't know why I hadn't imagined Karel with children and a family. Perhaps it was because he seemed so free-spirited. He had an ease about him, a lack of burden; he took joy in life. He didn't seem like an old, weary father but a Pied Piper, especially with this group. He told most of the jokes and kept people in stitches.

The jokes inevitably came with a *Švejk* theme.

He would start in his drawling way with something like, 'Have you heard the one about the Russian Special Minister of Defence and the Czech Next-in-Line Special Minister of Defence at the special parade at the Kremlin with their two helpful Good Workers of the Motherland . . .' He would then insert Švejk-esque characters and on it would go, with the Good Workers causing mayhem and madness until both Ministers were either (a) sent to Siberia, (b) sacked, (c) demoted, or a combination of all three, with the Good Workers then cheerfully going off to the pub. Each story could take a good half an hour, with the Gang wheezing and slapping their chests and falling about in hysterics.

Even to my uneducated ears the jokes were hilarious and Jarda confirmed they were really clever, not just in their themes but in the way the words were put together: the use of Czech wit, the play on words. Not everyone could tell a Czech joke cleverly, he said. If you got the emphasis wrong or one word in an incorrect place, it would fall flat.

Karel had the gift.

He was also a magical musician. As I watched his long, elegant fingers move across guitar strings and listened to his gentle harmonies, I decided I could adjust to the new Karel. The one with daughters. The one who would actually make things safer for me. There'd be less chance of me fantasising about romantic possibilities, and less risk of falling down that slippery slide of unrealistic hope.

I was also dealing with a growing sadness. The Czech-Australians were flying home the following week and Ludva was leaving for England. I'd felt so strong and safe with Míša and Jarda. Then I remembered Jarda's words as I'd left the restaurant at Benešov and blinked back the salty tears. I didn't want them to think me cowardly or not up to the job. I was an explorer, a foreign correspondent, a lucky traveller who had a passport to leave, and I knew I was morally obliged to make the most of my experiences.

The Gang dropped me off at the nearby railway station at the end of the weekend as Míša had to return directly to Prague. It would require four train changes to get back to Sedlčany but the boys had prepared the usual notes and this time I felt more confident.

'Last piece of advice for the train,' said Ludva, handing me my backpack. 'Don't talk to people you don't know! Look what happened when you did that last time!'

Much laughter, hooting. I hugged them all tight, struggling to get out the words.

'Thank you for everything. I will miss you so much.'

'Remember, Táničko,' Míša urged me. 'Let life touch you! But not too much our famous stinging nettles!'

'This will soon be nice memory,' Jarda warned, 'so make the best of your time here.' As usual, he'd read my mind. 'We will see you back in Australia.' It sounded so normal.

'You will have me now, if you so wish,' Karel said chivalrously. His lips swept my cheek. 'Try me by the special Sedlčany telephone when you are ready and I will meet you in Prague.'

How very Czech. How very relaxed. No forward planning, no dates or time. *Just call and I'll be there.*

I touched my cheek where Karel's lips had been. Leaning back against the train seat, I looked up into the sky and dreamed about the new life I was creating.

16

Last days

Resigning from Gymnázium Sedlčany was the hardest part. But once the dreaded deed had been done (and I'd shared a gasping, glacial glass of *slivovice* with Headmaster Zdeněk to seal the deal), I felt the burden slip away, replaced by a sense of freedom to plan my next steps.

I decided to throw a farewell party for the female teachers in my *panelák*. Having experienced such wonderful hospitality during my time in Sedlčany, I wanted to return the favour. The week before the party, I handed out invitations to the English teachers and some other women in the *gymnázium* I'd met since arriving: twelve invites in all.

'Ooh, Tanya!' Naďa's eyes lit up. 'Thank you. It is excellent idea. I am sure people will be very happy to come especially as a chance to say goodbye.' As she rushed out the door to a class, she added over her shoulder, 'No teacher has ever done this before.'

The pressure was on.

I went shopping to buy the kind of food I had seen others prepare. That meant I had to brave the supermarket, but fortunately I now knew the rules, so over several days I used the trolleys correctly and bought sufficient items until I had everything I needed. I focused on *chlebíčky*, small slices of baguette topped with egg, mayonnaise, onion and salami; quark cheese to spread on rye bread (a delicious and equally popular snack); packets of salted nuts and chips; Bohemian Sekt; and red and white wine.

On the day, puffing and panting up the hill with the last bag, I felt oddly pleased to be like the other women I had seen labouring along the streets with their provisions.

Twilight fell outside the window on the evening of my party. I rushed around trying to make my little flat look presentable, laying out the few plates and glasses I had in my cupboard. As 7 p.m. approached, I became increasingly nervous. To start with, none of my food was homemade, which meant the teachers would finally discover I couldn't cook.

That mattered because Czech women cooked brilliantly—all of them, it appeared. Indeed, no matter how hard the former regime had made them work, Czech women found time to be domestic geniuses in the kitchen. I had no such excuse. *Too late to worry about my reputation now*, I thought. I set the food out in neat little rows, put the nuts in bowls, and arranged the wine, Sekt and glasses in front.

At the last minute I rummaged through my case, trying to find something presentable for a party, and pulled out a cream, lacy, slightly scrunched top. It was pretty, I hadn't worn it here before, and it would do. I threw it over jeans and brushed my hair, even added a touch of lipstick. I was almost ready.

My last touch was to click 'play' on my tape recorder, and soon Smetana's *Má Vlast* filled the room with its soaring violins and Czech nostalgia.

Naďa arrived first, beaming, brandishing flowers and Bohemian Sekt. 'To celebrate your first of many parties in our country.' At my raised eyebrows, she added. 'Yes, do not worry, we will see you again. We will visit you in Prague and have parties there!'

Blanka, who lived in the castle, arrived next, looking as angelic as ever and carrying a tray. 'Czech delicacy—*ovocné knedlíky*,' she smiled, gently. 'I made them for you.' She put fruit dumplings down on the table. I knew they were delicious and thankfully I now had real food to add to the table. We opened one of the bottles of Sekt and clinked glasses.

Old Maruška entered carrying an apple strudel, for which I knew she was famous, and now I was truly overjoyed. The table was starting to look fabulous, full of beautiful things to eat. I poured more champagne and the bubbles and music fizzed through us.

The last three English teachers, Staňa, Maruška and Head Teacher Jindra, brought flowers and wine. Deputy Headmistress Lenka swept in, beehive as erect as ever, bearing a plaque of Sedlčany for me to 'take away and keep as special memento'.

Next came the final five women I had invited: smiling, dark-haired Jarka who had taken me to Benešov where I met the Czech-Australians; Helena, the classical music teacher who was happy to hear her music tapes in action; guitar-playing Lidka; and School Secretary Jana with her young assistant Iveta. They all brought flowers, more food, wine and champagne.

By now there was enough to eat and drink for months to come. My room, designed to hold one or two people at most, was crammed to overflowing. We sat on boxes, the floor, my bed and a window ledge. It was like a uni party all over again.

I raised my glass of Bohemian Sekt to the group.

'*Na zdraví*! Cheers! Thank you all so very much for coming tonight. I wanted to thank you all for welcoming me here during this term, for your generosity, for your kindnesses.' I looked around at them all and my voice faltered. 'I could not have made it without you and I will miss you all very much. And I'm particularly touched by your gifts—the flowers, the treats—I didn't expect them and this is such a special way to say goodbye.'

The English speakers translated my words to the others. They laughed, smiled. We clinked glasses noisily, drank to each other's health and refilled our glasses. We found the common thread of female connection through hands and laughs. We told stories in half-Czech and half-English, and I wanted the night to last forever.

'Do you have parties like this in Australia?' asked Naďa, squashed up against the heater, one long, elegant leg crossed over the other.

'In a way, yes. The world over, women are women. We are all the same.'

There was a slight murmur of dissent, a rumble of words, conferral.

Finally, someone asked, 'But no husband and children yet?'

Hmm. Just as it was back home, my unmarried and childless status was unusual here too. Czech women married in their late teens or early twenties at the height of their beauty, and had beautiful children, usually about two.

Not to marry and not to have children meant one (or more) things in this country: that you were a lesbian, or a spinster, you were not at all beautiful or, worst of all, you were a feminist. The last was so reviled that there were virtually no feminists to be found.

When I'd asked the teachers some months earlier why feminism had a bad rap, they'd explained that the former regime lambasted feminism as a product of the Wicked West, and therefore no one had dared support it.

I was shocked. 'But feminism is about liberation for women—more respect, challenging the unfair status quo, empowerment, good things like that.'

Apparently not. The regime had shouted from the rooftops that it represented resistance to authority, which was a punishable crime. More insidiously, the message was that feminism would make women harsh, ugly, strident, and no longer feminine or beautiful. Thus it became a self-perpetuating circle that no self-respecting or law-abiding woman would go near.

'We don't need some angry, unhappy label to tell us who we are, to make us feel better,' they'd said. 'We Czech women know who we are. We are confident in ourselves.'

Well, the propaganda had worked. Even women opposed it, without question.

I suspected the real reason the authorities damned feminism was that it questioned a system in which men were very comfortable: Czech women worked all day, and when they were not at work they ran the households, did the shopping and (brilliant) cooking, and looked after the children. Feminism might turn that comfortable scenario on its head. I remembered Kamila once saying that many men went to the pubs and there were many unhappy marriages.

But it was a fine line I was walking and I didn't want to alienate my friends by mentioning the f-word. Especially as the night had gone swimmingly so far.

Nor did I want to have to explain that the root cause of all my love-life problems was a fear of being trapped, and that marriage and children represented the end of freedom as I saw it—a view that was considered abnormal and unnatural by everyone I knew (except for my dear flatmate back home, who was gay).

The room of women waited.

Finally, I said, 'It's a long story. But I guess I haven't found the right person.'

That was it? Silence, wrinkled brows, narrowed eyes. So many men, so many opportunities. What was wrong with me? And what about my ticking biological clock?

Just as I was trying to work out how to escape this conversation, Helena stepped in and saved me with one of her wise-white-witch insights.

'Perhaps you are special case and your time has not yet been right.'

I smiled weakly as she patted my shoulder.

'Perhaps you will find special Czech man and stay with us in our country for always.'

Everyone laughed. Except me. As if riveted to the spot, I stared into her eyes, shivering all the way up and down my spine. 'Er—'

Deputy Headmistress Lenka clearly decided it was time to bring order to proceedings. 'As you say, Tanya, all around world, women are the same. We women hold the life together. We are the strength.'

She might as well have clapped her hands and brought a class back into line. Everyone nodded. They understood. In that moment, political, geographical, cultural and language differences did not exist, had never existed. We shared the desire to connect and understand and support one another. My lack of husband and children paled into insignificance next to the connection we shared as women.

Smiles and laughter echoed down the concrete corridor as my guests tottered towards the lift.

As I lay on my couch bed later that evening, I reflected that the evening had been a kind of coming-of-age party for me. I'd stepped into this world on the train of women's acceptance and kindnesses—women who, four years ago, I would never have met, who I would have been forbidden to meet; women who, years before, would have been described as dangerous enemies of the West, and who would have viewed me with the same mistrust. It was so ludicrous that I wanted to laugh and shout out loud into the darkness.

I drifted off to sleep, Helena's words going around and around in my head: *Perhaps you are special case and your time has not yet been right.*

On the second-last day, I approached School Secretary Jana. She spoke English well and I needed a *big* favour. Would it be possible for me to use the school telephone to call Prague?

'I will see.' Jana's brow creased. There was nothing in their rule books to tell them what to do when a foreigner asked to use the phone. Call the secret police? But they allegedly no longer existed. A lengthy conferral with two colleagues followed, and some phone calls to higher authorities, after which Jana returned to her office and pointed to a telephone on a desk from which I could make my call.

'You will be quick, yes?' she whispered.

Relieved, I nodded my thanks and pulled out the beer coaster Karel had given me in Prague. It was slightly squashed but his number was still visible. I dialled carefully, trying to keep my fingers steady. It took almost ten minutes and ten further attempts, but just as I was about to give up, I heard a male voice on the other end of the line.

'*Ahoj*, Karel,' I said quickly, in case the voice disappeared. '*Jsem tady* Tanya.'

'*Ahoj*, Tanya, and how are *you*?' His slow, lilting tones crackled down the wire. My heart thudded through my chest.

'Very glad to hear you!' I said, a little unnecessarily.

'I am pleased to know this!' His teasing voice rose and fell in that slightly formal way. 'And when will you come to the Prague?'

'In two days. I arrive at the bus terminal at 2 p.m.' I was gabbling. 'I should be at the Old Town Square about 3 p.m. Will that work for you?' Dealing with logistics like this even back home made me flustered. Here it was difficult to stop the panic rising. There was still a chance I could end up in Poland.

Karel's tones were soothing. 'I will be at main metro station at the three o'clock I will wait for you there. Do not worry, Tanya.' He paused. '*Měj se hezky.* Have a nice time until we meet again in the Prague.'

He hung up, and as the phone clicked it was followed by a series of clicks in other offices throughout the school.

Jana emerged from her room. 'Good news! You have friend to collect you.' Her brow had unknotted and she looked genuinely pleased, making no pretence of having done anything other than enjoy my conversation too. 'And a man?'

'Yes, just a friend,' I said, flustered all over again.

I thanked her and backed out of the room.

The former regime may have gone but its habits of surveillance were hardwired.

———◆———

On the morning of my last day, I stood at my *panelák* window. Outside, pale blue skies framed golden fields crisscrossed with dark woods that stretched beyond the town's outskirts. Through the glass I could see two old ladies with pinafores tied around their waists, cutting the grass next-door with scythes. They moved their scythes effortlessly, back and forth in a slow rhythm, as the yellow grass fell into piles. An old man piled the grass onto a horse-drawn cart and climbed up onto it, lifted the reins, called to his horses and ambled off. I tried to imagine a scene remotely like it back home and failed.

I thought of my first month or so in Sedlčany. It was difficult to remember how grim and grey it had seemed. Yet in my hand I held a reminder of those times, a letter that my great friend Michael had written to me from London urging me to 'get out and kick some edelweiss—whenever you're feeling sad!' I reread that and laughed. Most days now my little room was filled with the soaring strings of *Má Vlast*, like velvet caresses to my heart, played joyously to a wide sky and the promise of summer.

I stared out the window and thought of Peter Barr. He'd stayed a whole school year here. He'd done so much that I didn't and couldn't. But I'd given my all in these three months and hoped I'd contributed to the dreams and hopes of at least some of the students. Their wonder, naivety and hope for the world had enriched me beyond words and I'd been humbled by them. At times they made me even feel like I was one of them.

Eventually I'd even realised my *panelák* was a privilege and a gift.

I'd learnt more about myself in this lonely little cell than I would have done in the comfort and safety of a Czech home. Without distractions, I'd had to face myself. I'd come to Sedlčany to escape a place I didn't fit and just found another place I didn't fit. I'd come with fantasies and dreams I couldn't manifest at home and found I couldn't create them here either. I came carrying my loneliness as an unseen weight, but found some peace with myself and who I was in the silence of this *panelák*. I'd found that I was okay after all and I had many reasons to be happy. So what if I wasn't married with children or that I felt strange compared to everyone else I knew? I had music and I had friendships beyond anything I could once have imagined.

This growing confidence meant I'd taken up every single invitation offered to me by the school. I'd been helped by the quiet things too: the soaring lark in a Czech violin, fields of flowers, the trusting eyes of teachers and students, the kindness of strangers. In the silence of my cell, I'd started learning what 'I have confidence in me' really meant, as Julie Andrews had so joyously sung.

———

The last school ceremony was held in the main hallway of Gymnázium Sedlčany, with students hanging over the banisters, sitting on steps and the floor, and standing wherever they could find space. It was stifling hot but everyone had dressed for the occasion, the boys and men in their best nylon jackets and the girls in their best nylon frocks.

In honour of the occasion I'd worn a dress too, a sleeveless cotton one, and strappy shoes. It was comfortably loose, thanks to my strange diet over the previous few months. I definitely wouldn't have lost weight if I'd lived with Sedlčany families: all that *řízek*, for starters.

In my bag, I clutched perhaps the most precious gift I'd ever received—a farewell present from Pavel's class. It was a T-shirt signed by all the girls and boys that said, 'We love you—3A.'

'It is the highest kind of love I told you about—Czech friendship,' Pavel said. 'You are now one of us.'

They all hugged me. My eyes were aching from crying by the time I made it to the hallway.

The ceremony was very formal. Students from each year level were presented with plaques, certificates and flowers. Kamila stood next to me and Naďa waved from where she stood with the other teachers. Both Kamila and Naďa had promised to visit me in Prague and that was a comforting thought.

'Tanya,' Pavel's voice rose above the din. 'Please come forward.' He walked into the centre of the hall bearing the most enormous bunch of deep red roses. As he handed them to me and further clapping ensued, more tears welled in my eyes.

'On behalf of students, and also teachers, please play "Waltzing Matilda" for us. One last time.'

Slow clapping started. Michel, one of my favourite 3B students, put a guitar in my hands. I gazed out into the crowd, now cheering and hollering, and leant forward over my guitar as I'd done so many times here. I took a deep breath. I looked up again, barely able to take in the noise, the faces, the bright eyes, the applause. Trembling, I looked down at the guitar and my fingers. It was all a blur. I put my fingers on the opening chord and trusted my body would do the rest. I started singing and the crowd put their hands together over and over again in a cacophony of sound. I could barely hear myself and then I realised why.

Hundreds of students had joined in with me, slowly at first and then with gusto. They sang lustily, joyously, brokenly. They laughed as they sang. They clapped along in time, wildly, happily. They sang every verse and every chorus with me, right to the last note and the last breathless word. There was a lump in my throat that wouldn't go away.

After a flurry of farewells and kisses my time in Sedlčany was over, dissolving along with the distant blue hills on the horizon, shrouded in the midday shimmer.

17

Hello Prague!

As I waited for Karel on the platform of Staroměstské náměstí metro station, in the Old Town Square, I felt like one of the teenagers I'd just left behind: cotton frock, leather sandals, tattered and overstuffed backpack.

But Karel wasn't there. My palms sweated. Stomach squirmed. Had I done the right thing? Was this all a mistake?

Ten minutes passed.

What if he'd forgotten me?

If he had, where would I go? I hadn't even tried to look for hostels. Why didn't I prepare a backup plan? *Idiot.* Just as I was sliding into panic, I heard my name.

'*Ahoj*, Tanya.'

And through the crowd, a familiar voice. This time my heart leapt. Karel was pushing his way towards me. He leant down to kiss me on the cheek, his eyes smiling, his smooth, unlined cheek smelling of soap and spice. A rush of happiness drowned out my tangled thoughts. What had I been worried about?

'*Tak*. It is good to see you again! You followed my instructions very well.' He gazed down at me with those intense blue eyes. 'Welcome back to our beautiful Prague! I am sorry to be late, but it is always surprise with our special metro as to when and how we arrive somewhere.'

I remembered Jarda saying Karel was always late but smiled up at him before I could stop myself. 'No, it's fine, thank you.'

Of *course* it would be fine. I'd followed my heart and I was here, standing on the threshold of a dream come true. I'd searched all my life to live somewhere as magical as Prague and today I'd arrived. I was standing on this platform with my heart open wide, welcoming in my next adventure where the possibilities were endless—an exciting job, an artist's garret in the old cobblestoned part of Prague, and hopefully time with Karel and his city of stars on velvet.

Karel and I could go into the Old Town Square right now. We could drink champagne in a gorgeous café with a red-and-white-striped umbrella to celebrate my new life and allow the next steps to unfold. Finally, I'd found a man with a bohemian take on life; he was no threat to me, nor me to him. I was ready for some fun at last.

But before I could suggest anything, Karel hiked my backpack over one shoulder and led me down the platform, talking as we hurried along.

'*Tak*. We go to my home in our suburb Prosek. My daughter Radka is preparing the late lunch for us and my other daughter Šárka will join us with her little girl Veronika. We call her "Princess". My daughters are very much looking forward to meeting with you.'

The smile on my face turned lopsided, froze.

His daughters? This soon? And a *granddaughter*? I didn't remember any reference to him being a grandfather. As quickly and thrillingly as thoughts of enjoying an afternoon with Karel arose, they vanished with the speed of a water droplet under a summer sun. I trudged behind him along the platform, unable to think of a response.

The trip to Prosek took a long, hot and wearying hour, which involved climbing up and down many steps in many stations. Even though it was the first time I'd been with Karel on my own, and even though I'd been anticipating the moment, I lost my nerve and voice for most of the trip and sat mute, eyes shut between stops.

When we arrived at Prosek, I opened my eyes to a utilitarian bus stop surrounded by acres of concrete stretching into the distance, beyond which *panelák* blocks reared up like demons. I thought my legs would give way. Oh my God, no. Karel hadn't told me he lived in a suburb made of *paneláky*. No, no, no, not again, no, please . . .

'Yes, thousands of people live here, Tanya,' Karel confirmed as I followed him on a good ten-minute walk to his tower block, perspiration dripping down my back, my cotton dress clinging to my thighs inelegantly.

The air was heavy and stifling. The bitumen burnt and shim-mered with reflected heat. Each block was divided by more concrete playgrounds and more concrete walkways. The layout was virtually identical to that which I'd farewelled in Sedlčany— only it was much, much larger.

My pulse raced with panic and dispair. Time to change tack. I would have to escape. I had not come to Prague to repli-cate my life in another tower block. Admittedly, I'd learnt to appreciate my Sedlčany cell, in an 'I have no choice' way—but now I did have a choice. Tomorrow I'd go out and find some tiny bohemian nook in the Old Town, with views of the River Vltava, near the castle. I'd read in *The Prague Post* of others doing it, so it must be possible.

Fighting the panic and despair, I trudged after Karel into his foyer, up a lift and down a corridor. The entire building was a replica of my *panelák* in Sedlčany, only bigger. I thought if I knocked on the door down the end of the far right, I'd find myself opening it to greet me in some kind of sliding doors nightmare.

However, when Karel opened the door, we stepped into a cool oasis. His apartment was welcoming. There was a breeze. We crossed a tiny hallway into a small living room, neatly furnished with the ubiquitous wooden sideboards and wooden glass cabinets and central coffee table I'd seen everywhere in Sedlčany and that reminded me of Mum and Dad's 1960s wedding furniture. I'd never forgotten my shock at first seeing them, that night at Maruška and Franta's when I learnt that life under communism was more complicated than I had thought.

The centre of Karel's living room featured a squashy couch and two big armchairs; leading off the room was a tiny balcony from which I could feel the breeze. As Karel put down my bag, I thought perhaps I too might crumple with relief.

'This is Radka, my youngest daughter.' Karel puffed out his chest as he headed towards a dark-haired girl.

She was leaning over a stove in the kitchen next to the living room. It was a narrow space. She turned and smiled shyly, all dark eyes, Czech-pretty.

'Hello.' She put her slim hands around Karel's arms. 'I do not, cannot, speak the English . . .' She broke off and said to Karel, helplessly, 'Please, Father . . .'

He turned to me. 'Radka is eighteen and studying English but is nervous. Perhaps you will help her.'

Radka fluttered her long, lacquered eyelashes, released Karel, and then returned her attention to the stove. Expertly, she laid out slices of roast pork on a plate next to thick white dumplings. She was undisputedly the lady of the house. I smiled back, politely, not knowing what to say next. Perhaps some sort of reassurance, given Radka's rather possessive hold of Karel? Like: *Don't worry, I'm not your father's new girlfriend.*

The door flew open and a tall girl strode in, wearing tight jeans, a figure-hugging pink top and long dark hair pulled into a ponytail. Behind her ran a little girl, all blonde curls and eyes for only one person: Karel.

'And this,' said Karel, swinging the child up into his arms, his face lighting up, 'is our Princess. And my older daughter, Šárka. She can speak English.'

Šárka beamed at me, extending a strong hand and speaking in accented but clear English. 'It is very nice to meet you, Tanya! It is nice you come to stay. Welcome to our Prague!'

I felt an immediate rush of joy meeting Šárka. She reminded me of Naďa; glamorous, confident, headstrong, fun and potentially a friend. I beamed back. She was her father's daughter. But then I reminded myself—no matter which way I considered it, she *was* her father's daughter.

Šárka was a single mum and told me all about her busy world as we sat down at a laminate table at the edge of the kitchen. I quickly gathered that Princess Veronika's father was no longer part of their lives and that Šárka and Princess spent time with Karel and Radka as often as they could. I tried to get my thinking in order. This was the world Karel had alerted me to in Šumava. What had he said back then? 'My girls are the most precious thing in my life.'

Well, he hadn't made it up. I was seeing it now, writ large.

'We now have the lunch!' Šárka translated for her sister. Radka served us all with the traditional Czech dish she had made and I thanked her. I was now very hungry, and impressed that it was so beautifully cooked, particularly given my own lack of prowess in the culinary department. Karel opened beers and poured a glass for each of us. It was ice-cold and delicious. While we ate, Princess climbed all over him, planting messy kisses all over his face. He chuckled down at her and everyone laughed and chatted in Czech throughout lunch, with Karel and Šárka translating constantly for my benefit.

Karel told me he had lived in this *panelák* for nearly thirty years.

Thirty? Yes, once assigned a *panelák*, Czech families did not move—or, rather, *could* not. There was nowhere else to go. As I knew, the communist regime had herded them into living groups and taken away their family homes.

Šárka lived in a little flat nearby and usually drove to Prosek in Karel's car. Karel did not drive.

'Why would anyone drive in Prague?' Karel shrugged. 'It was not built for cars and is now very congested. But it is good for Šárka to have it and we go to the countryside often.'

The sun eventually set across the *panelák* city of Prosek, sending rays of soft tangerine and gold across the balcony and soothing us after the heat of the day. We moved to the lounge. Šárka asked lots of questions in English and wanted to know about Australia. Radka pulled out her drawing books and showed me some of her work. She was studying at art school and her pictures were stunning. Princess spent her whole time climbing all over Karel and gurgling happily. Eventually, I relaxed enough to think that this was nice. Weird, but nice.

I hadn't been in a family setting for a long time. The warmth in this family reminded me a little of my own—of Mum and Dad, and of M'Lis, Brett and Benny. Thinking about them brought an unexpected pain to my heart. It had been a long day, with all the emotions of leaving Sedlčany, and I suddenly needed some space and time to come to terms with it all. Excusing myself, I stood up and headed for the bathroom.

It was a tiny, cramped space but, like everything in the apartment, it was clean and neat as a pin. Even through my blur of emotions and fatigue, I felt a wave of gratitude to Radka. She had gone to a lot of trouble to prepare for my arrival. In the space of the bathroom, I wiped my eyes, pulled myself together and returned to the table, ready to express my appreciation for their kindness and friendship.

Outside I found Šárka packing up her bag and Princess smothering Karel in farewell kisses. 'We must go,' she said to me, sounding regretful. 'It has been so nice to meet you, Tanya. My father says you are staying for a while so it will be nice to see you again.'

I had a happy sense Šárka and I could be friends, no matter where I lived, no matter what my connection was with her father.

'Thank you, Šárka!' I said and hugged her. 'I look forward to seeing you too!' Her eyes shone.

Radka farewelled her sister and niece, then disappeared into her room to study for her next art exam. 'I say good night later,' she said, her eyelids lowered. She was very beautiful and I hoped that despite the language difficulties she wouldn't mind me in her space 'for a while'.

'*Tak*! We have some special surprise to welcome you to Prosek, Tanya,' said my host, heading for the kitchen.

My throat felt dry. I really was on my own with him, for the first time, properly.

He reappeared with a bottle of Bohemian Sekt and led me out onto the tiny balcony. The sun had set and the balcony was soft with dusk. He held two round crystal glasses in one hand and a dish of *mandle*—Czech salted almonds—in the other.

'Your favourite *šampaňské*, yes?'

'Yes, yes, it is.' I was surprised and touched.

He popped the cork and poured us a glass each. 'I hope you will enjoy your time here with us.'

The breeze across the balcony had picked up. Karel pulled my jacket off the back of the chair and draped it across my bare arms. I remembered that he'd done something similar at the end of our first night in Prague. Our eyes locked, then I lowered mine, suddenly shy.

'Tell me of your plans, Tanya,' said Karel easily, as he sat back into his chair.

'Well,' I said, regaining my composure, 'I've written three application letters to three schools, but I've not heard back from them. I hope you don't mind—I put your address in the letter in case they want to contact me.'

'*Není* problem. You are welcome to do so whenever you want.'

'Thank you!' I was yet again touched by his openness. 'I've also written to Prague Radio and *The Prague Post*. They need English journalists. Not that I am one, but I thought I might as well have a go.'

Frankly it would be the coup of the year if I got a job in journalism, especially given that it was my long-term dream to become one. I could live in an attic in the Old Town and sit at a café under an umbrella and scribble stories to meet deadlines for these exciting papers.

He nodded thoughtfully. 'You do have the courage, I think, Tanya. As you know, we do not try for different positions here. We start with one and we mostly stay in it all our lives. Where does this courage come from?' His eyes focused on me.

I felt a little breathless at his attention. 'I think growing up in the bush. Well, we had to learn to do things from a young age, give it a go. But I don't think of it as brave. It is a great adventure for me.'

'You are very unusual person, Tanya. I think you will find something in our city, in ways perhaps a Czech person could not.'

I grew hot with pleasure in the darkness.

'Are you applying for full-time jobs?' he added.

'Yes—I've only got three months left on my visa, but the Gymnázium Sedlčany told me my visa can be extended if I have a job. The employer has to tell the government.'

'Ah, the visa process.' Karel clicked his tongue. 'I am afraid that will require lots of time and patience and'—he paused—'special techniques.'

Panic re-emerged. 'Like . . . bribery? Anything worse?'

He shrugged. 'We are still in the world of Švejk, and the bureaucrats have special ways. But I am sure your employer will help you.'

'Er—right.' I didn't feel so confident.

'I will help you too.' His steady tone was reassuring. 'I work with bureaucrats all the time and we will find a way for it to happen. Do not worry!'

I tried to smile and he changed tack, perhaps to distract me. 'And what about your home? Do you not miss your family?'

'Yes, all the time,' I said without thinking. My rush of home-sickness this afternoon had been intense and I was having surges of longing for the land, *my* land, and friends and family. Then I shook myself. 'But this is an amazing opportunity and I want to try everything before I go back. I've a year-long plane ticket until March next year.'

He shook his head, musing slowly. 'It is surprise for me that you can stay away for such a long time. We Czechs stay most of our life where we were born.'

'I . . . I'm a bit of a gypsy.' I paused, emboldened by my own words. 'We don't all live with our families in Australia like you Czechs do.'

He shrugged. 'Perhaps you do not know yourself truly yet. I do not think you can ever really leave your country and your family. They will always call you back, in your heart, in your mind.'

I looked at him curiously.

Before either of us could say any more, Radka emerged in the balcony doorway. She moved like a shadow and said something softly to Karel. He turned and kissed her cheek with the tenderness reserved for a child. They spoke in Czech, after which she turned to me and said haltingly, 'Good night. I go . . . bed.'

'Good night, Radka! Thank you again so very much for the lovely dinner.'

Bed—what a good idea. Aided and abetted by the Sekt, the day had truly caught up with me. 'Karel, I'd like to go to bed too.'

'You will sleep in my bed,' he said.

I was stunned.

'And I will sleep on couch in living room.'

'No! No, Karel, that's not right. I am perfectly happy to sleep on the couch. I'm used to sleeping in all sorts of different places when I travel.'

He shook his head. 'You are a special guest and you shall have my bed. For as long as you stay. For as long as you wish to be with us.'

Nervously I crawled into crisp white sheets on a small double bed in Karel's room. The room was right next to Radka's room, which was smaller again. My head was about three feet from the toilet and bathroom across the narrow corridor. Everything in *paneláky* was small. It was a good thing I was small as well.

'There is no privacy in *paneláky*,' Karel said wryly, as he leant into the doorway to say goodnight. 'For example, we have many old jokes about our thin walls.' He lowered his voice conspiratorially. 'Best joke of all is about a couple lying in the bed arguing about the best way to make love.'

My mouth was suddenly dry again.

'Joke says that next morning the neighbours from *paneláky* above, and below, and each side, meet up with couple at the lift on their way to work, and offer them solutions to their problems.'

He closed the little wooden door behind him, chuckling. I lay there, wishing for a moment he had leant over and brushed my lips with his. Then I told myself I'd been on my own too long and was living in a fantasy land. He had children. He was much older. I was from Australia and, after his words tonight, I was sure he was pushing me back there. I thought of Radka sleeping only a few feet from me on the other side of the flimsy interior wall and shut my eyes.

Resolution time: I would find work and my own place. I would move out as soon as possible, far away from the *paneláky* of Prosek, and I would create my own beautiful, bohemian life in Prague.

18

Velmi starý pes—Grumpy old dog!

After a few days, however, all my good intentions were lost in the thrill and excitement of being with Karel in Prague. During those days he took me with him as he 'crisscrossed the Prague' and I carried with me my own fantasy of fairytales and fun.

Wherever we walked (and there was a lot of walking), we talked. I lapped up his company, his intelligent mind and his easy outlook on life. I was hungry for real conversation and regular companionship, and everything about Karel offered me that. He was older, yes, which gave him an assuredness and self-confidence that were enormously attractive. He made me feel safe and relaxed. I also found the difference in our ages simply didn't matter.

He also had a childlike way of embracing life and living in the moment, a boyish energy that more than matched my girlish energy. Although, to be honest, my energy was wilting some-what in the heat as he marched me here and there, exclaiming,

'You must now see this baroque architecture, Tanya,' or 'This is famous and romantic nineteenth-century building; let us go in and I will show you its ballroom,' or 'Up ahead now you see our Gothic towers. Would you like to climb them and see over all of the Prague?' His passion for and knowledge of the buildings and architecture of the city were born of a lifetime of loving every corner of it. I learned more in those first few days than I could ever have discovered in my faithful *Let's Go Europe*.

Quite simply, I'd never met anyone like Karel.

As we walked his city end to end, he told me stories of life under communism, patiently answering all my questions and offering up thoughts on the new regime. He was less fearful than most other Czechs I'd met, perhaps because life in the city had given him more opportunities and a broader outlook. There was a sophistication in his lightness and absurd humour, and he included at least three long and complicated jokes about the regime per day—more if he found time for them in between visiting the worksites he was project managing as part of the reconstruction of historic Prague buildings.

Perhaps best of all was how he treated me during our time together. He listened to what I had to say seriously. He commented thoughtfully. He respected the fact I had a law degree. He was interested in the law I'd practised. I knew I had the edge of being different and interesting because I was from elsewhere. And there was something else too: he'd picked up that I was a free spirit and that reflected his approach to life.

The days of talking and walking restored my soul. But by each evening my legs ached and my brain hurt and I was ravenous. On the fourth night when I said I couldn't walk *another* step he took me to a beer garden where we sat in dappled light and drank Pilsner Urquell. Basking in his attention, I forgot how tired and sore I was, and soon we were engaged in a passionate debate about world politics.

At one point Karel raised his glass. 'Here now is one of our favourite Czech toasts: to your youth and your beauty! And I should also say—your intelligence!'

'Ha! Every Czech has a sermon,' I responded, using one of his other favourite Czech quotes back at him.

He touched his eyebrows with a grin. 'Touché!'

The waiter brought us more beers.

'You've been so good to me, Karel.' I spread out my arms in the glow of the sunset across the garden. 'This is bliss. I know you're so busy at work and still you've taken a lot of time out to introduce me to Prague.'

Karel waved away my thanks. 'It is no problem for Australian girl who is going to teach me English soooo well.'

I couldn't help but laugh. He was outrageously charming.

He pointed to the Lesser Town slopes behind us. 'One evening in summer—if you stay, Tanya—we can climb to the Prague Castle and see where your famous Mr Havel lives, and visit the palace gardens below.'

'You are quite crazy, you know, Karel,' I said, emboldened by the atmosphere of the evening. 'You've got the passion for life of someone in their twenties, if not younger.'

'We Czechs keep young through music, beer and making love. You should try it one day, Tanya.'

I choked on my beer. I'd managed the first two and he knew it.

'I used to be much more with energy,' he continued guile-lessly. 'When I was young, I worked all day and played all night. I'd walk for hours under the moonlight to go to a party, play some guitar, sing some folk songs, meet some nice girl—but now I am *velmi starý pes.*'

'What's that?'

'It is name my girls give me from time to time.' He grinned. 'Grumpy old dog.'

I laughed. He gazed at me across the wooden table, which was now draped in dusk's colours of crimson and orange. I felt that I would remember this evening forever.

As I sat there and we talked some more, the energy between us changed in some imperceptible way. It was as though Karel was making up his mind about something. And then, as the moon rose and the moths fluttered under the lamps on our table, casting crazy shadows along the wooden benches, he decided. He traced the shadows with his finger, put it to his lips and then, slowly, touched my lips.

The shock was electric; my breath caught. It was as though the earth had thudded up through my body. His fingers were salty from the *mandle* we'd eaten and he let them linger on my parted lips. I couldn't move. Paralysed by the audacity of what he'd done and the intensity of my involuntary response, I realised that everything had changed with that simple act.

Then he took me to the metro and I leaned into him, drunk with beer and desire, rocked by the warm carriage, knowing that if there was any moment to turn back, it was now. But there was no turning back for me; I knew it.

Inside the dark and narrow hall of his apartment, I fell against him, found the warmth of his chest, felt his fingers trailing along my neck. And then I was in his arms.

His lips were in my hair, along my back, around my waist, and I stood on tiptoes and pushed myself into him, hungry for his touch, hungry for kisses after being alone for so long, every cell in my body reaching and expanding for a connection, no longer caring about anything, including the darkness. I knew he wanted my body; I was glad to give it to him, and I wanted his. His mouth was on my mouth, my clothes were on the floor, his body strong against me. Our whispers and cries rose and fell, snatches of laughter between kisses, a sense of profound release as we finally collapsed into twisted sheets.

If the neighbours from the *paneláky* above, below and each side were home, I hoped they slept soundly.

The next morning I woke to an apartment flooded with light. The pillow next to me was indented and still warm. I sat up dazedly and looked around. A bird sang outside my window. I got up and padded to the kitchen. On the table was a note on which was scribbled: 'Táničko, I have gone to the work. Radka is with Šárka and Princess. I will see you tonight. *Měj se hezky* (have a nice day) Karel.'

I looked at the note, felt a flutter of excitement, then folded it up and put it carefully in my purse. I also felt a twinge of guilt for sleeping in when everyone was up and working. But there was nothing to be done except follow instructions so I headed out quickly into the big world of Prague, smiling all over, humming to myself. I wanted to dance and swirl around this beautiful city and make every moment of my intense happiness last. It was as though I was the first girl who'd ever been loved.

In celebration I headed to my favourite place, the Old Town Square.

Feeling bold, I took a table at an open-air café where red-and-white striped umbrellas shaded tourists from the morning sun. There I ordered espresso in my best Czech—'*Jeden kávu, prosím*'—and pulled out my diary, scribbling down my thoughts.

ages with what I'd learnt from Karel over the pre-
and more than a few pages about how I was feeling
The coffee was bitter and the sun warm on my
ated in the pleasure of having connected to another
person who had so obviously wanted to connect with me.

Once I'd finished writing, I pulled out my tattered but faithful
travel guide, *Let's Go Europe*. I was fascinated with the martyr
Jan Hus, whose enormous statue towered over the southern
end of the Old Town Square. Karel had told me about him and
I wanted to learn more. This was the perfect opportunity.

Jan Hus was the great church reformer of the fourteenth
century, burnt to death for the crime—a depressingly common
one—of defending his principles of religious and political
freedom, for highlighting corruption in the Catholic Church,
and for trying to bring truth to the people. Karel had told me
Hus's statue was now a symbol of opposition against foreign rule
and represented the Czech's cry for independence.

'Look at the foot of the statue,' Karel had said. 'There is famous
quote from Hus: *Pravda Vítězí*. It means "Truth Prevails".'

One of the most tragic things about the numerous despots
who had occupied Karel's country over the centuries was their
fear of individual thought, and in particular, truth—in any form.
Brilliant minds and ideas had been regularly crushed, destroyed
and lost because political and religious powers feared them.
Truth was stamped underfoot as corruption gathered pace and
power. The only person whom the Czechs collectively really
considered truthful was The Good Soldier Švejk, which was
ironic in itself.

And, I thought (and hoped), Václav Havel.

My eyes went to Havel's castle on the hill. Thank God he'd
survived; he was now advocating compassion and acceptance

for all, and was finally free from personal risk. I envisaged myself, notebook on knee, pen at the ready, poised to take down his words of wisdom. I'd decided to ask Karel if he thought there was any chance of a meeting.

The air on my skin was soft, the light translucent, and I realised I was looking out at where Beethoven had once walked, and Mozart before him. Each had once trod the cobbled stones of this great square.

I saw them in my mind's eye, in wigs and gowns flowing, proclaiming the beauty of Prague, the city in which, it was asserted by the Czechs, that each felt most at home (even though neither was born here), musing upon their latest compositions and creative endeavours. Here each composed some of their greatest magic and grand theatres were built in their honour. *Amadeus*, the movie about Mozart's life, was filmed right here, among the pastel hues and silver spires and golden palaces. That was the incredible thing about Prague. Despite the brutality over the centuries, creativity still flourished, and the Czechs were now reclaiming it for themselves. They were a resourceful people, despite the abuses that had been heaped upon them during those centuries, and Karel was one of those working day and night to rebuild and re-beautify the ancient structures of the city. I felt a thrill, a sense of pride, that I was here and a part of this.

Offering Hus one last respectful look, I paid for my espresso (including thanking the waiter in Czech, which made me feel like a real local) and headed happily off to explore the other side of the river and Havel's castle.

Before long I was in my own fantasy world. There were little back lanes and alleyways and old shops to discover, achingly beautiful architecture to muse over, bridges, spires, intricate patterns in the stonework, and hidden gardens. Down Golden Lane under the Castle, for example, there were ancient men in little shops that could have been straight out of Grimms' fairy-tales. If I closed my eyes, they danced before me, fashioning horseshoes over hot forges, hammering metal, spinning gold, stirring pots, making spells. Alchemists and magicians once lived in this street; it was a place known for magic and fables and seemed the perfect setting for Grimms' stories and characters.

As did any narrow laneway or crooked street or hidden pathway where, just around the corner, the lands at the top of the Magic Faraway Tree came and went, enticing me to enter for a glimpse but hinting also at the risks if I stayed too long. Magic had its dark side. Prague's history offered a stark reminder of that.

Life back in Australia faded, slipping into the recesses of my mind. Prague was where I wanted to be: learning and absorbing a new life; jumping excitedly from the top of the tree into another land; taking on a new language, love and culture. Right now I didn't want to be anywhere else.

—————

But by the time I arrived back at the apartment that evening, footsore again and very tired, I was harbouring my first twinge of concern. Perhaps it would have been useful to have a discussion with Karel about our 'frisson' before we'd thrown caution—and day-to-day living arrangements—to the wind the night before?

Had we just indulged in a one-night stand (hopefully not, but always best to be prepared for the worst) or something that would repeat itself? (Hopefully, it would.) What did it mean for us and the household and the girls? What did it mean for me and my new life in Prague? What if everything was suddenly, terribly awkward?

I opened the door cautiously, heard Karel whistling in the kitchen and saw Radka watching television. Karel turned towards me and grinned, and in that moment any concerns vanished. His charisma filled the entire apartment, as usual, sweeping me into its wide embrace, reminding me that last night had occurred because every part of my being had wanted it to, and that things tonight looked equally promising.

'How was your day, Tanya?' he inquired as Radka looked up and smiled absently before returning to her program.

'Good, thanks.' I was a little breathless. *What now?*

Nothing, as it turned out. *Should I be worried?*

No. I need not have been concerned about the effect on our home life. The evening passed as normal—I prepared more job applications, Karel and Radka talked at length in Czech about the program she was watching—and then, when it came time for Radka to go to bed, Karel kissed her cheek tenderly and she disappeared.

I stood up. 'Does Radka—know?' I asked awkwardly.

'She was not here last night, so no.'

There was silence. I suspected that meant he wasn't going to tell her either. I didn't know what to say. But Karel didn't appear awkward—on the contrary. He whistled some more while turning down the lamps in the living room and put on some soft Czech music. Then he invited me to join him on the couch, his current bed. He draped his fingers along the back of my neck and found my mouth. Pulling me down on the couch, he whispered Czech words I couldn't understand but I went with him, no longer interested in talking either. He tasted so good and I was hungry for him. If he wasn't worried, why should I be?

Later, much later, I found myself wrapped up in his bed/my bed. He lay looking at me, touching my cheek tenderly, tracing his fingers along my breastbone.

'Are you sleeping here tonight?' I whispered.

'Yes, Táničko.'

I trembled. He'd spoken my diminutive Czech name for the first time.

—————

Karel slept soundly, peacefully. My eyes, however, stayed wide and glued to the ceiling. Despite Karel's reassurances, I couldn't help worrying about what Radka would say when she woke up. I'd come here as a visitor for a short stay and ended up in her father's bed. Was that *normální*? Would she disapprove? Would she tell me to pack my bags and leave?

I remembered Pavel telling me that it was *normální* for hormonal teenagers to stay at each other's homes. He'd looked at my surprised face and shrugged. 'Where else would we go, if not our own bed?'

Perhaps this was the bohemian way of relationships all over this country. We were in Bohemia, after all.

Finally I slept too, hoping the rule applied to this household as well.

19

Looking for work

My life over the next few weeks became a blur. I wasn't sure whether Karel ever spoke to Radka and Šárka about my sleeping arrangements but they appeared relaxed about my presence in their home. It quickly became fun living in a ready-made family (something Peter Barr, no doubt, would attest to), and Karel was the most exciting and alluring man I'd ever met. I couldn't get enough of his energy and his time. Kisses at night, conversations that stimulated my mind, the chance to learn about a whole new city, history and way of life—it was my idea of the perfect holiday romance.

My time with the family was made easy because the girls were lovely. Radka was generous with her space. She and I spoke almost nothing of each other's languages but we shared smiles whenever we passed in the hallway and used finger language when we needed to converse about something. She was also very shy and as a result we led quite parallel lives, with little in common other than Karel. He acted as our go-between. He also (I think deliberately) made no overt displays of affection towards me in front of Radka, or in front of anyone for that matter; he was the same courteous and charming man wherever he was, and he never played favourites.

Šárka visited often with Princess and brought great energy with her. She actually came out and said, 'We are glad you are here! *Táta* is happy too! He was becoming too much grumpy old dog!' And she and I giggled, opened a bottle of wine and toasted the moment. It was the closest thing to an acknowledgement of my current liaison with her *táta* that I'd had. How long it would last, none of us knew, but I realised Šárka had long ago learnt to simply 'go with the Karel flow'.

As I'd surmised in Šumava, Karel was a Pied Piper—in a good sense. Friends, family and even strangers queued up to see him. There was always much backslapping and many jokes to be shared (mostly told by Karel), cold refreshing *pivo* to drink at any time of the day or night, sloping palace gardens dappled by summer sunlight to visit, old parts of Prague to explore, guitar nights in old pubs—and people wanting his attention, everywhere. I even met a few of his foreign clients who spoke reverently of Karel's 'very impressive project management' of the 'exceptionally diffi-cult bureaucrats'. People really *liked* him. He was kind and funny and generous, and in turn they sought out his time and company. I realised quickly I was on the end of a very long list.

Karel introduced me to everyone as 'our visiting *Ohhhh-strahhh-lian* teacher'. His friends were charming and welcoming. They also tried to size up my relationship with Karel. I could read their thoughts as the men smirked at Karel and the women stood back, arms folded, trying to get a measure on what a young traveller was doing with their Karel.

Their Karel was always busy, so to compensate he took me with him often in those first few weeks. But when he didn't or couldn't, I spent time exploring the city on my own. I ambled and daydreamed, lost in my own world of magic and musing, and only when I'd walked too far or for too long would the bump of the cobblestones under my feet—and my sore soles—bring me back to the moment. I felt an occasional stab of guilt, too, when I remembered everyone else was working. In turn that reminded me I only had funds for about a month in Prague unless I found work too.

———⟫●⟪———

Despite my best efforts, however, the Great Work Opportunity refused to manifest itself as I 'crisscrossed the Prague', either with Karel or on my own. I sat broadcast writing exams at Radio Prague and I waited in vain for the three language schools to contact me. When the responses finally came, they were negative. The media outlets wanted a real journalist, not a pretend one, which was fair enough. The two schools with unpronounceable names simply said, 'No TEFL qualifications'. Well, I knew that already, and that was also fair enough. I didn't have any qualifications in teaching English as a foreign language (TEFL); I'd entirely winged it in Sedlčany.

The third school, English House, did not reply at all.

Karel sought to reassure me each time. 'Just take it easy, Táničko. Everything takes time in our country. You must remember we are run by former communists.'

'How have you managed to create your own consultancy then?' I challenged him.

'It is not so easy. I must work very hard to make up for all my years of lost time—and at the same time, still not to expect too much too soon. It is, how you say, a balancing act.'

I'd of course lost no time with my career back home, ever, and in the West we were expected to quickly raise our sights high. It was all very confusing and back-to-front.

'What made you want to be a businessman in this new world, then?' I persisted.

He shrugged. 'A chance finally to make some money. I need money to keep my girls and one day I dream to build them a family home.'

'A family home?'

'Like Jarda and Míša have.'

Ah—a standalone house on a block of land.

'But to tell you my honest thoughts, Táničko,' he sighed, 'it is not likely to be possible in my lifetime. No matter how hard I work. A family home in Prague is almost impossible for a local person. Only foreigners and corrupt former communists can afford one.'

I thought how commonplace a family home, a backyard and a Hills hoist clothesline were in Australia in 1994, and how we took them for granted. I thought of sun-streaked afternoons, kids running around on dry lawns, backyard cricket, endless sunlit days for play. I thought of big houses and little houses, inside and out. Plenty of space—there was always space in Australia. That was my 'normal', yet Karel's girls might never know it.

Then he brightened up. 'But perhaps one day I will renovate my Prosek palace instead.' At my surprised face, he nodded confidently. 'I have some plans, some ideas. I cannot make it bigger, of course, but I can make it nicer—not look so old, perhaps more modern. But that is a big project too and I need time.' At this thought he sighed again. 'I do not have that at present and do not know when.'

I saw a string of emotions cross Karel's face when he talked about his desire to succeed in this new world, the difficulty of doing so and the reality of the limitations he faced. I saw hope mixed with a sad fatalism. But just when I was starting to feel despondent myself, he laughed.

'But we must find time to do the things that are important—that is Czech survival strategy. *Tak*! Shall we call my girls and our friends to share a sip of *pivo*?'

Every Czech problem was solved by *pivo*. And any spare time was spent with his girls and friends. I fitted in where I could in the curves of his life, holding on to the hopes I had for my own.

———————

At the end of the second week I wandered alone towards the trams. The setting sun sent splashes of orange and gold along the rippling surface of the Vltava. Pigeons darted and fluttered in the dying rays, and the faint strains of an accordion from Charles Bridge floated across the water. I took in the burnished sky, the music from the bridge, the sparkle of spires overhead. Soon Prague Castle would be ablaze with lights and the city a glittering fairy-land. I felt overwhelmingly, joyously at home and at peace.

I sent out a prayer to the Gods of Prague.

Please, please, pleeeease find work for me so I can stay.

Arriving at the apartment an hour later, I saw an envelope addressed to me on the hall table. It bore the name 'English House' on the front.

I ripped it open with trembling hands, then shrieked. 'Karel! It says they have nine hours work for me! I'm to ring them to discuss! Oh Karel! I can stay! *I can stay!*'

He came into the hall and I threw myself into his arms.

He kissed me.

I kissed him back.

Something had changed. Everything had changed.

20

English House

English House!

The name evoked a three-storey Victorian house covered in ivy with wide wings and a sweeping drive out the front, a house where mysteries and the odd scary murder had once taken place.

However, as I would soon discover, the Prague version of English House comprised two cramped, overstuffed rooms behind an unmarked door just beyond the outskirts of the Old Town. The dark lane in which it sat smelt of stale cigarettes and rising damp. It was there that two young and clever business partners, Scottish Anne and Czech Richard, ran a burgeoning TEFL business.

Their strategy was simple: offer employment to young, hungry foreign teachers, contract them out to teach English to Czech government departments and businesses, and endeavour to make a profit. The brutal tax system and inefficient bureaucracy made this difficult, but they were optimists.

And I was their next recruit.

———»●«———

I went to meet Anne and Richard several mornings later. As the tram rocked towards Karlovo náměstí, the transport hub nearest to the school, I sat very still, my stomach in knots, a reference from Headmaster Zdeněk in my bag.

I had a lot riding on this: my future here, my future with Karel, my future as a teacher.

Anne met me at the door with a firm handshake and a warm smile. 'Good morning, Tanya,' she said in a soft Scottish brogue, rolling her 'r's like the Czechs did.

With her blue eyes, long blonde hair, corduroy trousers, T-shirt and Doc Martens, she fitted neither my image of businesswoman nor of a headmistress. But she sounded like both.

'Unfortunately, you are neither a teacher, nor trained to teach a second language, so we cannot offer you full-time work,' she told me. 'But despite your lack of qualifications, we have secured a contract with the Ministry of Justice and the High Court, who have agreed to accept you as a legal English consultant because you are a lawyer.'

I stared at her, stunned.

The Ministry of Justice and the High Court?

When I found my voice, I fell over myself to assure her that yes, I would love to represent English House as a 'legal English consultant' and could certainly manage part-time to start with. And once I had my foot in the door, I thought, surely other opportunities would open up. In the meantime, who were the players and what would I do, exactly?

'You will have individual lessons with the Minister for Justice, the Deputy Minister, the head of Legal International Relations, the head of the Courts, the Chief of Legislation and anyone else they suggest. You will teach advanced, intermediate and beginners in accordance with British TEFL textbooks.'

As I was trying to get my head around this remarkable development and look confident, Czech Richard arrived. He was tall and thin with a shock of black hair and charming smile. He passed me a number of documents.

'So now, please Tanya, you must execute these papers.'

Oh dear God—not more documents that I didn't understand to sign. But I had to trust these two people if I wanted to stay here. I felt the usual frisson of fear, took a deep breath and signed my life away. We shook hands and I hoped I could pull off this next daring adventure.

'Now we go next door to official opening of fishing tackle shop,' said Richard. 'Please, would you care to accompany us?'

The fishing tackle shop was through another dark entrance off the seedy lane. An excitable Czech who had more rods and packing boxes than available space was distributing heavy, acidic red wine in cracked cups and already doing a roaring trade. Richard networked and Anne giggled and dimpled. She spoke fluent Czech to the gathered punters. Overwhelmed by the morning's events, I sculled the wine, choked and gazed at them in complete awe.

When it was all over, Anne answered my many queries with more dimples and great modesty. She had taught English in China and Turkey, among other places, and spoke several languages. 'Not long after I came to Prague, I met Richard, and we both had the same idea: why not pool our skills and start our own business, rather than work for someone else?' she explained. 'We wanted to set a standard that was higher than any other TEFL business here and secure the cream of the client crop. I manage most of the teaching side and Richard does most of the business development.'

Not a bad effort for someone who was barely twenty-six.

Taking off her Headmistress Hat, she asked, 'Are you doing anything this evening?'

I found myself accepting an invitation to join her for a rock concert. It would be held at the famous club Legenda, the artistic home of the underground movement during the Soviet era. One of Anne's friends from university, Richard 'Dickie' Lyst, had travelled across Europe in a van with his band The Exploding Buddhas, and Anne had organised gigs for them all around Prague.

I left the meeting in a daze, which seemed to be par for the course for my dealings in this country. Matters weren't helped by a growing headache from the truly awful wine. But I did find the right tram stop, which gave me a sense of achievement, and I sat mesmerised as the tram rumbled alongside the grand River Vltava. Life stretched out before me like the tantalising, shimmering waters below, heading onwards to who knew where, bright and bold and beautiful.

———⟫●⟪———

It was late when I made my way back to Prosek after The Exploding Buddhas' high-voltage performance, but I hardly noticed. Dancing and partying with Anne and her friends felt like being back at university. Speaking English with native English speakers made me feel normal in some wild, free way—the way

I *used* to feel. The whole evening was liberating. I had taken the
first independent step towards creating my own life in Prague and
I felt greatly emboldened.

Opening the door to Karel's apartment, I tiptoed into the tiny
squashed passage overflowing with jackets and long coats and
boots, hoping I wouldn't trip or bang into anything.

'*Dobrý večer.*' Karel's mellifluous tones floated out from his
bedroom on the right. 'Good evening, Táničko!'

A smile widened across my face as I peered around the door
to his broom-cupboard–sized boudoir. Karel sat perched on
a chair at the end of the room. He was working at a new desk
that he'd recently built into the wall. Czechs had little space in
their apartments so they made the most of every bit available.
Engineering plans and documents were spread out over the
table and bed. It looked completely chaotic. My smile died away.

He held out his arms, as though embracing him in such circumstances was the most normal thing to do. Then he paused
and murmured some words into my hair. 'I was worried about
you this evening. It is now so late.'

I pulled back and looked at him suspiciously but his eyes
were soft. A rush of warmth tingled the back of my neck and
then I felt ridiculously glad. I couldn't remember when anyone
last knew or cared where I'd been during the evening.

'Don't worry, I've had the most amazing night,' I said breathlessly, then told him all about it. 'I've been at your famous
Legenda!'

His eyes crinkled with pleasure. 'I am happy for you. And
now that you are at home, would you care to look at some legal
document for me and give me your special advice?'

He pushed a wad of papers across the table. 'I am preparing for
big negotiation tomorrow with our special Czech bureaucrats.

I need to get permission for Dutch client to reconstruct some nice Prague building. You said yesterday you would like to help me so this could be a perfect start, yes?'

What—*now*? It was nearly midnight. But delivering to Western clients took precedence over pretty much everything for Karel. Plus it was true that I'd made the offer, as helping Karel would be one way to pay him back for his generosity. It would have the added benefit of teaching me about Czech documents too, which would be important in generating more work. After all, documents were a lawyer's bread and butter and the sooner I got to understand Czech legal documents, the better.

'I will get us each one *pivo* to help,' Karel suggested. He got up and padded towards the kitchen, returning with two cold bottles.

I decided to read the document quickly, tell Karel what he wanted to know, and then escape to sleep. But the document was extremely complicated. Drafted mostly in Czech, it included paragraphs of mangled English and terms I didn't understand relating to construction and property development. My head ached.

Sighing, I put down the document. 'First, tell me about your negotiations. What are you trying to achieve?'

'Ah. Well, it all boils down to simple psychology.' Settling back into his chair, Karel looked at me sideways, mischievously. 'You must understand the special way that people in bureaucracies think. As you know, most of these people are still in the same jobs they had under former regime. For them, nothing has changed. The rules are still the rules to be followed, even if they are without meaning or even if they make hardship for people. You have to be clever to get around such stupid rules. And number one thing is they must think that they have created the solution. It takes a lot of time and careful strategies.'

'Doesn't it frustrate you?'

'Yes, of course. But I am patient man. And when I get that important piece of paper or authority for next step of my project that no one else can get, and everyone else says is not possible, then clients are always very happy.'

'So—give me an example.'

'Okay. You must look at the person and work out some strategy for them. Should it be a compliment to a bad-tempered woman in front desk about her hair or nice blouse? Or should I make a lunch with the important secretary? Or do I give a promise of some necessary favour to high-up chief? Or is it clearly and simply about money that they want from my client?'

He refilled my glass of *pivo* and went on cheerfully, warming to his theme.

'When they finally reach brave decision to let you proceed under some difficult and technical law, or step over it alto-gether, you must praise their vision and courage. Then also you might offer some champagne or flowers or a dinner, or perhaps just money.'

'But . . .' The implications of his story were slowly dawning on me. 'Isn't this all . . . bribery? Isn't it dishonest?'

'No. It is survival. It is the only way to get outcomes in this country. If you wish to work here, it is only way. You have to know how to be more clever than them.'

My puritanical Protestant principles registered a protest. But then again, what did I know? I hadn't spent a lifetime behind the Iron Curtain under a communist regime where the common view was that if you didn't steal from the government you stole from your family.

'So what would you say is your secret to success? To flirt with the women and charm the men?'

Karel nodded seriously. 'Remember, I did not make the rules. You will find out, soon enough, that it is necessary to know some tricks if you want to stay here.'

I suddenly felt very tired. English House had advised me that I needed three visas: living, working and residential. They would sort out the working one and I had to organise the other two. 'Karel, I have to go to the Department of Foreign Police this week. English House tell me I have to go early and it will take all day. They also suggested'—I now bit my own lip—'that I might have to pay extra money for the privilege.'

He shrugged. '*To je normální.*'

Now I was also depressed. Back home, laws were clear, obeyed, and bribes forbidden. At least in the home I knew. Putting down my pilsner, I decided it was time for sleep. There was nothing I could do to help Karel with his document tonight, or my visa situation for that matter. My ardour had definitely cooled.

The day of the first teachers' meeting at English House arrived. When I walked in there was standing room only, and the room buzzed with the noise of a first day back at school. Bags and textbooks were squashed into every conceivable corner. The majority of the occupants were in their mid-twenties and everyone spoke with a different accent.

Anne made introductions and everyone said a little about themselves.

It was a veritable United Nations and it made my head swim.

Jo, pixie-like, punk-looking, hailed from inner London. She lived in an apartment just off Wenceslas Square (I was immediately envious and wondered how soon I could score an invitation). Next was James, a tall, blue-eyed, brooding Welshman, accessorised by a glamorous Czech girl who wore cheap jewellery and smiled dazzlingly. Then came Mark, tousled and scruffy, locks of sandy hair falling over his face, who'd come straight from County Cork in Ireland. There was Rose, a weathered sixty-year-old ballet dancer from New Zealand; Andrea, a Frenchwoman with a gorgeous mass of curls who taught the French expat community; and Vera, half-English and half-Czech, a teacher and lawyer and an enigmatic beauty.

Then there were the two 'right hands' to Anne and Richard; blond and bespectacled English Alistair, who was jovial and charming and spoke fluent Czech; and Canadian Carolyn, stout and primly dishevelled, who wore round glasses, beamed around at us all and offered up her home-baked pumpkin pie.

And Lisa from Tasmania!

The only other new teacher to English House.

The only other Australian in town, as far as I could tell.

She looked up with a face almost as anxious as mine. We clutched each other's hands, ecstatic at meeting, promising friendship, exchanging common experiences in garbled undertones.

Anne called us to order and handed out relevant textbooks, timetables and school details. Then both she and Richard briefed us on what they expected from the group in the coming term. It was a lot.

Anne had previously told me everyone she employed had a TEFL degree. Most had taught in various parts of the world. Some taught in other Prague TEFL schools as well. Most spoke one if not two foreign languages. Many studied Czech at night classes. I squashed myself in behind a bookshelf at the far back of the room, hoping no one would ask me anything.

Once the briefing was over, Anne came towards me and said, 'I will draw you a map, with transport stops, so you know how to get to the Ministry of Justice and High Court.'

She stopped and relaxed, her eyes smiling. 'Did you enjoy the other night?'

'Yes, thank you so much.' I relaxed too, and we hugged. 'It was fabulous. Did you?'

Her dimples gave it all away. 'Dickie is staying on for a few days without the band. Fancy dinner in the Old Town with us? There's an old pub where the meat comes in different weights—a relic of wartime rationing—and I want to show him.'

'Yes, I'd love to!' I couldn't believe I was so lucky and sensed a bourgeoning friendship with Anne lay ahead. She was my first friend here who linked me back to the West and I found that hugely comforting.

Vera walked towards us, smiling, and Anne reverted to Headmistress mode. 'Vera will give you some more details about your new role, Tanya. She worked in it last year but is now starting at a law firm.'

I nodded quickly, hoping my enthusiasm would make up for my lack of everything else.

Richard called out to the group, 'Okay, I now pronounce the autumn term of English House 1994 open!' There was much laughter and cheering, and he added, 'We will now go to the Obnoxious Pub for lunch.'

Feeling like a tongue-tied student again, I joined my young, groovy colleagues as they adjourned to an evil-smelling pub across the dusty courtyard that effortlessly lived up to its name. The place was smoky and filled with drunken men, and the service and food were appalling. However, it boasted three redeeming features: proximity to the office, excellent beer and cheap prices.

As I settled into conversation with my new friends, an unexpected ache grew inside.

If only I could tell my family all about these thrilling developments! If only they could wander alongside me and experience firsthand the beauty of this city; experience my new life 'by my side', as the Czechs were fond of saying. In that way they would understand why I was so captivated. But my family were on the other side of the world and could not feel the magic of this place in their veins. And to the locals it was all *normální*.

Fortunately, Karel had recently bought a fax machine for his business and although it was expensive to use, he'd generously invited me to send letters home on it. I was thrilled because the Czech post was slow and unreliable. I decided to fax once a week, like I had done at boarding school, although back then we'd communicated by letter. I also hoped it would alleviate the ache that was starting to feel like a mulga stick in my leg, niggling, painful, unrelieved.

I finished the cheap beer and floated back to Prosek, composing a letter home in my head, the mulga stick ache blessedly numbed for the moment. Karel's kisses waited for me and for now, that was enough.

21

Finding the Ministry of Justice

Mr Svoboda—Deputy Minister of Justice, lawyer and rising political star—was my first English House student. He was also the most handsome man in Czech politics, not to mention the most unusual. He did not drink, he was honest, and he had no affiliation to the former regime. Not for Mr Svoboda the early morning vodka, garlic soup and gossip sessions with colleagues in the basement restaurant (which, according to the locals, was the norm for every other minister and bureaucrat). No—he spent every free moment studying French and English before dashing off to The Hague or Geneva on international legal matters.

And from 8 a.m. to 8.45 a.m. each day, he studied English with me.

On my first day, I wore the two smart things I'd brought with me to the Czech Republic, a dark-blue court dress and blue court shoes. But they were designed for an office, not for the cobbled streets of Old Prague. It was a hot morning; my toes pinched, my knees hurt and perspiration dripped down the back of my neck. When I finally made it to the entrance of a long and incon- spicuous Ministry building, a large guard jumped out at me.

'*Zastavte!*' he shouted, brandishing his weapon.

I stumbled backwards. Did I really look that dangerous? But I didn't want to get the guard offside on my first morning so I quickly handed over my documents and looked deferen- tially at my feet. He spent some time reviewing them before nodding, reluctantly it seemed, and pointing me through the revolving door.

On the other side, a metal box-like contraption barred my way. It looked like something the Russians would have made James Bond enter in order to extract the obligatory confes- sion. Tottering inside, I waited to be zapped or electrocuted or imprisoned, but I got through unscathed and immediately encountered another guard, who descended with a buzzing handheld device. She ran the device over me, coming peril- ously close to my nether regions in her zeal to find whatever James Bond–type devices she suspected I'd secreted in my crevices. Sporting a large moustache and even larger eye- brows, she inspired a fearful flashback of the guard in the Sedlčany supermarket. My attempts to smile were met with narrowed eyes.

Finally, I was through, sweating all over by now, and put before guards at a counter who reviewed my documents again, stamped them and directed me through a further glass door, after which a female guard led me up several flights of wide, con- crete stairs. We turned right and entered a large waiting room. Groups of besuited men with briefcases sat on chairs around the wall and stared at me. The guard spoke to a receptionist, who turned to me and said in broken English, 'You are new teacher? Please sit, wait too.'

But I'd barely sat down when several men marched out and the receptionist pointed to me and instructed, 'Come!'

I leapt to my feet and followed her through the inner door into a long olive-green room that reminded me of the Oval Office in the White House. It was very grand, with paintings along the wall and a long desk in the middle.

A tall man raised his head from some papers, politely gestured me towards a seat at his long table, and said in a courteous tone, 'Good morning, Tanya. I am Mr Svoboda.'

My heart somersaulted. Black hair that curled into crisp, grey-flecked locks around the base of his neck. Crisp, pressed shirt. Dark tailored suit that hung elegantly off his tall, slender frame— they were all bought in Paris, I later learned. Immaculately groomed. Discreet eau de cologne. Early forties, at a guess.

'Good morning, Mr Svoboda,' I gulped. Was that the right way to address a Deputy Minister who looked like a film star? Were there any telltale signs of perspiration on my dress? I shook his hand, trying to appear calm and professional, trying to focus.

Mr Svoboda spoke in perfect and lightly accented English. 'I have many people who wish to meet with me. They are not happy to be sent away or to have to wait because of my lessons.' He gave a wry smile, and I smiled back, nervously.

Mr Svoboda explained he had been recently appointed to represent his country at the European Court of Human Rights. It was the Czech Republic's opportunity to show it had moved on from communism, had improved its record on human rights, and was ready for admission to the European Union. His immediate superior, the Minister of Justice, did not want to learn English, and wished for his Deputy to carry out the international missions.

'*Tak*! We need to make sure I am prepared well for these meetings and to have enough in English to contribute.' He looked at my copy of *Advanced English* irritably. 'Do you have anything else—more relevant?'

'Er—yes, well . . .' My mind emptied. My new student's grasp of English was going to challenge mine. In a rush, I suggested, 'Why don't we review documents you need for your trips? That way we can make your lessons practical and useful.'

He raised one elegant eyebrow. Letting a foreigner like me look at confidential documents wasn't quite what he'd had in mind. I added, as authoritatively as I could, 'As a lawyer, you can trust me to keep this all confidential. Why don't we try it and see how it goes?'

He looked taken aback but after a moment nodded. 'I am writing a speech for the next UN meeting in Brussels. We wish to make our laws the same as European Community laws and this speech expresses our intention. I need the English words to be perfect.'

'Let's work with that, then,' I said, breezily, as though I did this kind of thing all the time. 'We can focus on how it should be written. It will be a practical application of grammar and spelling and you can take away a finalised document.'

'Very well, Tanya. This once, we will see.'

But, as in Sedlčany, here I knew instinctively that I'd found my way in. I'd learnt I was better at practical teaching than theoretical approaches, and I knew this would work. I'd just substituted a guitar for a political document.

By the end of our lesson I'd learnt a great deal, and Mr Svoboda had seemed to enjoy it too. When he said, 'This was very good and very useful', I glowed from head to foot. I would conduct all lessons in the future based on his material. But I wouldn't tell Anne just yet that we'd discarded *Advanced English*.

I picked up my bag and was ushered out while the next round of besuited men with briefcases was ushered in. It all happened in a whirl.

'Thank you very much. See you tomorrow!' I said politely to the receptionist.

She watched me go, her face closed. I was starting to get the message—I was an interloper here. But I didn't care. I swept out of the waiting room and bounded down the wide stone staircase. Tomorrow we were going to look at another UN document. It was history in the making—legal history, in fact. Not even a foreign correspondent would be able to do this!

The future was full of stimulating opportunities waiting to unfold. *Thank you, thank you, thank you*, I called out to the grey morning sky with its pale slants of yellow light. To think I could still be in Australia dealing with wills, divorces and disputes about fences.

———————

One floor down from Mr Svoboda was the Ministry's Office for International Relations.

And the Head of International Affairs.

Mrs Wurstová, my next student.

When I arrived for my first lesson, I was told Mrs Wurstová was running late and that I should take a seat in her office. I looked around in some alarm; in contrast to Mr Svoboda's streamlined, elegant surrounds, this room overflowed with papers, books, paintings and coffee cups.

As I tried to squeeze my bottom onto a chair piled high with files, my student steamed into the room like the *Queen Mary*. 'Oh, my little kangaroo.' She shook my hand up and down, beaming. 'So glad you are here! We are going to be a wonderful team! Coffee, we must have coffee just now. Dana, please bring some and meet our new kangaroo. Oh, this is going to be great fun and you are going to be tremendous help to me!'

Mrs Wurstová was generously proportioned and had fiery red hair. She wore a vibrant red silk blouse with ruffles, matching red lipstick, a black skirt and high heels. She trailed an exotic perfume in her wake, along with a line of people who were falling over themselves (and the files and books on the floor) to finalise matters with her before our lesson began.

The phone rang as they put more documents before her. Mrs Wurstová picked up the phone and called out instructions while busily signing papers. Another assistant rushed in with several overflowing files. The assistant looked anxiously about the desk, no doubt trying to find a spot for them, and when she couldn't she piled them on top of a large dictionary where they teetered precariously. Mrs Wurstová signed more documents while talking to the assistant. Dana brought coffee. The phone kept ringing. Mrs Wurstová kept giving instructions.

I drank my coffee fast.

'So, Taaaarnya.' Mrs Wurstová finally turned her dazzling gaze back to me, as I tried to refocus. '*Tak*! You are here to teach me everything I must know so I can do the best work possible. Yes! This is new role for our country and it is important that we make our mark in the international relations and especially the UN Commission on Human Rights.'

The phone rang again but this time she ignored it, shouting instead to the secretary in the adjoining office. Seizing the opportunity, I pushed forward my carefully prepared lesson.

'Now, Mrs Wurstová, shall we begin? I have prepared a lesson based on—'

'But you must know, I am not interested in the grammar.' Mrs Wurstová pushed away the papers just as firmly. 'No, I will not be good at this thing called grammar and don't intend to be.' Big peals of laughter.

'But . . .'

Mrs Wurstová leant towards me, speaking confidentially in warm, honeyed tones. 'Oh, but I want to learn to speak better. That is most important. You will talk with me and you will come with me sometimes to meetings if I need a help and you will find interesting things for me to read and learn about.'

I stared, open-mouthed. That was a worse deviation from English House's strict rules than the rewriting of Mr Svoboda's curriculum. But Mrs Wurstová waved her hand dismissively at my concerns. 'And sometimes we will have a little glass of wine and chat. I want to hear all about your country with its beautiful kangaroos and funny wild animals.'

And with that, she beamed me out of her office.

From that moment on, our lessons involved lots of conversations and glasses of wine, but I quickly understood Mrs Wurstová's style was to learn by osmosis. I also learnt that although Mrs Wurstová was now important enough to have a driver and a car to bring her to work, she still lived in a little *panelák*, just like the rest of us.

'It is normal,' she chortled. 'Only President Havel has the castle.'

Mrs Wurstová had a huge heart and an unyielding will.

'My intention is to create international respect for our Czech position on human rights,' she said, proudly. 'And I will do whatever it takes to make that happen. And *you*, my little kangaroo, will help me!'

Every night I rushed home to tell Karel about my day. And once a week I crammed small words into every conceivable space of an A4 page, stories pouring out in a jumble like the roofs that tumbled from the castle down the hillside, my excitement bubbling out into disjointed sentences. I pressed 'send' on the fax and waited anxiously for my family's responses.

When the machine burst back into life, usually between eight and thirty hours later, I would rip the paper out and devour the familiar cursive letters of Mum that had filled so many pages to me at boarding school; the rounded words of my sister, who seemed as close to me as if we were still in the schoolroom together; and sometimes even a short note from Dad that brought a lump to my throat.

Inevitably I felt waves of homesickness as I soaked up their responses, which were a mixture of tenderness and love as they tried to understand my strange descriptions and support my adventure. There was day-to-day information from them too: the dry weather, the difficult cattle sales, the mustering camp, the endless work. And then there were stories of M'Lis and her husband Chris's baby Mitch: his new tooth, his angelic smiles, the joy he brought them all. There were phrases that tugged on my heartstrings—'we miss you'—and, from Mum, 'Please thank the kind family you are living with'. I hadn't mentioned my liaison with Karel. I didn't dare; I wasn't ready.

When Karel said, 'This weekend the girls and I will go and stay with some friends in their cottage in the country. We will also see Standa and Ivana, and Growing Boy and Vladěna. We will walk by the river—there will be full moon—and play some guitar, drink special local *pivo*. Would you care to join us?', I said yes, quickly, gratefully. Family *was* important, as Karel had pointed out on my first night in his *panelák*, and I missed it more than I was prepared to admit.

22

Love is for nothing

I couldn't put off my visit to the Department of Foreign Police any longer. One morning the following week I left Prosek at 4.30 a.m. to get the right combination of bus, metro and tram in order to reach the Foreign Police by 6 a.m. My strategy was to beat the queue, but that strategy, like most in this country, didn't work.

On arrival I found a large, soulless concrete building with a long queue already pushing out around the corner. People had obviously slept there all night. My fellow queuers were the saddest people imaginable—mainly Romany Gypsies and refugees from Yugoslavian and Baltic states, all of whom looked far more fraught than this well-fed Westerner. Children wailed while mothers clutched them to their hips; thin, gaunt men with shadows under their eyes smoked cigarettes. When the doors opened finally opened at 8 a.m., I found a building awash with smoke haze and grime and human misery.

That included my own, as I stood in wrong queue after wrong queue all day. There were no signs in English and no one spoke English to translate (not that I'd expected otherwise). And I lost my place every time when either I could hold my bladder no longer and had to rush to the one stinking toilet, or, having eventually got to the front of a queue, was sent to the back of another one. This Kafkaesque crisscrossing of the room took all day, and it starred a series of bored, greasy-haired bureaucrats who might as well have been characters in Kafka's own stories. Nine exhausting hours later, I tottered home with some documents I couldn't read and my purse significantly lighter, having parted with more money than I thought was legal.

'I'm never doing that again,' I wailed to Karel, looking for sympathy as I collapsed on the couch back at Prosek. 'It was dreadful.'

'On the contrary! You had success! Did I not tell you the other night this was how the system worked? Besides, five years ago you might not have even been allowed here.'

'You are unbelievable,' I said, throwing up my hands. 'Don't you ever get frustrated?'

Appearing to consider my question, he eased himself down onto the couch before turning to look at me, his face only centimetres from mine. I nearly stopped breathing. He was close, very close, and I tried to move but couldn't.

'Sometimes, yes,' he said finally. 'It all depends what about.'

His blue eyes were intent on mine and I could smell his musky scent, almost taste it. As I registered what he was saying, butterflies squirmed in my stomach and fluttered up to my throat so that I forgot to swallow.

But before I could think of any way to respond, Radka walked in. She looked thunderously at me, then at Karel, and burst into tears.

Karel leapt to his feet. I cringed and hunched back on the couch, mortified, wanting the room to swallow me up. When I finally managed to look up again, they were both in the kitchen, Radka's words coming out in choked fits and starts. Karel's voice was calming and soothing.

I crept to my feet and started edging towards the safety of the bedroom, but before I could get there Karel led her back to the couch and spoke in English.

'Radka has some boyfriend problems.'

My legs went wobbly, my whole being flooded with relief. It wasn't me! It was a boy!

'He has gone off with someone else. And I have told her my "old truth".' His tone was weary. 'Never run for a bus—or a girl, or a boy—because there will always be another one around the corner.'

Radka stood next to her father, white-faced. She didn't look as though she'd bought his old truth. And in the rush of adrenaline that accompanied my relief, I blurted out: 'That's a bit hard-hearted! Radka might be in love.'

Karel looked at me askance. 'Radka is too young to know what love is!'

Radka burst into a fresh wail. Perhaps she understood more English than she let on.

'That's ridiculous, Karel!' The day had been long and exhausting and this situation was becoming increasingly irritating. 'Love has nothing to do with age. Love can exist at any time of your life when you meet the right person.'

'*Tak!*' Karel now looked exhausted himself. 'Love is for nothing. It does not last. It is of no use for her to destroy her young life now for something that will leave as quickly as it came.'

Love is for *nothing*?

'You and Radka are young. You will know this one day too.'

'That's insulting!' I snapped, adding before I could stop myself, 'You sound old and bitter!'

As soon as my words were out I regretted them. 'Maybe, yes,' he retorted, 'but this simply means we are destined to be, how do you say, at cross-swords with life.'

Tears seeped afresh through Radka's beautiful dark lashes.

He turned to her again, murmuring softly in Czech, and said to me, 'I will now put Radka to bed.'

I grabbed my keys and ran downstairs. Everyone told me there was no crime in Prague and women could walk safely everywhere at night. That was lucky. I pounded along Prosek's floodlit concrete, upset and angry, yet knowing I had no reason to feel this way. Irrespective of Karel's negative views about love, what did it matter? There were no bright lines drawn around our liaison; it could vanish by tomorrow morning. As might I from this city, if I didn't get more work. What did I expect from Karel? Love, too?

I thought of the fun dinner I'd shared with Anne and Dickie several days earlier. We'd met in a 'locals only' restaurant tucked into a side alley just off Staroměstské náměstí, and I'd watched Anne and Dickie glowing with the radiant blush of new love. They'd held hands under the table, gazed into each other's eyes. The only impediment between them was distance—Dickie was about to return to England—but in every other respect they were, to use a Czech expression, 'on the same board'. They intended to have a long-distance relationship until Christmas and then 'work out next steps'.

Karel and I were not on the same board. We were two people who had connected, passionately I thought, but did we have a future? I might be trying to create one, but he was a busy man with a busy present, which was where he put his focus. There was something else too. He was also constantly surrounded by women. No surprise: he was charismatic and handsome. But I'd discovered surreptitiously that he'd had many girlfriends over the years. I was sure I'd already met several of them—gorgeous, glamorous women, all tall with high cheekbones.

Rage and fatigue after my long day burned hotter.

When I stomped back into the apartment, Karel was sitting at the table. He got up stiffly.

'Where have you been?' He could hardly keep the anger and anxiety out of his voice.

'What does it matter?' I sounded childish, churlish.

He came over to me and pulled me to him. I stood, hands by my side, unwilling.

'I wish to tell you something, Táničko. I have never had any woman live in this apartment before. Since my wife left fourteen years ago, I have invited no one to live. It was my rule.'

I blurted out, 'But women—there were always women, yes?'

'Yes, of course,' he said irritably. 'I'm not some monk. But not to live. This is all new. For me and my girls. But it is okay. You are different—and my girls are happy. We just need to take it easy. We don't need to talk about big words that only cause problems.'

By 'big words', I assumed he meant 'love'. I breathed out, heavily, trying to get perspective. For fourteen years the girls had had their beloved father to themselves. I was here, and allowed to be here, presumably because I was no threat; they no doubt thought I was sure to leave soon enough. But I *was* here. More than that, Karel had said I could stay as long as I wished. Every time I talked about leaving he talked me out of it. Perhaps I did need to take it easy. Perhaps I was worrying too much.

'But the girls, and Radka particularly—I'm in her space.'

Karel shrugged. 'It is good. We are all happy. Just come to bed.'

There was nothing more to say, no further answers, other than the infinite tenderness of Karel as he took me to his bed. I lost my sense of self as his hands came back to my face and waist. With the practised ease of a much older lover, he undressed me through kisses, and made love to me through more kisses, until finally I lay curled up in his arms, satiated.

I was falling in love, in every way, and there was nothing I could do about it.

But I had to hide it, not tell Karel, stuff it down deep.

23

Bowing before the High Court

Across the river from the Ministry, several tram rides south of Lesser Town in the direction of Petřín Hill, the High Court towered over a cluster of ancient buildings and churches that encircled its grounds and sloped away towards the River Vltava.

The High Court was the second-highest court in the land, equivalent to Australia's Federal Court. It was an enormous building with three storeys of courtrooms and offices. Each floor was linked by sweeping staircases; and its rooms boasted high ceilings and big windows. Surrounding the building was a wide expanse of green lawn, perfectly cultivated roses and gravel paths.

Within that building awaited my next set of students: their collective Honours, the Judges of the High Court.

I'd been told by English House there would be three classes— beginner, intermediate and advanced—comprising twenty students in total.

There was just one problem.

While I'd assured Headmistress Anne that I was up to the job, I hadn't told her that judges terrified me. I'd spent most of my legal life trembling whenever I stood before those esteemed creatures. Admittedly, mine hadn't been a long legal life but there had been sufficient excruciating moments during that time for me to put judges on the same platform as God.

Going to court had been the most nerve-racking part of my previous life. Judges, wigged and gowned, ruled the courtroom with their probing questions and brilliant minds. I would usually rush into court, disorganised, papers all over the place, my own wig at a dishevelled angle, gown hoicked up with pins because it was too long and I was too short. A bad day in court was akin to having my appendages pulled off with pliers, one by one. I'd leave as I'd begun—a wreck—and head home to hide away.

Now, on my first morning at the Czech High Court, I had more pressing matters to worry about. First, there was the usual panic to find the right metro and tram stops, and time my arrival accurately. Next, I had to try not to think about Karel, or the fact I had a limited wardrobe of business clothes and would really have to do something about buying some new ones. If only I had the courage to go into a Czech shop.

Fortunately, the High Court's security arrangements turned out to be almost identical to those of the Ministry so I settled into the lengthy *Švejk*-like process like a local. Once the guards were satisfied I wasn't a saboteur, I was led up several flights of stairs. We entered a side room with many desks, and long windows that overlooked a courtyard filled with flowers. Before me were ten men and women with expectant looks on their faces.

Women? What a lovely surprise! I didn't know any women judges. Maybe no glass ceiling here, then? I blurted out 'Dobrý den, jsem Tanya.'

The judges looked startled at my attempt at Czech, then stood up and introduced themselves slowly in English.

'I am glad to be here with you,' I plunged on, nervously. 'We can study from the *Advanced English* textbook if you'd like, but first I'd like to get to know you, understand what you're interested in, and see how I can make our classes relevant. I'm particularly interested in your law. Perhaps we can work our time together around the kind of legal issues you are dealing with.'

Before I could say anything further, a woman in the front row spoke in exquisite English. 'That sounds excellent,' she said warmly. She had beautiful, shiny dark hair swept back in a short bob, and wore elegant designer clothes. 'I am Marta, Deputy Chief Justice of the Family Court,' she added, then laughed—a great, rich laugh. 'We need a lot of help in the Family Court,' she said. The room rocked with more laughter.

Relief filled me and another judge, Vladěna, spoke.

She said she was one of several judges who presided over the criminal and civil courts. Shy and softly spoken, she nonetheless spoke fluent English and she said, with some urgency, 'I am very interested in international law.' She had recently received permission to attend a legal conference in Geneva and, like Mrs Wurstová, was excited to play her part in legal matters beyond the border.

During the first lesson we agreed to talk about law in the Czech Republic generally. 'Being a judge here is very difficult role,' they all said, 'especially in this new world.' To my joy, the conversation flowed and I started to relax.

They wanted to know about my legal background too, and why I'd left the law to come here. I was chuffed by their interest and gave them a summary of my career, which, to be honest, sounded much more impressive in the telling than the living. And to my delight, the conversation had real depth, because we shared a profession, albeit with some differences.

They told me the Czechs had a civil system, similar to France and much of Europe, rather than a common law system like Australia's. They didn't have juries for criminal matters, and judges ran the cases and interrogated the parties. They didn't wear wigs and gowns.

By the end of our session, I'd learnt more than they had, yet everyone said they were looking forward to the next lesson. They promised to bring printouts of recent European Court of Justice decisions to work on. As I packed up my books, my head was spinning. For the first time I'd met colleagues here on an equal footing and that was empowering. Marta and Vladěna appeared at my side while the rest of the class headed out the door.

'Tanya, we wish to invite you to our local wine bar. Are you free to join us?'

I fell over myself to say yes. My Ministry lessons were in the morning and the High Court in the afternoon, so the timing could not have been more perfect. I tripped after my two new friends around the corner to another grey building. The venue didn't matter—I would have gone to a grotty old parking block with these two judges, such was my thrill at being asked to spend time with them. I hadn't realised how much I'd missed having colleagues.

Inside, the bar was busy and cheerful. We found a table in the corner and huddled in like three university friends catching up. Marta ordered Rulandské *šedé*, an expensive dry white wine. I kept thinking: *If my friends could see me now . . .*

As we sipped and shared stories, I asked them to tell me more about life as a judge here and why it was so difficult.

'Many reasons.' Marta's response was prompt. 'A lot, lot of work, the pay is not good and we are not well-respected. The parties can yell at us and we have little authority to control this. This is because the government will not give us support.'

I was aghast. 'Why not?'

Vladěna sighed with the melancholy air I had come to associate with the Czechs. 'Reason, of course, is political.'

Of course.

She explained: 'The former regime was "unofficial" main court. They made the big rules about important things like treason and crime. And if people behaved in criminal way, the secret police usually dealt with them first. We were left to solve arguments between people, which government did not think important.'

'By "arguments between people", do you mean civil law disputes?'

'Yes, problems between neighbours, meaning of contracts and so forth.'

'What about family law?' I asked Marta.

'People wanted divorce, of course, but there was no free accommodation anywhere, people had little money, so not everyone tried for it. Even today it is not easy because finding accommodation is still a big problem. You might know this.'

I certainly did.

'Restitution is the biggest problem facing the courts just now,' Vladěna added. 'The cases are clogging up the courts and taking much time and money. Do you know of it?'

The new government's policy of handing back property that had been illegally taken from families? Yes, I did know about it. Czech-Australian Jarda was still working to get his property back, and Ludva luckily now had his cottage up in the Šumava mountains.

'What are restitution disputes about, though?' I was curious. 'I thought people would be glad to have their properties back.'

'Disputes are mainly about who are correct owners. Most property was taken by the Nazis in the 1940s or the communist regime in the late 1940s and 1950s. Memories from that time are not good. Documentation has been lost or destroyed.' Vladěna frowned. 'My own family, we were handed back old family home near Letenské sady, but other family argue it is theirs, and have taken us to court. Luckily, we have all the necessary documentation to prove our case. But other family wants to make us run out of money in the courts and force us to surrender. We had to vacate our *panelák* last year to move into the house, and have nowhere else to go if we lose our case.'

We all sipped our wine in mournful silence. If judges couldn't even get a leg-up through a system that was inherently corrupt, what hope was there for anyone else?

'Although,' Vladěna added with a weak smile, 'perhaps other family deserve it if they get it. The house is so cold and in such bad repair, and we have no money to heat or fix it.'

Marta filled our glasses. 'But Tanya, I am optimist. We now have a new Commercial Code and that means there will now be commercial cases that need to be solved. There is much corruption here—the former communists who still hold the money—and foreign companies take advantage of our people. We have no experience in commerce, we have no background. Court problems like this will bring publicity and so perhaps government support and money for us.'

Who would have thought that sending high-profile corrupt companies to court would finally grab the government's attention? I decided Marta was a visionary.

Vladěna agreed. 'This is reason why we must learn the English better and have chance to travel to other jurisdictions and learn how law is managed there. The more we can find out and bring back here, the more chance we have to make a difference.'

'You must always remember to be glad you can practise your law in the West, back in your own country. It is great luck for you,' Marta finished, draining her glass.

As I crossed back towards the Old Town on the trundling tram, the river sparkling beneath the city's many rows of bridges, quivers of delight ran through me. I'd felt validated today; my own story had been given meaning. If I'd had my stock hat handy, I'd have ripped it off my head and waved it joyously in the air. I couldn't wait to send a fax to my family about all these new experiences and share my excitement with them. For the first time in a long time, I felt proud of myself and my career.

———❖———

My next student at the Ministry of Justice was Dr Holub.

Once the Chief Justice of the High Court, Dr Holub had been seconded to the Ministry to advise on International Affairs. He primarily assisted Mr Svoboda and Mrs Wurstová with his 'excellent expertise' and 'excellent English'. I could attest to the latter. It was formal and perfect.

I guessed Dr Holub was in his late sixties. A thin, sparse man whose threadbare suit hung down from his gaunt shoulders, he wore black glasses and combed his thin wisps of hair neatly back. He loved to avoid grammar by starting each lesson with a detailed history lesson based on his life, which had involved terrible suffering under both the Nazis and the communists. Stories included that of his mother in a German labour camp, the repressions he had suffered and observed, and his views on the fruitlessness of war.

By the third lesson, he obviously felt confident enough to set some war records straight. He told me the West betrayed the Czechs to the Nazis and then to Stalin. Did I know that?

I looked at him, appalled, insulted. We, the West, we were the good guys—the Allies. Weren't we?

Dr Holub told me that during the 1930s, when Czechoslovakia was enjoying its second decade of independence (after centuries of occupation), Hitler's popularity was also on the rise. As part of his power play across Europe, Hitler urged the Sudetens (ethnic Germans living along the northern and western Czechoslovakian borders) to publicly agitate for the return of their lands to German control. Czechoslovakia suddenly found itself a pawn in a much bigger game between Eastern Europe and the Western powers at the time—Great Britain, France and Italy. The Western powers had been World War I allies and were desperate not to go to war again. Under pressure, they capitulated. They signed the Munich Agreement. This gave Hitler permission to seize the Sudetenland area. They might as well have given Hitler the keys to all of Czechoslovakia. Within a year Hitler's troops had rolled into Prague and were rounding up Jews, communists and anti-fascist resistance members from one end of the country to the other.

By the time the West realised that Hitler had no intention of stopping, it was too late. The Czechs had been sold down the river, Hitler had seized most of Central Europe, and war broke out anyway.

I frantically searched my memory for Mrs Howe's Year 11 Modern European History lessons. I dredged up a vague recollection that British Prime Minister Neville Chamberlain had come back to London after the Munich talks, victoriously waving an agreement that he claimed would prevent war. Now I remembered it was a hollow victory as Hitler did not abide by its terms. I'd not known the other side of the story—that the West sacrificed Czechoslovakia for that short and hollow victory.

I remembered my conversations with Pavel in Sedlčany about what the Nazis had done to the Czechs. I felt sick.

'There is more,' Dr Holub pressed on. 'By the time war was over, Hitler had nearly destroyed us, which you would think should have caused great shame among the Allies. But no, because as part of a deal to finish the war, the Allies then handed us over to Stalin.' Dr Holub looked as though he couldn't believe it either. 'Our resistance fighters flew for you, for Britain, they were so loyal, and when they came home here, as heroes, Stalin's thugs killed them.'

'Why?' My head snapped up. 'Russia was on the same side as us in the war.'

'Stalin and his people were insane. They killed people because they considered them a threat to their power.'

I remembered Míša and Jarda telling me about those terrible years in Czechoslovakia after World War II under Stalin: trumped-up charges, thousands killed or disappeared overnight, hauled off to uranium mines. I felt even sicker as the pieces of the puzzle fitted together.

'It is the same story throughout history,' said Dr Holub. 'Governments only want to make their people happy so they can be re-elected. The West did not care about us. We were so small and, how you say, dispensable.'

No wonder the Czechs hated the West. The reasons kept piling up.

He tapped the table grimly one more time, for good measure. 'We just want our country back to ourselves. Now, have I told you about the latest problem with the Romany Gypsies?'

Arriving for Mrs Wurstová's lesson, I could see it would be difficult to keep her focused between phone calls and a 'Top-Secret and Very Urgent' missive that was flying around the Ministry. In an effort to put Dr Holub's details out of my mind, I thought I'd concentrate on something happier—The Life and Career of the Fabulous Mrs Wurstová.

'Ah.' Her sharp eyes drilled into mine. She put down her pen. 'That is not a great story. There were bad times.'

'I'm sorry,' I said, immediately contrite. I wasn't doing well today. I took a deep breath and tried again. 'But I am very interested in the career path you took to get to your current role.' That was true, particularly as I had now met the female judges. 'We have the glass ceiling in the West, which often means women don't get into positions of power, like you are in.'

Mrs Wurstová frowned, confused.

'What is this thing, your glass ceilings?'

I explained the concept to her. 'There are of course women who have reached the top positions in Australia but the numbers are few. Pitifully few, given women represent half the population. But there are women judges here—and then there is you!'

Mrs Wurstová's response was immediate and to the point.

'All women were all made to work under the former regime so that is nothing great. And my new role is'—she paused—'very new. I was granted it because of what happened to me under communism.' She sat back and looked at me, as if weighing up whether or not she should disclose what happened. Decision made, her eyes darkened.

'In 1968, I was young lawyer and—how you say—*ambitious*. I had big dreams. President Dubček had brought in a more liberal regime and I was going to be young diplomat abroad.' She paused. 'But you know what happened then, of course— the Russian invasion of Prague, August 1968. I was taken from Academy, my place of work, with forty of the forty-three other lawyers—marched out like a prisoner—and charged with crimes against the state. Do you know what they were?'

I shook my head.

'I was charged with not being sympathetic to the invasion, to communism, and to Russia. Only three lawyers kept their jobs. Like President Havel, and thousands of others, we were punished for the rest of our careers. Just because I wanted to be a diplomat abroad.'

Her voice shook, momentarily.

'My father was Vice-President of the Supreme Court in 1968. Most respected man, excellent lawyer. He was my hero. He refused to vacate his court for the use of the Russian troops. They stripped him of his title and rights, his court, the right to practise law. They made him a "no one".'

I remembered that also happened to Tomáš in *The Unbearable Lightness of Being*.

Mrs Wurstová didn't lose her law ticket altogether but spent the next twenty years of 'normalisation' paying her penance in boring, soul-destroying work in a planning department. She was a 'marked woman' within the regime, never allowed to apply for promotions, never able to advance her study of law; all her dreams of an international legal career destroyed.

'The anger burned, burned hard inside,' Mrs Wurstová said, looking fierier than ever. 'When miracle of Velvet Revolution came in November 1989, it was too late for my father, but not for me. This is my chance now, Tanya,' she said, leaning forward. 'After these many years, I can join the outside world, and use my legal skills to benefit my country. And you will help me.'

The air was electric. In that moment I wanted to give her my all, to stay forever and assist her with her dreams. I wanted to help the women here everywhere—to use my legal training in the West to assist them. To help make amends for the past, to secure retribution for their previous betrayals. I saw a future where I was bold, vocal and independent, finally finding my real place in law—using it for good, and encouraging local and international forgiveness.

But our lesson was up. My starry visions dissipated in the chaotic wake of Mrs Wurstová's departure for her next meeting. I quickly collected my bag and a large box.

The box caught her eye. 'What do you have there, my little kangaroo?'

'Czech crystal—some glasses, for my Czech family.'

She looked at me sagely, then murmured, 'You talk about this family a lot. This Karel especially . . .'

I blushed and departed hastily, with her laughter ringing in my ears.

———————

On arriving back at the flat with my box of glasses, I found Karel home early.

He was delighted. 'Our famous crystal!' He ran his long fingers slowly across the neck of a glass. He pulled a bottle of

Bohemian Sekt from the fridge. 'Thank you, Táničko. They must receive a famous Prosek welcome, yes?'

Karel was relaxed as I joined him in the kitchen. He had changed out of his suit and was wearing his usual blue denim shirt and jeans. They brought out his blue eyes.

Cracking open the chilled bottle, he poured its bubbles into the two glasses; it sparkled through the delicate crystal. To aid the celebration, I lit candles and placed them around the kitchen. Then he put out *mandle*, toasted almonds, which we both agreed were a drug: once you had one you couldn't stop.

As he handed me a glass, Karel told me Radka was with her new boyfriend tonight. Had Radka moved on to a new boy—a new bus—so soon? I didn't want to raise the subject. Besides I was also achingly glad to have Karel all to myself for the whole evening.

'Have you heard of this special Czech song by famous folk group Brontosaurus?' Karel pressed 'play' on a song on his tape deck. The music enveloped the room. He put my glass down and took me in his arms. 'And now, Táničko, may we dance?'

Could any Australian man I knew match an offer like that? I doubted it—no Australian man that I knew, anyway—and I melted. We slow-waltzed around his tiny kitchen in the glow of the candles, Karel whispering a translation of the folk song as we swept and turned: a story of the moon and forests and rivers; of boy meets girl, boy wants girl; of love and passion and longing.

Only the moment mattered as he kissed me, then swept me off my feet and into bed. I wanted to be nowhere else tonight.

I was in love.

24

Finding language and music

I had also fallen in love with Prague's trams. During the day they rattled and swerved and hummed around the old city, offering up glimpses of hidden alleyways, the grand National Theatre, bridges lined with statues, palaces adorned with angels, and the baroque towers that loomed over the Vltava. At night you could glimpse the castle sparkling, its reflection glittering in gold along the length of the river, rippling and skidding over the water in a fantasy swirl of skirts and tulle. I would sit mesmerised, my breath falling and rising as the tram rocked underneath me.

I spent a lot of time on trams because my various classes were located on both sides of the river. That gave me chances to discover new places—an art gallery, a Renaissance café, a tucked-away park, a walled palace. It was during those rides I noticed the colours of Prague starting to change. The thick plane trees lining both sides of the river turned to russet and rouge, deep gold and blistered orange. The parks took on a deeper, richer hue. The air became crisper and sharper. I felt filled up with energy and the joy of life.

My challenges, however, grew in equal proportion to the delights. Language difficulties headed the list. Not being able to speak more than a few words of Czech meant ever-present anxiety and frustration. The lack of language meant nuances, meanings and connections with places and people were limited. Worse, Karel and I had regular misunderstandings that arose from the meaning of words and the endless cultural differences between us. If I was going to make a success of my foreign liaison and working life, I would have to take the plunge and learn how to speak Czech.

Fortunately, by now I was smitten by the sound and pitch of the language. My whole body resonated with its singsong quality, the way it curved up and over the end of the sentence like a wave that peaked and then crashed. I found it extremely sensual. Singers crooned its complicated words around musical notes, people flirted with it in the street and radio announcers exaggerated its nuances. When Karel spoke Czech, I would sit silently, absorbed, obsessed even with the soft lyrical quality of his conversations. It was music after all that had helped me so far in this country. But the grammar and the words remained enigmas.

I decided to enrol in a language school. But which one? Headmistress Anne said Státní jazyková škola was the best in Prague but it was well beyond my budget. I looked around at other options. None suited for a variety of reasons.

Karel came to my aid. 'If it is important to you to learn our language, then I would like to help you go to Státní jazyková škola.'

I couldn't believe it. Karel had consistently argued that the best place to learn language was in a pub, where local words and phrases and expressions flowed with the beer. But perhaps he had also realised that a better grasp of the language would benefit us both. Despite my protests, he therefore paid for my entire first term: 2900 Czech koruna, nearly A\$147. This was a lot of money for any Czech and the stakes were high.

He shrugged off my gratitude. 'You are very intelligent, Táničko. I tell you this often, so I think it is good investment for me, yes?' He grinned cheekily.

With *Czech for Beginners* and *Do You Want to Speak Czech?* stuffed into my briefcase, I determinedly headed off to class.

'*Dobrý večer. Jsem Jiří.*'

Those were the first words spoken on the first night of our first lesson.

I looked around triumphantly. I knew he had said, 'Good evening. I am Jiří', but most people's brows were furrowed and their eyes screwed up. Not me. I was a local. I knew basic Czech terms. I was having a wild affair with a Czech man. I was going to be *just* fine.

Teacher Jiří then bounced into an unbroken stream of Czech at breakneck speed. Earnest scratchings of unrecognisable words on the blackboard were followed by voluble exclamations, meaningless to the class, and so it continued for the next hour. My rush of self-congratulation was short-lived.

In retrospect, what had I been thinking? I'd only studied one year of languages at school—Year 8 French—and that had been a long time ago. Naďa and Peter Barr had told me Czech was similar to Latin and full of complex, archaic rules.

By the end of the lesson, with eyes glazed and head aching, I'd learnt precisely four new Czech words in total and missed all the grammar. As I packed up my books, I muttered to the English accountant sitting next to me, 'Complete waste of time and money', and he nodded gloomily. We shuffled out into the evening darkness, heads bowed, each lost in frustrated (and, in my case, humiliated) thoughts.

The lessons did not get any easier.

In fact, they reduced me to impotent fury. I spent most of the time with brows knotted, and migraine pending. I was not alone. My English accountant friend began carrying a hip flask and took long swigs before and during lessons.

At the end of each lesson I said I was going to quit. Then I remembered that Karel had paid for the entire term. Given that he had thought the whole process was a waste of time in the first place, I couldn't pull out.

Finally, some of the class started to get the hang of it. They were the clever ones already skilled in European languages, or those who had studied Latin. Or the Scottish among us who naturally rolled their 'r's, like Headmistress Anne. The English accountant and I remained in the back row, a shameful disappointment to ourselves, the class dunces.

I would go home and weep bitter tears to Karel, berating him and his forebears for creating a grammatical structure so impossibly difficult. His helpful response was to revert to form and suggest that I ought to spend more time in a pub if I *really* wanted to learn Czech.

As a way of filling the grammatical gaps, I became obsessive about learning vocabulary. While waiting for the metro or in between my students' lessons, I would pull out my language books and recite words to myself. I devoured lists, billboard text, shop names, instructions on the inside of buses and trams. I also focused on learning the names of the many 'set' Czech meals. My frustration at not understanding the Benešov restaurant menu, on the night I had first met Míša and Jarda, was never far from mind. And, as the Czechs would intone: 'Without work there is no cake.'

Eventually, I started having some wins, especially with menus. Once I started registering the patterns in the clusters of words, and memorising them, I became better at recognising and knowing the difference between, for example, the umpteen different ways of presenting cabbage, or the squillion methods of preparing pork: boiled, stewed, fried and baked.

Finally, painfully, excruciatingly, I began to get a handle on words and useful phrases, if not the grammar. Each time I translated something correctly, I thrust my fist into the air and felt like I was a kid again, rounding up and returning to the cattle yards the last of the would-be escapee scrubber bulls, my horse and I galloping along in victory, my long blonde plaits flying out behind me.

Fortunately, my ability to teach language surpassed my ability to learn it. News about my English classes spread by word of mouth throughout the Ministry and the High Court. Before long, class numbers expanded. Headmistress Anne and Richard were pleased. My probation period was over. My hours had extended to fifteen per week.

I was both chuffed and relieved, but I'd done the figures and it still wasn't enough. I needed a minimum of thirty hours in order to live here long term.

On Karel's advice I advertised in Prague's English newspapers: '*Legal consultant experienced in Western business negotiations. Will help companies negotiate English business deals, improve oral or written communication skills, and assist with business presentations.'*

Karel let me put his phone number in the ad and took me out to celebrate. I couldn't believe my daring. I'd never have had the audacity to do something like that back home. And I wasn't even sure I could deliver on what I was offering in that advertisement.

But I had a reason to be bold. Karel and Prague were now intertwined for me. It was both of them, or neither. I couldn't imagine being here without Karel and I was hungry to make my own mark in this city, to carve out my own exciting career, to make the kind of life I couldn't make back home. And if I missed my family too much (and I did miss them, very much and often), I could keep on faxing them and then visit for holidays. I knew I had a way out: a Qantas return ticket.

———⋙●⋘———

Prague continued to change, which continued to thrill me. Burnt brown, smudged apricot and vibrant yellow now tinted the trees across the city, bringing something new to its dimensions—a softness, a mystery, a different kind of magic, a deeper and richer hue. Its Gothic splendour draped in dying colour was mesmerising. The baroque palaces took on darker lines and shadows, and the gentle afternoon light set elegant renaissance buildings along the river boulevard aglow. I took every chance I could to wander the city, enchanted by its capacity to bewitch and seduce with its scents and light and promise of more.

But autumn came with a downside. The chill factor.

Afternoon temperatures plunged below 0°C, creating silent fog and wreaths of mist that veiled the city. Some days I could barely see a foot in front of me. White vapour wrapped itself around winding stone staircases and daylight struggled to penetrate the tiny, narrow cobbled streets. Thick mist blanketed the sound of voices and muffled the rattling noise of the trams. On mornings when the Prague basin was filled with condensation, the bridges across the River Vltava looked ethereal.

It was exquisite—and freezing.

My ears and nose were constantly bright red and my fingers and toes bright blue. Inside court shoes that I wore to classes, my toes felt like they were going to snap off. The icy winds sweeping along the streets bit viciously into my thin jacket and little black dress, freezing my bottom into a numb block.

As I stumbled, shivering, between tram stops, I started to think longingly of the intense heat of Central Australia, of bare feet and bare arms, and of warm, caressing sunlight on my face and shoulders. I thought of autumn in Alice, where the days were glorious with huge blue skies and endless sunshine. I momentarily lost my mojo.

'Karel, I am so cold and I don't know how to survive in this weather!' I wailed.

Karel responded in true pragmatic engineer fashion. 'You do not have proper clothes. You must get some. That is more useful than being cold.'

The next day I begged Mrs Wurstová for advice.

'Of course I will help you, my dear Tanya,' she tut-tutted, looking at my hopelessly ineffective skirt, blouse and jacket. 'Also'—she removed her glasses and waved them up and down— 'there is no use to ask the man for assistance in this regard.'

Sweeping documents aside and calling out to the long-suffering Dana for coffee, she proceeded to give me a rapid-fire account of her local knowledge.

'First, you need the boots. Ones that have—how you call it—some thick stuff inside to keep rain and cold off your small foots. You can buy them in our number one department store on Václavské náměstí.'

To assist matters, Mrs Wurstová scribbled a request for boots in my size on Ministry paper and instructed me to present it to a store attendant. I rushed off that afternoon, and between my hand signs, limited Czech and Mrs Wurstová's note, walked out delightedly with one pair of black waterproof knee-highs. They cost me A$10. Mrs Wurstová nodded in satisfaction when I stomped into the Ministry the following day, my 'small foots' finally warm and snug.

'*Dobrý*! Good.'

Next, I needed a coat. Mrs Wurstová sized me up, Dana hovered with coffee, and the two of them entered into an animated discussion, aided and abetted by a tape measure miraculously produced from the depths of Dana's desk.

After some examination they stood back, appraising me. There were a number of 'tch-tch' murmurs and some head shaking. I felt like Cinderella being fitted out for the ball, still largely uncertain whether or not I'd make it.

Finally, Mrs Wurstová announced, 'I have one coat at home that my daughter once wore. She is grown-up now and can't fit into it. You are so small, my little kangaroo, I'm sure it will do perfectly. Coats are too much expensive at shop.'

'Oh—are you sure? Thank you, thank you!'

True to her fairy godmother role, Mrs Wurstová waved away my dribbling gratitude, saying, 'I will make the coat arrive for you tomorrow.'

And indeed, the very next day she presented me with a long, thick beige coat and scarf. She and Dana dressed me and I felt like royalty. They both then beamed like Cinderella's fairy god-mother (and assistant) and I headed fearlessly into the day's chill. Not only did I feel warm again, I felt terribly grand. The coat brushed the tops of my boots, and I completed the outfit with a woollen hat and gloves.

I twirled around in it like Dr Zhivago's Lara.

I was going to the ball after all.

However, no sooner had I worked out how to stay warm on the streets, I had to work out how not to overheat inside. In the colder months the Czechs pumped gallons of hot air throughout their buildings, hot enough so that when it was –10°C outside, workers could walk around inside in shirt sleeves. I had no idea how to get the balance right.

Most days I'd barely be through the front door of any building before a blast of boiling hot air would bring on a hot flush. Frantic, I would start ripping at my clothes, pulling off layer after layer, messing my hair and smudging my make-up. By the time I staggered into classrooms, barely visible above books, coat, scarf, hat and gloves, hair sticking up at all angles and perspiration dripping down my back, I looked more like a vaga-bond than a teacher.

The next challenge of the changing seasons was coordinating night-time public transport, especially as darkness now came early and the nights were freezing. If I got the timing wrong, I would miss key tram, metro and bus connections. This would mean a wait of an hour or more, huddled in the corner of icy, windy, poorly lit transport stops, trying to avoid the mumbles of leering drunks and chain-smoking old men.

Late trips did have one redeeming feature. I would see concert musicians fresh from weaving their magic in the lavish Prague theatres where no doubt they'd been lauded with accolades; heroes and heroines of the concert hall. It was surreal and thrilling for me, a girl from the bush, to travel each night with the stars of the Prague stages. I would spend much of my trips gazing admiringly at them from out of the corner of my eye and wishing I had the courage to ask for autographs. They seemed so humble, so *normal*. Up close, their black-and-white outfits were often threadbare and dated. Their instruments were usually held in scratched and battered music cases. They would often sleep standing up, holding the inner rail, cases between their legs, anonymous once out of the spotlight.

'I want to go and see a real classical concert,' I announced to Anne, anxious to see these musicians close up in all their glory and especially hear them play the works of Smetana, Dvořák and Suk. The city was abuzz with recitals and crammed with recital halls, musicians and mansions, so it would be easy to find a show. Concerts took place in chandeliered salons and Renaissance palaces and chapels, in grand opera and theatre houses and ancient churches—pretty much everywhere. All I needed was for Anne to interpret the schedules and agree to join me.

'Right, there's a performance at the Rudolfinum,' Anne said, consulting *The Prague Post*. 'Dvořák's Ninth Symphony is playing this weekend. I'll get us tickets at the—woohoo—special local price!'

Woohoo, indeed!

Only locals, and people who were sufficiently fluent in Czech like Anne could buy 'local' tickets to Prague's varied forms of entertainment. 'Tourist' tickets were exorbitant and beyond a teacher's budget. But Anne would chat in her soft and charming

Czech to the ticket dispensers at the various theatres, and—bingo!—return brandishing fistfuls of tickets we could all afford. I was so impressed she could pass herself off as a local.

I was especially thrilled we would be hearing Dvořák's Symphony No. 9, *From the New World*. Helena from Sedlčany had introduced me to the work; in fact, she'd watched tears pour down my cheeks as I soaked up Dvořák's homesickness and felt my own so keenly.

That Saturday night, swirling around in my Lara coat and feeling like a movie star, I waited for Anne to join me on the steps of the Rudolfinum. The gold-encrusted nineteenth-century theatre gazed imperiously over the River Vltava and was home to the famous Prague Philharmonic Orchestra. Theatregoers swarmed up the floodlit steps, flanked by the statues and carved golden lions that led to the building's ornate entrance. Everyone wore fur coats, long gowns and black tie, and looked like royalty.

'*Ahoj!*' Anne's smiling face emerged through the crowd. We hugged, took each other's arm and stepped through stately etched glass doors into paradise. Attendants took our coats and put them in a cloakroom, which added to the sense of glamour.

'It would be perfect if Dickie was here,' said Anne, slightly wistfully, as we sipped champagne in crystal at a long marble bar with the other beautiful people. 'But this wouldn't be his kind of music anyway. He's a punk rocker!'

We laughed at this. I knew it wouldn't be Karel's music either; his first and last musical love was the folk music from the forests of Bohemia, played on guitar and preferably by Brontosaurus, the group to whom we'd waltzed on the night I'd brought home the Czech crystal.

The bell went and we sailed up a wide marble staircase, through the plush richness of red velvet curtains, past curving balustrades and gleaming gold trim, and into the Dvořák Hall itself. I forgot about Karel and instead thought how lucky I was, a girl from the outback, about to experience an event people at home could only dream about.

The orchestra warmed up, the conductor in tails strode across the stage, and the crowd erupted. Emotions swam in my eyes from the first note of Dvořák's *New World*.

As the orchestral strains rang through the rafters, I sent Helena a silent thank you for introducing me to these soaring expressions of sky and bird, of field and river, of forest and flower. Outside the night sky fell into the River Vltava. I felt the waters wrap me in their embrace, enveloping me with their magic. I belonged here in a way I couldn't explain.

And those musicians—at a distance, they looked every bit as glamorous as I knew they would.

⸻⟫●⟪⸻

'You want real music experience, Táničko?' asked Karel when I told him about the concert. 'Next weekend we go to historic town called Mělník—in countryside north of Prague—for *burčák* wine fest. It is the annual fest for young white wines released at this time of the year. And Brontosaurus will be playing there!'

'Ooh-er! Really? How exciting. And what is *burčák*?'

'It is . . . how you say . . . partly bubbling juice from grapes.'

Did he mean *fermenting*? It sounded something like the release of young new Beaujolais wines at the beginning of autumn in France.

'*Tak!*' said Karel. 'And we will dance to Brontosaurus in the main square with many, many other people.'

It all sounded perfect. I imagined myself whirling round in his arms, wandering along, sipping wine, kissing among the autumn colours.

'We will go with some friends—and the girls and Princess.'

I smiled wanly, reminding myself that Karel came as a package and that I was lucky to be included in that package. Besides, the presence of lots of people gave me more chances to practise my Czech, to meet others, to assimilate. That was important to building a life here.

Pushing down the mulga stick ache that months ago had wedged itself down in the hollow inside me, I focused on how lucky I was. Then I went and faxed my family and told them all my news. It was a bit like being at boarding school again, torn between two places. Having a foot in each place meant I didn't fully belong in either one, but I had to make this work.

I wasn't ready to give up. I didn't *want* to give up.

25

A-networking we go!

When I next turned up to English House, I found Canadian Carolyn pinning a flyer to the noticeboard.

'Hi Tanya,' she said over her shoulder, pins in her mouth. 'There's an international group in Prague called "Women in Business". They meet and network. Want to go?'

My heart turned over. More people to meet—and women in business, no less! Surely this was serendipity with a capital S.

There was one catch. I didn't know how to network. That's what people did in American films where they handed out business cards and wore jackets with padded shoulders and made deals over cocktails and did each other favours.

'It's easy,' said Carolyn. 'Just take lots of business cards. Introduce yourself to lots of people. Ask them what they do. Get them to talk about their work.'

I knew Karel used business cards so I sought his advice too.

'Yes, Táničko, to hand out a card is *normální* in Prague. It is how people do the business here. You can make them at machine at the Old Town Square metro station. Best printer of all the metro stations. Just use some words similar to your newspaper ad. And yes, you can use my telephone number again.'

After a long and complex negotiation with a strange machine at the metro, I rushed back to English House with fifty white cards in my money belt. 'Okay, let's do it!'

The next Tuesday evening Carolyn and I met by the tram in the Old Town Square and headed towards a Viennese-style café called Gany's. The night was frigid and I pulled Mrs Wurstová's coat close, the chilled wind nipping at my heels and slicing through my collar. The blue court dress underneath provided little protection. We walked fast. Carolyn talked as we walked.

'I've found out a bit about this group. The president is half-British, half-Czech. Her name is Irena Brichta. She is well-known in the Prague business world.'

Gany's was a gorgeous Art Deco café, abuzz with noise and smartly dressed women: suits, high heels, coiffed hair. For a minute I wanted to turn and run. I'd never had the nerve to do something like this back home. Why did I think I could do it here?

Carolyn was having none of my weak-kneed behaviour. She took my sleeve and pulled me towards the middle of the room, grabbing us each a glass of wine on the way. I clutched my glass and wondered how, when and to whom I should hand a business card. In the distance was a woman I couldn't take my eyes off.

She was tall with short dark hair, trim, toned and smartly besuited in tailored linen. Working the room, she was handing out business cards, smiling brightly and welcoming people.

Clapping her hands, she called the meeting to order.

'*Dobrý večer* and good evening to you all!' She beamed around the room. 'I am Irena Brichta, president of this group, and I welcome you all. We are many women of diverse nationalities living in Prague together. Tonight we will network, share those issues we have in common, and discuss business in the Czech Republic.'

Murmurs of assent, support.

She continued. 'A little about myself. I am Czech-born, with a Czech father and English mother. Raised in Britain. My career involves managing executive search businesses all over Europe. I run the Prague branch of Heidrick & Struggles. I speak fluent Czech so that gives me a great advantage.'

'Upmarket headhunter,' Carolyn murmured. 'Seriously impressive.'

Indeed—not just because Irena was so capable of self-promotion, but because she was living the dream. Well, *my* dream, at least. She combined two worlds, the West and Eastern Europe, and she could do this because she was both brilliant and bilingual.

Irena pointed out that the room of women comprised bankers, architects, lawyers, accountants, editors, marketing managers, small business operators, diplomats and even members of the Peace Corps. The common language was English but women from every nationality imaginable were present.

'Please, give a brief bio of yourselves,' Irena continued, 'and then you are all free to network and make the most of this evening.'

When it came to my turn, my throat was dry, but I got through my story—Australian lawyer teaching English in Prague, looking for work—and hoped somebody in the group might want to help out. But it seemed that to be successful here one had to be an expat with an expat firm, or bilingual like Irena, and I was depressingly aware of my lack of options.

After it was over and we were released to find more wine (which I now required desperately), I spotted Irena bearing down upon me. Panic struck my already parched throat but Irena didn't seem to notice my mumbles. Instead, she thrust a strong hand into mine and passed me a card with the other.

'I was so *interested* to hear you're from Australia,' she said. 'Most of my family now live in Sydney and I go out there for Christmas every year. Please give me your card and I hope to talk to you further.'

Really? Australia? And a card? Oh yes, a card! With a damp palm, I ferreted around in my money belt, then remembered the cheap metro-machine paper on which it was printed and hoped Irena wouldn't look too closely at it.

'Come to my office next week and we can talk about Australia and you can tell me about your experiences here.'

I nodded mutely, stunned, thrilled.

'Totally amazing.' Carolyn kept shaking her head on the way home. I wanted to skip with joy but my court shoes prevented it. I also thought of Irena's final comment: 'Also, I'm a Hash House Harrier and we're heading next weekend to a rather beautiful park south-east of Prague. Would you like to join us?'

I'd blinked confusedly but she'd explained.

The Hash House Harriers, or HHH, were an international running group and the Czech version involved some running and a huge amount of beer drinking. *Beer?* Looking at Irena's trim figure, it was hard to imagine, but I expected she was brilliant at everything.

'It's beautiful this time of the year in the forests. And remember—bring your business cards. You will meet lots of people!'

I couldn't bring myself to say no although it sounded terrifying. Fortunately I'd started running at night around Prosek (inspired by my recent 'love is for nothing' enraged stomp) but I was really doing it to stave off the autumn stodge rather than because I enjoyed it.

When I got home I told Karel.

'Have you heard of "hashing"?' I asked. 'It involves beer, lots of it, and some running.'

He looked nonplussed so I filled him in on the details.

'Er, no, Táničko . . . it does *not* sound nice for the beer. Not at all.'

The following weekend I left Prosek and headed to meet Irena and her crowd of 'hashers'. It was a two-hour journey from Prague by bus and train, with lots of stops and starts en route. I arrived weary and overheated. The last of my goodwill evaporated completely as I took in a large and very excitable group gathered on the edge of the platform.

I expected these were the HHH reps; if so, this was no amateur's picnic. Where were the gentle walkers and overweight beer-drinkers I was expecting? Most in the crowd were lean and fit and engaging in an assortment of stretching exercises. In the chilly afternoon air, their breath hovered in clouds. The majority had muscular runner's legs. Almost all were wearing proper running gear: bright, skin-tight lycra tops and leggings with top-quality running shoes. I looked down at my own dilapidated and muddy sandshoes, not to mention my unfashionable brown jogging bottoms and thick pink parka. My stomach turned over as I realised how embarrassing I looked.

But before I could scuttle back on the train, Irena spotted me and strode over. She was elegantly attired in a matching outfit of emerald green lycra.

'You made it. Excellent!' she breezed. 'We're about to head off. Join in as best you can. Bring your business cards?'

I shoved my hand into my pocket and wriggled it around. There was only empty space inside. My stomach twisted. 'Er . . .'

Irena didn't have time to wait for such inefficiencies. 'I'll be at the front as one of the leaders, but if you have any problems, you can tell me when we stop for beer. We'll stop quite often.'

She was interrupted by a tall, strapping German of indeterminate age and bulging biceps blowing a horn and shouting: 'So! I am Heinz. We will go. You must all have map. We will make five beer stops in this run. You all know the penalty for failure to drink beer at each stop. *On, on!*'

I looked around anxiously. My clothes didn't match. I'd forgotten my business cards. I didn't have a map. I didn't know what the penalties were. I was certainly unable to drink beer at five *pivo* stops.

But before I could find a map—or, better still, a strategy for escape—the German blew his horn again and about forty people tore off after him. This was a lot like a hunt and we were a mix of horses, dogs and fox.

The next hour was a blur. I tried to keep up with the stragglers of the group and follow the distant shouts of 'On, on!' as Heinz and Irena led us up hill and down dale through the forest behind the railway station. Irena was right—the forest was beautiful, a mass of bright gold flecked with crimson and brown. As I ran and panted and sucked in snatches of sharp, clean pine-scented air, I told myself, through agonised breaths, to enjoy it. Tall conifers stretched high overhead and their leaves made a soft carpet underfoot for the runners. We cut across steep rocky slopes and then downhill towards a series of rushing, crystal-clear streams, pounded across several narrow footbridges, and puffed up the hills on the other side only to do it all again. Yes, it was truly beautiful and I would never, ever have found this place alone.

I thought of the times I used to run from our homestead to the nearby water bore. I remembered a bowl of blue sky that ringed a flat red landscape, the air turning my skin crackly dry, straggly mulgas lining the low hills and thick dust caking my running shoes. The bore windmill always creaked as it turned slowly in the wind, crows cawing overhead.

Back then I could never have imagined being able to run in pristine beauty like this—in soft greenery, with water everywhere. But while I knew I should be enjoying it more than I was, it was clear that neither my jogs back home nor those around Prosek were sufficient preparation for running with the HHH, and I was struggling.

Heaving and wheezing, I ended up as one of the last runners trailing behind the others; for all I knew, the walkers were ahead of me too. It was hard to keep focused on the glorious surrounds when my only focus was making it to the finishing line.

After twenty minutes or so I clambered over a rise towards a little wooden hut and staggered to a halt. I hacked and breathed and sucked in air. A stitch in my side threatened to cripple me. I thought I might just stay there and die. Then I lifted my eyes to the most bizarre sight imaginable.

All around the hut, grown men and women were downing litre jugs of *pivo*, splashing beer all over themselves (despite the chilled afternoon air), shouting and challenging one another, throwing down empty jugs as soon as they were finished and racing off again, roaring, 'On, on!'

Irena was fitting in a few short stretches as I came to a ragged halt. 'This is a great way to keep warm, isn't it?' she called out. 'And then, just when you need it, the beer cools you down! See you at the next stop!' She waved gaily and dashed off.

A stout Czech man was distributing the beer in the little hut. He passed me a huge glass jug frothing over with amber liquid. I staggered under its weight. Out of the corner of my eye I saw a small group watching. Someone jotted down notes on a small writing pad. Dear God—were they the modern-day hashing equivalent of the secret police?

The pressure was on. I heaved the glass up to my lips but couldn't manage any more than two gulps. The note-taker shook his head at this cardinal sin, wrote something rapidly, tucked his pad away and jogged off. I put the jug down quickly, thanked the man in the hut and ran after the note-taker, hoping he'd already forgotten me.

As the hour wore on, the back of my legs burnt with lactic acid and my lungs were ready to burst. Each *pivo* stop offered short-lived relief but I couldn't manage any more than a few sips each time. Irena, who threw back *pivo* jugs with the best of them, shouted a warning at me as she sprinted past: 'You may be called upon at the end to scull a jug if you can't do better than that, my dear!'

Alarmed, I put on a spurt for the last leg of the hash and finally staggered across the finishing line in a blur of nausea and pain. I collapsed at the bottom of a nearby tree.

The rest of the runners swarmed backwards and forwards, slapping each other's backs and cheering. The winners had to scull large jugs of beer, as did the losers; everyone appeared to take it in their stride, with much hooting and laughing. I remained in a heap at a distance, hoping the note-taker had forgotten me.

Irena, though, had not.

'Well then!' she shouted cheerfully, extracting herself from a gaggle of men and women and jogging towards me. She shoved her business cards into her running belt as she did so. 'How did you like it then?'

'Fabulous, thank you!' I wheezed, struggling to breathe.

'Excellent!' said Irena happily, then called back to me as she jogged off towards another group. 'Luckily you weren't forced to scull this time. But next time we won't be as easy on you!'

———❊———

Hashing the Czech way was clearly an acquired skill and possibly required Czech genes. I did go with Irena whenever I could, though, spurred on by my desperation to find work and spend time with this extraordinary woman. I hoped some of her brilliance and success might rub off on me. It didn't, although hashing did give me the chance to find hidden pockets of magical countryside around Prague I would never have discovered on my own.

And I never did manage to hand out a business card.

26

Love is for nothing (part 2)

A week later, Radka was having more boyfriend trouble.

'It is too much for me to survive,' Karel said, shaking his head after trying without success to talk to his daughter. 'Things should be light, easy—not with problems at her age.'

From my bitter experience I knew that age was irrelevant to whether love was easy or not. Being younger often made it harder. But I'd been waiting for the opportunity to raise the 'love is for nothing' issue and decided this was as good a time as any. I took a deep breath.

'Karel, what's so wrong with hoping for love?'

I realised this was dangerous territory but I wanted to draw out Karel's real concerns. If I knew what they were, I could work out how to address them. Surely he didn't really mean 'love is for nothing'. How could he? That was not *normální*. And for the first time in a long time, I had something riding on this: my Qantas ticket deadline, looming in late March. It was just over four months away.

'Love?' Karel's eyes turned wide with shock, as though I'd asked him what was so wrong with life under Stalin. 'Do we have to go through this again?'

'Well, *why* don't you believe in it?' I persisted.

For a moment I thought Karel might have a heart attack. He paced around, spluttering. 'You are beautiful flower, Táničko, and you live in a daydream. I need to tell you: there is no "happy ever after" for love, except in fairytales.'

I was momentarily miffed. Why couldn't fairytales be real? Growing up, I'd been told that the full version of Tanya— Tatiana—meant 'fairy princess' in Russian. Tatiana was also a Fairy Queen in *Midsummer Night's Dream*. Fairytales could be as real as you wanted them to be, dammit. I'd also staked a great deal of my life's hopes and dreams on finding love and wasn't letting this drop.

'That's not true!' I said defensively. 'Lots of people around the world believe in love.'

Karel breathed heavily. 'I need *not* to keep enduring this conversation, so I will tell you why I do not believe in it.'

He folded his arms, his voice grave. 'I once loved very much, very deeply, my wife.'

What?!

In my wildest nightmares, I'd not anticipated a response involving his *wife*.

'I collected from her the "down" . . . the special covering on a butterfly . . . that is Czech expression for when we find and take a true love. We take that special covering from the butterfly and it becomes our own.'

Butterfly 'down'?

'But eventually my wife left me. I took my girls and raised them myself. It has taken me and my girls many years to recover from this. Yes, I have had other women, as you know, but I said I would never let that hurt happen to me again.'

Oh my God.

'The only thing that matters is some nice friendship. That is what I want with you. It means no one gets hurt.'

This was worse than what I'd expected—far, far worse. I wanted the floor to swallow me up; I wanted to catch that Qantas flight out of there tomorrow morning. I turned away, tears welling, ashamed at myself and my stupidity. I'd ignored the first rule of cross-examination: don't ask a question unless you know the answer.

Karel pressed on. 'Czech *friendship* is the one thing that lasts forever. It is the highest of all feelings between people because it does not die or get broken.'

I remembered Pavel saying this to me in Sedlčany. Czech friendship was so special and important it had its own name— *přítel* or *přátelství*.

But I didn't want some noble Czech friendship with Karel. I had fallen in love with him and I wanted him to love me back. I wanted more than a flaky holiday romance, a happy fling. I wanted a relationship with him that could grow and mean something, where we were on the 'same board', like Anne and Dickie.

True, I'd not wanted this before. But I'd never met anyone like Karel before. I'd never lived anywhere like Prague before. I'd never felt so alive and happy before. For the first time I'd met someone with whom I felt free to be who I truly was, and I felt empowered by the possibilities and potential of a future life with him.

I pressed the tears back into my eyes, wanting to curl up and die.

He went on, relentlessly, far beyond what I'd intended, perhaps reading my mind.

'Táničko, if I love you, I will marry you and have children with you here—and then one day you will leave me and return to Australia. It is *normální*. Then I will be broken again. Completely. And I will never recover.'

'You'll never recover?' I heard my anguished voice as though from a distance.

'The truth is, one day you will have husband your own age and children in Australia—yes, I know you will, because your family is there, you have good career there, and the chance for this so-called love you talk about. That is *normální*.'

Finally, my voice came—rushed denials and heated words— but he put his fingers to my lips. His voice was weary. 'You can stay with me forever if you want. I've told you before now. But that is your choice. This is the highest thing that I can do for you. Do you want to keep arguing with me?'

———————⟶•⟵———————

The following weekend included a public holiday so I went away by bus with Headmistress Anne and Czech-English lawyer Vera.

Anne had suggested a girls' long weekend in the beautiful medieval town Český Krumlov and I couldn't take up her offer fast enough.

I needed time apart from Karel to tend to my wounded soul and regain my sense of self. As we were heading somewhere new, it would be a distraction from the stark realisation confronting me. I couldn't have what I wanted with Karel and I was a fool.

Perhaps if I had that special butterfly down, things might be different, and Karel would, *could*, love me. I'd seen a photograph of his former wife. She was beautiful, just like Radka—slim waist, dark hair, high cheekbones. I couldn't even begin to compare, with my small, dumpy Celtic genes. Instead, my hopes of finding love with Karel were dashed—which, according to him, was the inevitable consequence of love anyway.

Once with the girls, I shared my sorry tale with them. And over mulled wine they were both sympathetic and supportive. God, I loved my girlfriends.

The weekend was fun and I jammed my despair down inside me, not wanting to miss out on the new adventure, and nodded in agreement when they reassured me that I just needed to meet the right person and everything would fall into place. At night I breathed through the hot, heavy ache in my heart and thought sadly that Radka and I weren't that different after all.

At our prompting, Anne also filled us in on her letters to and from Dickie. When she said, 'He's coming back to Prague to see me', with her cheeks pink, eyes bright, I was thrilled for her but wanted to cry for myself. After all, that was what real love looked like, wasn't it?

I was so thankful to have these girlfriends. I reminded myself that it was one of the best things about boarding school. Those years had taught me about the beauty of friendships between girls and women and I treasured my connections with these two.

What lay ahead was unknown. The worst-case scenario was surviving four more months, then flying home to forget all about Karel, my hopes and my dreams.

I thought about a recent conversation with Dr Holub. When I'd told him of my attempts to find more work in Prague he'd looked sad. 'I am very sorry to tell you this, Tanya. This will not be possible because you are not Czech.'

'But I'm learning Czech, I'm trying really hard, I'm studying Czech, I could be a real help to the Ministry and the courts. Surely anything is possible?'

He'd looked even sadder. 'Not in our country. Surely our history should tell you that.' He sighed. 'You must return to Australia if you wish to work in law.'

My heart had sunk. Was this payback for the West's betrayals? Why were the Czechs so wretchedly pessimistic? But I hadn't lived through two world wars and communism like Dr Holub had, where virtually no dreams had come true, ever.

With a jolt, I remembered him saying, 'We just want our country back to ourselves.'

27

A toilet in the kitchen

Arriving back at Prosek after my long weekend away in Český Krumlov, I opened the front door and stopped, stunned.

The interior walls of the apartment were gone.

The kitchen, living room, toilet and bathroom had been turned into a one-room building site.

Remnants of walls were lying in untidy, chaotic piles all over the cramped space. Ugly grey pipes, once well-hidden, now crawled visibly over the floor, ceiling and walls. It was like a basement boiler room that had been freshly bombed.

The only rooms left standing were the two small bedrooms at the back.

And there was dust, dust, dust everywhere.

Not a fine layer, but thick, choking wads of dust—over the pillows, the ancient lounge suite, the lino floor and carpets, the kitchen sink and rusty stove, the bathroom cabinets, the old television and the ubiquitous long Czech living room dresser filled with glassware. The bedrooms hadn't escaped either: the bed linen, duvets and pillows were all smothered in dust. Every inch of space in the tiny apartment was littered with hammers, nails, drills and buckets. Rows of bricks were stacked in each available corner, as were pieces of timber of all sizes and shapes. The furniture had been moved, stacked high, and anything with a level surface had become a workbench.

And, most astonishing of all, the bathroom and toilet were now the centrepieces in this one-room construction site. Without walls around them, they were barely a metre in any direction from whatever else was left standing—the kitchen stove and cupboards, the lounge suite and the bedroom doors. They brazenly boasted a 360-degree view of the entire apartment.

I dropped my backpack, speechless.

Then I saw Karel. Standing in the bath, presumably because there was nowhere else to stand, he was caked in dust and hammering at some pipes. A tape measure was draped around his neck; one hand held a power tool, the other a beer. He was wearing grey baggy trousers that were filthy and held up with ancient braces. His reading glasses were coated in dust and pushed high on his head, and there were huge dark rings under his eyes.

'Karel, what is going on?'

'Ah yes . . . Táničko,' he said distractedly. 'I have one reconstruction project that has been delayed so I decided to take this time to renovate our apartment. As you know, I have wanted to do it for a long time and now seems good opportunity.'

'Now? For how long?'

'Perhaps one month.'

'You must be joking! How can we live and sleep in all this . . . this . . . dust? And what about cooking? Privacy?' I choked on the last two words. 'The bath? The *toilet*?'

'*Ano*, and what about them?' Karel stared at me, perplexed.

I couldn't believe I was the only one who saw a problem.

'There are no walls! Or doors! You can see the toilet and the bathroom from everywhere in the apartment!'

Karel started to sound agitated. '*Ano*? And what is wrong with that?'

'Well, privacy, you know!' I burst out, equally agitated. 'There are three of us who live in this tiny space . . . and visitors come here . . . and . . .' I trailed off.

Karel looked exasperated. He climbed out of the bath and walked towards me.

'You Australian girl! When I was in army as young man, we were lined up once a day and had to squat together over ditch latrine that we built with our own hands.'

I shuddered.

He shook his head. 'If some sort of privacy is important to you, next time you want to use WC, you tell me and I will go and stand on balcony for as long as you need. Now, I must get on with this. I have very little time and much work to do.'

The fractured apartment, crumbling around us, was a metaphor for our lives.

Worst of all was the toilet and bath set-up. Every morning became a frenzied dash to get to the toilet before Radka opened her bedroom door or Karel wanted to use it. I huddled down, trying not to be seen, trying to feel normal (which proved to be almost impossible). During the evening, I would ask Karel to go out onto the balcony, but given how cold it now was, he was usually back after a perilously short time, ignoring my feeble protests and grinning as he marched past to carry on with his next project: 'Just pretend I am still out there!'

In every spare moment I had, I did what I could to help. I thought it might mend things between us. Since my return, our conversations had been limited to all things logistical, and Karel mostly slept on the couch because he worked through the night. But eventually, I'd had enough. A helpful friend from Australia faxed me with advice.

'My dear, he's in his cave and there's nothing you can do about it until it's over. Isn't there a nice hotel you can go to?'

Huh. At A$200 per night, only tourists could afford to stay in hotels in this country.

After a week Radka sensibly moved out into Šárka's apartment. For the sake of my sanity and my blood pressure, I decided I also had to go. But where?

The wonderful Irena Brichta, Upmarket Headhunter and Hash House Harrier Extraordinaire, came to my rescue. After hearing my traumatic tale, she said briskly, 'You can come and stay with me for a few days.'

'Really? Oh, thank you, thank you, thank you!' I repeated inanely.

Irena lived in a quaint village that was once miles from Prague but now part of the outskirts. And she lived in a real 'family home' (the first I'd seen in my time here), with a private garden (unheard of in *panelák* suburbs), on a quiet street of other family houses, flanked by a forest. Oh joy!

The house itself was two-storeyed, spacious and beautifully appointed. Every room featured high ceilings, elegant fittings and furnishings, and fresh flowers in vases. Glossy magazines—in English—were piled on the oak table in the living room. Gold frames and stunning artwork covered the walls. Stylish curtains hung from wide windows. Comfortable, squashy chairs filled the house. The kitchen was modern, equipped with the first microwave I'd seen in this country. By Czech standards, it was a mansion.

On arrival, I plonked down my backpack and collapsed with relief into the gin and tonic Irena offered me. It was the first one of these I'd seen since arriving in this country as well.

'Drink it,' Irena said dryly. 'Then straight to the bath with you.'

Irena's home opened up another world to me. I had my own bedroom, clean linen and access to a beautiful, gleaming private bathroom. I luxuriated in the bubbles and felt dazed by my good fortune. The chaos of Karel's life drained away with the warm soapy water. For the first few days, I didn't even miss him. In fact, I didn't even want to think about him. I felt like a Westerner again and revelled in it.

Every evening I asked Irena about her life. How had she become so successful? What could I learn from her? I couldn't believe my luck at being here with a real female success story. I didn't want to miss the opportunity to learn what I could. Even if I had to leave the country later, I was sure I could apply her wisdom back home.

Irena's responses were straightforward. Simply, one must work and network. 'Out every night', she said firmly. Really? It sounded exhausting. But Irena had enough drive to power ten Czech electricity stations. Her entertainment included Rotary International (a non-paying gig that gave her great networking opportunities), and she exercised by hashing (a further net-working opportunity) and galloping horses through Czech fields. She zoomed around Prague in a groovy English sports car and never took the metro. She lived alone, happily.

Irena's life struck me as terrifying. While I'd always shied away from commitment, I'd also gravitated towards community, family, people. I loved living with others—the more the merrier—and I'd happily shared large, rambunctious houses throughout my university and working years. No doubt it was why I had missed family so much when living alone in Sedlčany, and why I had been drawn to Karel's life.

After talking with Irena, however, I learnt that she was rarely alone because she hosted endless visitors from all around the world and her house was usually overflowing. But I wasn't sure I had even a pinch of her toughness or focus. Irena realised that. 'You must work on your shyness,' she said, briskly. 'And practise meeting new people.'

Against the backdrop of these opportunities available to me, it didn't take long for guilt to emerge. I realised that while I was luxuriating in this mansion, Karel was single-handedly trying to upgrade the only place he could ever afford. Irena had told me that the monthly rent on her house was approximately the average *annual* Czech wage. It was rented for her by her company, and its value and luxury were beyond the comprehension of the average Czech.

After a few gin and tonics on about my fourth night, it dawned on me that Karel was creating his own version of a 'family home' within the confines of what he had. Even though he was not a builder, he was doing it alone. He was his own draftsman, builder, concreter, tiler, plumber. He had no backyard shed to store things in or tray-top ute to collect things in or hardware stores to buy things from (as we did back home). He was 'criss-crossing all over the Prague' by foot and public transport to find his materials, after which he had to haul them up and down stairs and stack them wherever he could in the apartment.

Grudging respect replaced my frustration.

The anger started to dissipate in the waters of my many baths. I acknowledged Karel hadn't ended our liaison—in fact he'd said I could stay forever if I wanted. He wasn't a cad like some of those I'd dallied with in the past; he was kind, generous and hospitable. It wasn't his fault we wanted different things. He was scarred by love and had said he wanted to protect us both from future scarring. Perhaps I'd overreacted, wanted too much too soon. After all, this was the man who hadn't had a woman living in his apartment for fourteen years. Change was unlikely to come overnight.

The thought of leaving Karel now was too painful anyway. Maybe I had to take things a little more easily, relax, have more fun. My new strategy, born in the bath, would be to ignore Karel's dismal predictions, and continue to work hard—just as Irena did, but in a different way. If I was successful in finding more work, perhaps Karel would come around. If I could help him believe in love again, he might decide he could love me after all. No marriage or children were necessary—simply love. Surely that was possible?

———————

By the end of the next week, Irena would have friends arriving for a visit from London. I had to leave. Thanking Irena with all my heart, I hoicked up my backpack and trudged back to *Panelák* Hiroshima (as his friends had taken to referring to the apartment).

I'd left a phone message telling Karel I was returning, but I still hesitated outside, unsure what awaited me.

Eventually, I took a big breath and turned the key. And came face to face with half a door propped up against the pipes and the bath. Lo and behold, it obscured the toilet! The living room dresser had been dragged in front of the bath. Although, anyone sitting on the throne or in the bath could be seen from both bedrooms and from the corridor, there was no doubt about it: the area was partially enclosed.

'Yes, I made some improvements. It was for some strange Australian girl who seems to think we need a wall or door around WC.'

Throwing down my backpack, the suppressed emotions of the last month welled up inside me in a rising tide. Karel walked towards me, his blue eyes alight, and I rushed into his arms, tears brimming. Soon I was covered in dust but it didn't matter. I didn't care.

'*Tak, můj miláčku,*' he murmured, casting his eyes around at the chaos and kissing me absent-mindedly. 'It is very good you are back. Have you seen my glasses anywhere?'

Dickie arrived in Prague and Anne was delirious with excitement. We all met at the Obnoxious Pub for celebratory beers. When Dickie enquired how I was going, I told him I'd been living in a building site for some weeks.

'Really? I'm a bit of a renovator myself,' he enthused. 'I'd love to have a look at how the Czechs do it.'

'No, Dickie!' I immediately regretted my revelation. 'It's horrible out there.'

'I like horrible!' Dickie was unfazed. 'Anne, when can we go?'

Anne looked at me and shrugged helplessly. It was on.

As we left I whispered to Anne that Karel and I were back together although my future remained a muddle. She gave me a squeeze and said she'd support me no matter what. I hugged her back.

When I told Karel about the impending visit, he was delighted. '*Tak*! Some special English renovator will come and look at my work? We can share the ideas!'

I was not at all delighted. The apartment no longer looked like *Panelák* Hiroshima but it was still a way off completion. I also felt nervous. It would be Anne's first visit to the *panelák*, it wasn't my home, and I was unsure of the Czech rules of entertaining.

Karel was oblivious to my anxiety. With several hours up his sleeve on the afternoon of their visit, he decided to slap a new coat of paint on the living room walls. It was on his list of things to do for that day and he saw no point in delaying because of guests. Besides, he told me, Dickie was a renovator too, and would understand perfectly.

Anne and Dickie arrived, holding hands. We exchanged hugs and kisses. There were gasps of admiration all round at Karel's handiwork. In celebration Karel pulled a bottle of Bohemian Sekt from the fridge with a flourish. He wiped away the afternoon's dust from the champagne glasses and bowed deeply to Dickie.

'Please, Mr Dickie, I would like you to open the bottle. It is in honour of your return to our beautiful Prague.'

'Well,' grinned Dickie, 'let's pop the cork and get on with it, shall we?' In his exuberance, he inserted his fingers under the cork and let it rip.

Like a homing missile under instructions, the cork headed directly towards Karel's new paint job. Bubbles sprayed from one end of the wall to the other. A long silence ensued. Karel seemed paralysed, as did Dickie. Anne's ears turned crimson. I was undone by the tension and stifled giggles.

Dickie was the first to break the tableau. He rushed forward and tried to wipe away the mess of bubbles now dripping onto the floor. It didn't work. Anne put her head in her hands.

A few agonising moments later, Karel recovered his equilibrium. Being the consummate Czech host, he suggested we forget about it and drink the champagne. The wall could always be repainted.

Several bottles later, Karel was feeling no pain, and nor were we. He had taken to calling Anne's beau 'Dickie Pickie', taking pleasure in the rhyme, and feeling affection and amusement towards his English Renovator Colleague. Dickie in turn regaled us with the best of British humour.

As the night wore on, the effect of so much champagne meant Anne needed to use the toilet. I had warned her what to expect, but even she was not prepared for the intimacy of perching on the throne in such circumstances. With only a makeshift door propped up against it, barely two metres from the table around which we were all gathered, it was too much for my Scottish rose.

She crossed her legs and held on, her face growing redder as the evening progressed.

As they left, she managed to whisper, 'He's a really nice man, Tanya. *Really* nice. You two do seem happy together. Perhaps it *will* work for you.'

Her words filled me with some strange sort of hope.

———◦———

A week or so later, piles of bricks started to grow next to the bath. Karel mixed cement in an old orange bucket and, brick by brick, laboriously built a wall between the bath and the toilet, until he was standing on a ladder and had nearly reached the ceiling. Radka assisted, having courageously returned to the fold from Šárka's sanctuary. The entire apartment was filled with the overpowering smell of wet cement, grey grit and bits of brick, but I was past caring.

Privacy was on its way!

Finally, and not a month too soon, the new kitchen and bathroom took some shape. And eventually, we had three walls around the toilet.

'What about a door?' I pleaded with Karel.

'I give you three walls. What now is your problem?'

'But a door . . . it can't be too hard to put a door on? Surely . . .'

'Time is not yet right. That is obvious, yes?' Karel the engineer looked at me pityingly, shaking his head.

'But . . .'

'*Tak*, Táničko, this is how it goes. We order all doors for new bathroom and new toilet and new kitchen at same time. Then I have to go by bus and metro and by Šárka's car to collect them and bring them back and install them. This is long difficult process.'

He drew a long, weary breath.

'I told you, *můj miláčku*, it is not easy to renovate apartment in Prague.'

Finally, the apartment was finished.

We now had a brand-new bathroom complete with tiled walls in muted grey and pink tones. There were enormous mirrors on two of its walls, flanked by stage lights that made it look like a professional backstage dressing room. Best of all, there was a brand spanking new bath and basin with shining gold taps and handrail. For a tiny space that was really not big enough to swing a cat in, the bathroom now looked and felt large and luxurious.

The living room had new furniture, including a soft, comfortable couch in bright tones and a freshly painted wall. The kitchen was fitted with new wooden cupboards, built and installed by Karel, and smart wooden benches.

In a very small area, Karel had created the effect of an upmarket, spacious and airy apartment.

But best of all, the toilet now boasted a brand-new door.

———⟫⟡⟨———

Having achieved his long-held dream, Karel returned to his normal self, heading off to his real day job in his strangely endearing purple suits, changing into blue denim shirt and jeans at night. The dust-and-plaster-caked clothes were packed away and friends invited back in. Radka presided over proceedings and Šárka and Princess joined the fray. The apartment had a new lease of life and so had Karel.

And so had I.

A decision about the March ticket could be made closer to the time.

28

Carp and Christmas

I'm dreaming of a white Christmas . . .

Growing up in the bush, I had thought the true setting for Christmas was snow. The pictures on Christmas cards depicted idyllic villages coated in white, nestling in snowy mountainous valleys; merry families decorating real Christmas trees, with stockings hanging over roaring log fires; rosy-cheeked children bombarding each other with snowballs; forests glittering with ice-capped pines. I'd always longed to see it and experience it myself.

Christmas Down Under was a second-rate experience, I'd decided—certainly not the real thing. How could it be? In the red heart of Central Australia we sweltered through December droughts and bushfires and flies, without a speck of snow or flash of reindeer or drop of mulled wine to be seen. I always thought it amazing that Father Christmas made it so far down to the bottom of the globe without melting.

So I was incredibly excited as my first Northern Hemisphere winter approached. There were sparkling decorations all over the city and shops stuffed with Christmas cards promising a season of magic. My bubble burst, however, when the irrepressible Mrs Wurstová told me that white Christmases were a thing of the past.

'We have not had snow at Christmas in the Prague for some time,' she said. '*To je škoda*. It's a pity. No snow. It is from—how you say—global warming.'

My jaw dropped. Global warming *here*? She nodded, but added, 'Snow will come. In the new year, in the countryside, in the mountains especially. Everyone will go to ski. So just now we must pretend with our cards and decorations . . .'

She waved expansively around at her office, which was brightly decorated with gold and silver mistletoe, dried apples, fresh pine cones, holly, traditional Christmas biscuits and candles.

The rest of the Ministry had likewise been transformed. There was even a real fir tree in the foyer, festooned with sparkling lights and colourful presents, and propped incongruously next to the grim, silent guards with their protruding guns who examined my pass with the same sceptical and distrustful gaze every day.

The Prague judiciary had also got into the decorating swing. In the High Court grounds across the river, a 100-year-old fir tree stood ablaze with lights and colour. It looked exactly like a Christmas tree should, complete with those perfectly proportioned triangular rows of green pine needles that we'd drawn and painted from our storybooks as children. In most Australian cities, people erected plastic artificial Christmas trees; in the outback, we dug up straggly mulga bushes or tired gum trees and decorated them with tinsel and a handmade star on the homestead verandah.

So Mrs Wurstová's news came as a terrible shock.

'I can't believe it!' I wailed, dropping the books and documents I'd been neatly arranging on the desk. 'I've been waiting all year for a white Christmas!'

Mrs Wurstová shrugged. 'When you live under communism long enough you can believe anything. There is probably some directive still from the Kremlin forbidding the snow.'

We both giggled.

'Do you know, Mrs Wurstová, when we were growing up in the outback, we used to buy cans of white foam at Christmas time and spray it over our windows and trees? Perhaps you need some of it here.'

Mrs Wurstová threw back her head and roared with laughter. When she laughed, it felt like the whole room vibrated with her energy and joie de vivre.

'Dana,' she called out to her long-suffering secretary. '*Pojď* sem! Come here and hear what our little kangaroo has to say.'

Fortunately, Dana was busy on the phone.

I opened my books. 'Alright, let's get started. We have a very busy morning ahead of us . . .'

Mrs Wurstová beamed. 'Ah, but you are such good teacher, Tanya. Today I don't need extra study. Tell me, how do you celebrate Christmas when it is sooooo hot in your country?'

I gazed at her severely. It had no effect.

'Well, it's very different,' I said, continuing to spread out the documents purposefully. 'It's more than forty degrees Celsius for most of the summer. The land is brown and bare. Some Christmases have been so hot I have spent much of them standing inside our large cold room, where we normally hang slabs of beef.'

'*Opravdu*? Really?' Mrs Wurstová was incredulous. She stared at me with her large brown eyes, apparently fascinated.

'*Prosím tě*, tell me more. For example, what kind of Christmas songs do you have?'

In response I pointed decisively to the books on the table, but she waved them away. 'Grammar, grammar . . . blah blah. I am tired of this grammar you force me to study. All I need is my tremendous—how you say—bluff—and the wonderful English expressions that you have already taught me—and that is enough.'

It took some effort not to laugh.

She went on cajolingly. 'So *pleeeeaze*, kind Tanya, tell me of your songs. This kind of information could be very useful when I am abroad. I will be known as very clever and special Czech woman because I know international stories.'

I wanted to say that if I could go abroad with her and be 'at her side', as the Czechs were fond of saying, I could help her even more. But the Ministry bureaucracy was not going to allow any such indulgences with foreigners like me—not on their watch. Defeated, I sat back.

'Well, as a young girl, I learnt this . . .' Then I proceeded to sing to her an Australian carol about a typical Christmas in the bush: brown earth, dust in the air and a hot wind throwing up dry leaves from the paddock. 'We call the song "Christmas Day" or the "North Wind". . .'

The image was as far from a European Christmas as possible but Mrs Wurstová was captivated, laughing and clapping her hands. She was, to her credit, an appreciative audience.

'More!' she demanded and called out yet again to the hapless Dana who was fighting her way through mountains of paperwork in the antechamber, a large room she shared with several other secretaries. 'Dana, *musíš přijít' sem*. You must come here! Come and hear our little kangaroo sing Australian Christmas songs! Tanya, *ještě jednou, prosím tě*! Another one please!'

By now a small crowd had gathered in Mrs Wurstová's office. I told them about 'Six White Boomers', the song in which the role of Father Christmas's reindeer is taken over by large white kangaroos who bounce all over the bush, delivering presents to children in far-flung desert regions. The crowd loved it. They demanded more. Someone brought coffee. A plate of spicy gingerbread biscuits appeared. Several of the secretaries began a few rounds of Czech Christmas carols and the party revved up.

I only hoped that Deputy Minister Svoboda could not hear all this revelry from his oval office, one floor up. Earlier that morning, I'd worked with him on a complex document for Brussels, and he was preparing to head out to the next round of UN talks the following day. Of all days, this was not the day for disturbances and noise. Even Mr Svoboda's usual round of grumpy advisers had been dismissed in short order before and after me.

Fortunately, no one appeared to reprimand us, and after a while Mrs Wurstová clapped her hands and the crowd dispersed as quickly as it arrived.

'You little kangaroo,' she chortled fondly. 'Thank you for very special lesson. Your country has such funny songs for the Christmas and it all sounds so exotic. You are best teacher I ever enjoyed. *Tak*! Now I must prepare for my next meeting. I see you again tomorrow.'

Well, she was the boss.

With an unexpected hour up my sleeve, I headed for Staroměstské náměstí, which fortunately—snow or no snow— had been transformed into a picture-perfect Christmas setting. I wandered through it, childlike excitement rising again; even Mrs Wurstová's news about the snow couldn't dampen the pleasure I always felt entering the Old Town Square.

The Square's enormous fir tree centrepiece rose above the crayon-coloured houses and baroque churches, hung about with glittering lights and shiny presents; old men roasted chestnuts over fires; people queued up for *svařené víno* (hot mulled red wine) and *grog* (hot water and rum) served from giant, steaming cauldrons; and the smell of cinnamon and other spices and the sound of laughter filled the air. Outside the metro, a brass band and carol singers in matching blue-and-gold braided uniforms sang 'Good King Wenceslas'. Mrs Wurstová had told me the so-called king was actually a duke (but who wants to quibble?), that he was actually from here—Bohemia—and that Wenceslas Square around the corner was named after him. That was the kind of delicious, pinch-myself stuff that I loved stumbling across in this city. Every time I thought I might not be able to do this kind of thing after late March, I pushed the thought back down again. I wasn't ready to face that yet.

Besides, I had to survive Czech Christmas fare first. Karel had told me—and Mrs Wurstová confirmed it—that the Czechs celebrated Christmas with a traditional supper of fresh carp and potato salad on Christmas Eve.

'No roast turkey and trimmings on Christmas Day?'

'Roast turkey? No . . . that would not be nice celebration food for us,' said Karel.

Instead, the equivalent of the Czech fish mafia (or so it seemed to me) caught carp during the week before Christmas (by draining every main river they could find) and then sold it fresh and at great expense to hordes of Czechs from specially erected carp markets at every tram stop and metro station.

Mrs Wurstová was happy to give me the whole story at my next lesson. 'Tanya, it goes like this. After you buy fresh carp, you must take home and put in your bath full of water for whole day to clean it. Then on 24 December, you cut at its throat'—at which point she paused and made a dramatic thrusting action across her neck—'and cook it.'

I was aghast.

'Yes, you cannot have bath for more than twenty-four hours because carp must have lots of washing before eating.'

I couldn't believe my ears. And I thought the Czechs were a civilised race.

'*Tak*, if you need bath for your own cleaning, there is other way,' Mrs Wurstová sailed on. 'You can ask carp man to chop off head of fish for you and you take home on bus and metro without head.'

'Where do you keep it then?' I asked in increasing revulsion.

'Wherever you have the space. In bucket on balcony, perhaps, or in your fridge.' She narrowed her eyes. 'But you must take care, because without head, there is much blood.'

'Let me tell you, Mrs Wurstová . . .' I was starting to feel nauseous, 'carp is a menace to our river systems in Australia. It's certainly not a delicacy and we would never consider eating it. In fact, we try to get rid of it. We'—I paused dramatically—'turn it into liquid fertiliser for gardens.'

Mrs Wurstová looked slightly faint. Dana, who had been collecting papers from the desk, nearly dropped them.

Mrs Wurstová recovered first. 'It is late afternoon and I think it's time we all had a sip of *svařené víno*, yes?' she announced briskly. 'We can continue our studies in our favourite *hospoda*.' Then she added, in case I was about to protest, 'And Dana can come too. She needs more practice on the English.'

Accepting the proffered truce, I followed them for steaming, fragrant glasses of warming brew at Mrs Wurstová's local around the corner. As we shared more stories, my boss threw her auburn head back and laughed heartily and Dana's shy grey eyes lit up. I leaned across the table and talked passionately, heady from the rapid effect of the mulled wine and easy camaraderie between us all.

'There would have been no Cold War if political relationships between the East and West were driven by women,' I argued. 'Not if women from both sides had been able to meet and get to know each other.'

'As long as we didn't discuss carp!' Dana added helpfully.

'*Máš pravdu.* You're right. You're both right!' Mrs Wurstová pounded the table in fervent agreement and called for more wine. 'Our leaders used much fear and propaganda about the West.'

I thought of all those John le Carré books and James Bond movies, of Mrs Howe in Year 11, and Dad's fear of Reds under the Bed. 'I guess it was how the leaders were able to control us all, keeping each scared of the other,' I agreed. 'Of course, you can't do that if a relationship already exists between the people.'

Dana thoughtfully refilled our glasses.

We drank more wine, healing past wounds, putting the world to rights and building bridges as only women can. It was as though we were of the same skin. Our bond as women transcended politics, culture and language. I wanted to shout these truths from the rafters. I wanted everyone else in the West to know what I knew. I wanted to tell the world that our ties were universal and, leaving aside the Czechs' propensity for carp, we should build bridges and get to know each other. We had decades upon decades of lost time and friendships to make up for. And I didn't know how much time I had left.

The next day I saw the blond, bespectacled English House teacher Alistair. He had survived four carp Christmases and knew the ropes. So I asked him to help me understand the Czech obsession with carp.

'We'll go down to the markets together tomorrow,' he said with a wink and a grin. 'Once you see how it works, it won't be so bad.'

I wasn't convinced, but the following day headed to meet him at the market closest to the school, tržiště Karlovo náměstí.

The trees lining the streets were bare and tangled against the dull grey sky, but the market had gone all-out for its customers and erected a huge tinsel sign surrounded by tinsel stars exclaiming *Veselé Vánoce* ('Merry Christmas') in an attempt to bring some cheer to the process.

But as soon as I saw the rows of large plastic containers set up between the buildings along the tram line, my stomach churned. The containers were filled to the brim with water, and within their murky depths, the carp competed for room as they awaited their fate. On the top of each pond lay what looked like a large butterfly net, which was used to scoop out the next victim.

Queues of ferocious-looking women and their harried husbands pressed against rows of trestle tables, behind which the carp vendors haggled, pulled large grey fish from the icy ponds, and struggled to hold their thrashing prey. Once a punter had made a decision—live or dead carp, sir/madam?—the vendor grasped the squirming fish and weighed it, or, less attractively, pushed it into an aluminium execution tray, raised a knife and unceremoniously chopped the head off (resulting in blood squirting in every direction, just as Mrs Wurstová had promised, accompanied by people ducking and diving in every direction), then weighing the limp body. Business was brisk.

My outing with Alistair did nothing to allay my distaste.

Fortunately, Karel had taken care of the carp-shopping in another market closer to Prosek, so I was spared the actual handling of the fish business. But when I returned to Prosek that evening, the bathroom had been turned into an aquarium, just as Mrs Wurstová had briefed me. I stared in horror at the sight of a large, filthy creature flopping around in muddy water at the bottom of the brand-new bath. Karel appeared around the bathroom door, his eyes gleaming like a militant fanatic.

'Lovely, yes?' he asked happily, reaching into the water and patting the newcomer. 'Now then, little one, time for your water change. Just take many deep breaths and I will be quick about this. You'll be glad to have fresh water, I am sure.' And on he went, talking soothingly and cheerily to his conquest as he drained the disgusting water and refilled the bath to the top.

Karel straightened up, face wreathed in smiles, duties complete for the next hour or two. He was completely oblivious to my revulsion. '*Tak*, Táničko, you are lucky to see real Czech Christmas tradition in the live,' he said. He obviously thought he'd given me a great treat.

I knew I should try to enjoy the carp experience. It would make Karel happy. Not liking it simply demonstrated I didn't belong here, and might never belong.

I hadn't expected to find the festive season difficult, given the excitement of finally celebrating a European Christmas, but my life was empty once English House shut down and all my friends left town. The teachers boarded buses for Britain. Headhunter Irena flew to Australia, much to my envy. Favourite students disappeared to their country cottages. No one would return until after the new year. The days became increasingly dark and bleak. Alone with a handful of Czechs, mainly Karel's older friends, I realised how very alone that made me feel. It was almost like the early bad days in Sedlčany. My sense of unhappiness lengthened as each day shortened.

It was a conundrum. The closer we drew to the big day, the more I longed for my family. Their absence from my life felt like a raw gash across my heart. I'd wanted to be openly curious, grateful and excited about this season behind the former Iron Curtain. The markets and the ancient squares and real fir trees were thrilling; I'd waited a lifetime to see a real Christmas tree. But I realised, with a stab of longing, that for me nothing came close to our straggly mulga on the verandah, propped up in a four-gallon drum, adorned with homemade sparkles and a star on top.

On Christmas Eve, both Karel's daughters and little Princess gathered excitedly and participated in the decapitation, scaling and cleaning of the carp. I hid away, chiding myself as I did. What about all those years ago when we went out to get 'killers' every month? When rearing our own food was normal? When cutting it up and bringing it home and cooking it was de rigueur? Perhaps I'd gone soft.

That evening, Karel took charge of the kitchen and fried the carp in a great deal of flour, salt and butter. The process involved all the girls and there was much laughter and chatting. I emerged at the last minute. The family and their close friends gathered to eat it with cold potato salad smothered in thick, sweet Czech mayonnaise, washed down with even colder beer. As I joined them, I did my best to appear cheerful and glad to be experiencing my very own Czech Christmas Eve.

I tentatively raised a forkful to my mouth and chewed.

'You like?' Lots of anxious faces.

'Mmm. Lovely, thanks.' I did my best to be appreciative but to be honest fried carp was a bit like fish and chips, without the best bit—the chips. I also couldn't help thinking of succulent roast meat with wine-laced gravy and all the trimmings, and lots of Christmas carols, which reminded me how far I was from the symbols and people that *did* mean Christmas to me.

Luckily the post from Australia had arrived in time and I proudly wore a thick green-and-gold jumper Mum had sent me. I couldn't bring myself to cut off its tag: 'Made from Australian Merino Wool'.

My beloved sister M'Lis sent me photographs of her baby Mitch, who'd grown up so much since I'd last seen him. She added a beautiful homemade card that said: 'I love you, Tanya, and miss you so much. It won't be the same without you this year at Christmas but I hope you're having a wonderful time wherever you are. You're always in my heart.'

I found myself physically aching for brown earth and vivid blue skies and the scent of eucalyptus hanging in the scorching afternoon air. I thought of Mum bustling around the homestead kitchen, wiping beads of sweat off her forehead as she pulled crusted baking trays laden with hot turkey and vegetables out of the oven.

I heard the voices of Dad and the boys in their endless rounds of cricket under drooping gum trees—'He's out!', 'Howzat?'—as the ball hurtled over the washing line. I saw our dining-room table decorated with colourful crackers, sparkling streamers, Mum's precious, polished silver cutlery, and Dad carving the turkey.

Karel finally sensed something was wrong, perhaps because I kept disappearing into the bathroom and returning with puffy eyes. My attempts to eat his fried carp probably didn't fool him either (avoiding the bones was a laborious process, and despite being brought up to eat everything on my plate, I left a good portion on this one).

'Are you well?' he asked carefully. 'Do you need some nice *pivo*? Or a good joke?'

I laughed, assured him I was fine, refused to let him know I was struggling. That would only give him the ammunition to say, '*Tak*! I told you it was only a matter of time before you wanted to return to your own country.'

After the celebrations were over, we headed outside to fare-well Karel's friends. He stood next to me and casually put his hand around my waist. Then he pulled me towards him and held me there. For a moment I stopped breathing. Karel didn't usually show me affection in public. His friends grinned at us as they left. Radka raised her eyebrows and walked back inside.

'How is it that me, sensible Czech man, hugs you in public space of my own free will?' Karel shook his head and laughed. 'You are very bad for my reputation.'

With that he took my cold hand in his and put something in my palm. It was a bundle of tissue paper. I unwrapped it, fingers trembling. Inside lay a tiny gold necklace. He laced it around my neck and kissed me tenderly. My heart did a thousand somersaults.

We walked back to the *panelák* hand in hand. The tears froze in my heart.

29

Snow, glorious snow!

Snow, snow, snow everywhere.

Finally it came, transforming Prague into a magical fairy-land of soft, glistening white. Every nook and cranny of the ancient city was turned into a scene from those traditional Christmas cards I had coveted in early December. Heavy snowdrifts carpeted the cobbled squares, winding staircases, palace turrets and buildings. Thick, pristine white layers muffled the city's sounds; the jangling sound of the tram bells, the clickety-clack of horses and carriages promenading across Staroměstské náměstí, and the deep booming church bells that echoed across the still, near-frozen waters of the Vltava disappeared into the silence of snow.

Karel was ecstatic too, but for less romantic reasons. '*Tak*, Táničko, the Prague is full of snow, everyone is in the mountains for holidays, and now we can ski.'

He rubbed his hands gleefully and headed outside to the tiny balcony to extract a bottle of beer from a large stash covered in mounds of snow.

'Snow is much better for beer than is fridge.' He opened it with a flourish.

'How can you drink freezing beer in this freezing weather?'

'Táničko, you know very well we Czechs cannot leave beer bottle alone too long in case it dries out. Now, let us talk about skiing.'

'I've only skied twice before, Karel, and you've been skiing since you were a boy.'

Karel dismissed my hesitant tones with a wave of his hand. '*Není* problem, Táničko. Unfortunately, on my special mountain we have no beginner slopes, but you will ski very well alongside me. Besides, we Czechs have special life-saving weapon that helps us ski with great success.'

'Yes?'

'All over the mountains are many *grog* stands. You can ski to one or another for sips of hot *grog* and *svařené víno*.'

I was nonplussed. 'You can buy alcohol on your ski fields? And drink when you ski?'

Karel stared back at me, equally nonplussed. 'Do you think Czech person can ski *without* it? In our country, no one skis *cold sober*.' He chuckled enormously at his little joke. 'It would not be good for our health to do so.'

Terrifying images filled my mind: drunken Czechs careering out of control from one ski slope to another, yelling and laughing and falling over and abusing one another all day long, crowding in their hundreds around these tiny stands, fighting in the freezing cold to be first in line to be served. Hashing was bad enough. Was I up to this?

Karel headed to the hall cupboard where he pulled out boxes and bags and thick jackets and Russian fur caps and ski boots and, finally, the pièce de résistance, two long dusty brown planks of wood. As he propped them up carefully against the wall and lovingly ran his long fingers down their sides, I gazed long and hard. I could only assume they were skis but they didn't bear any resemblance to the sleek polished equivalents I'd seen whizzing down Australian or American slopes.

'Er . . . are these your skis?'

'*Ano*, I *made* them. I have had them for many, many years.'

He turned them over gently and then looked up at me, beaming like a little boy showing off his favourite toy.

My desire to go skiing was waning by the minute. I imagined myself ashen-faced and frozen, staggering to the top of a high mountain on huge unwieldy planks of wood, watching helplessly as Karel and his mates sailed blithely to the bottom of the slope and disappeared in pursuit of another *grog* stand, quite forgetting they'd left me behind. What if I was lost forever in the white Czech wilderness? What if I ended up succumbing to the warm allure of the *grog* stands and crashed drunkenly into a tree or plunged over the side of a cliff?

Fortunately, any immediate threat was removed when Karel discovered there was not enough room for me in the smoke-billowing Škodas and Ladas that he and his friends had pooled to get them to their favourite ski spot on the coming weekend.

'I hope you do not mind this time,' he apologised after the car seats had all been counted. Hiding my relief, I assured him it was absolutely fine. I was in no rush to test the veracity of my imaginings. It was more than a six-hour drive to the Šumava mountains and the television news kept flashing real-life pictures of cars queued up on narrow winding mountain roads, slipping on the ice and crashing over the edges. Each day we read about more holiday-makers being carted off to hospital with broken limbs.

Besides, I had a hot date on Saturday night with my High Court judges Marta and Vladěna. They had invited me to a 'special Czech-Indonesia restaurant'—a cooperative venture between some Indonesian immigrants and Czech entrepreneurs—and I couldn't accept fast enough. I started dreaming of fresh, spicy, flavoursome delicacies, coconut cream and coriander and lemongrass and herbs and spices, steamed mounds of fresh greens, delicate water chestnuts, slivers of corn, florets of broccoli and cauliflower, string beans, chicken and beef and chilli and garlic—all the food and flavours I hadn't tasted since I left Australia. I couldn't *wait*.

So on Saturday night I headed off, filled with anticipation, excited about the snow, excited about being with two independent, professional women I admired, and enormously excited about the prospect of food I'd missed for so long. Leaving the metro, I walked briskly into the freezing air, joining streams of people wrapped tightly in long winter coats and thick scarves and hats heading for Karlův most, the pedestrian bridge leading to the castle.

As we approached, my heart did its usual leap. The bridge never failed to thrill. Even at this hour, it was alive with painters and accordion players and postcard sellers and spruikers, and people like me, mesmerised and enchanted. Candles and high lanterns cast long glows over the pedestrians as they crossed from side to side. A soprano's rendition of *Rusalka* floated above the bass growl of an old man calling for people to buy his wares, and the laughter of people rose and fell, the buzz of different languages infusing the scene.

Below me the dark and beautiful River Vltava was hung with pockets of mist and danced with fantastical reflections. It looked like a gleaming jewelled necklace as it wound its way between the seven hills of Prague that rose steeply from its banks; I touched my own gold chain that lay against my neck. Spire after spire thrust themselves into the air like frozen witches' fingers, glittering and sparkling under an icy, star-studded sky. Uneven silhouettes of chapels and ancient mansions completed the jumbled skyline.

My ribs hurt, so intense was my joy at being here, now, experiencing this. My body wanted to expand through my layers of wrapping and become part of all the images that surrounded me, to connect with the sense of oneness that Prague invoked in me.

What was it about Prague? Why did I feel this? From almost the first moment I'd laid eyes on the city, I had felt a deep connection here, but still could not explain it. Just why did my soul feel such a deep sense of belonging in this city, so far from my bush home?

Perhaps it was the perfectly curved lines and golden colours of the castles and palaces. Or the constantly shifting kaleidoscope of images, and the reflections and beauty of the river. Or the ever-present clang of church bells; roar of honking traffic and rushing water. Or the fragments of evocative classical music that floated out of windows and doors at every turn. Or, perhaps most fundamentally, the city's stoic, brave spirit, having survived decades of oppression and decay and isolation from the rest of the world. Was it a combination of all of these things—or something more?

There were no words to fully describe, even to myself, how I felt or why. I knew only this: that somewhere deep in my heart and soul I belonged here. It was a spiritual knowing. An inexplicable truth. And on nights like this, I couldn't bear to think about leaving, couldn't imagine not being here. Fairytales had led me here, offered me the soul of this city, and now Tatiana belonged. The paradoxes of my own life collided—reality versus fantasy—and blurred the truth of where I really belonged and what I really wanted.

But I had to go or I'd be late. Above me, lights gleamed through tiny square castle windows and embraced the golden towers of Národní divadlo, the beautiful National Theatre. I hurried across the rest of the bridge and under the stately towers, down the narrow, cobbled roads that led towards Betlémské náměstí and then turned east. Soft lamplight threw shadows from the dark buildings, set in hard relief against pallid yellow walls. I found the restaurant, an unremarkable square building with a newly painted sign swinging over the doorway.

Marta arrived just after me, looking like Sophia Loren with a thick dark-blue woollen coat and matching scarf sweeping out behind her. Vladěna followed, shaking the snow out of her long hair and laughing like a young girl. This was as much an adventure for them as for me. We entered and handed our coats to the Czech doorman. I looked around with high hopes. Although it looked and smelt in every way like a classic Czech restaurant, I was optimistic.

Once seated, Marta ordered Moravian red wine. As we sipped liquid that looked like it had been siphoned out of a bull, they asked me what my plans were for the coming year. I told them how much I wanted to stay but I needed more work. I told them about Dr Holub's dire predictions. They nodded regretfully and agreed that he was probably right. The Czech bureaucracy was too conservative, narrow-minded and fearful of outsiders to allow one into their Ministry in anything but a limited teaching role.

That made me feel despair, so I cheered myself up by telling them about the conversation I'd with Mrs Wurstová and Dana before Christmas. 'Isn't it brilliant we can sit here together, as women, and learn about each other and enjoy each other's cultures and stories, without fear of repercussions?'

Marta agreed, taking the proffered menus and passing them around. 'Back then, if we were caught, you would be ordered out of this country. And we *would* have been caught of course because everywhere were spies—especially in nice new foreign restaurants. We could have been arrested for crimes against state, depending on how dangerous they thought our meeting was. Then they might have stopped us working as judges.'

I thought again of the privileges enjoyed by judges back home; respect, excellent pay and working conditions, and, best of all, the separation of powers, that wonderful Westminster doctrine that prevented the executive arm (the government) from controlling the judiciary.

Marta was on a roll. 'You tell us you have a ticket to go home in late March. Will you go? It will be loss for us all but we understand you have your law to return to and that is very important.'

Her eyes held mine, as though she needed to impress upon me the gravity of this moment. And she was right. I had a career I could freely enjoy, where I also received (mostly) respect, (mostly) excellent pay and working conditions; best of all, I would never need fear the arrival of the secret police on instructions from the state to prevent me from doing my work freely and independently.

'Yes,' I said, returning her gaze, acknowledging my luck, acknowledging I should not waste the gifts and benefits available

to me back home. To do so would be the act of an ingrate. Both
Marta and Vladěna, not to mention Mrs Wurstová, would have
probably once given their left arm and right leg to practise law
as freely as I did.

Vladěna broke the tension, smiled gently. 'But you can always
come back. We will always be here. We will always be happy for
you to return as a teacher.'

I blinked back tears. It was an emotional discussion for me.
Many options, many confused thoughts. Marta took charge.
'What about the food?'

Gazing optimistically at the menu, I looked for something
recognisable—such as the Czech words for 'spicy' and 'chilli' and
'fresh vegetables'. But there was nothing.

Marta adjusted her half-rimmed glasses over her fine nose
and read aloud for my benefit. '*Tak*! We have:

pork in the peanuts,

pork on, how you say, little stick, with peanuts and without
the peanuts,

pork with, how you say, the noodles, with peanuts and
without the peanuts,

and pork without the noodles.'

She looked at me over her glasses.

'These are very good warm dishes, yes? Is this what you have
in your Indonesian restaurants Down Under?'

'I am sure there are similarities,' I said as brightly as I could.
'Why don't you order for me?'

Most Czech restaurants served meals quickly because food
was prepared well in advance. However, this menu spoke of
'special preparation', which meant we were in for a long wait.
We solved the world's problems and our own, and had almost
finished a second bottle of wine before three laden plates were

delivered to our table. Famished, I looked down in hopeful anticipation. Pierced by a skewer, three pieces of fatty pork balanced on a watery heap of yellow noodles, surrounded by congealed grease and many crushed peanuts. Not a vegetable to be seen.

'What do you think of our Indonesian kitchen?' Vladěna studied my face intently. 'Is it good?'

Both women waited for my answer. Silence crackled between us. I picked up my knife and fork, hacked away at the first piece of pork I could prise free from the skewer, scooped up some crushed peanuts and raised it all to my mouth. I chewed carefully and responded just as carefully. 'It's very tasty.'

They beamed.

International relations were at an all-time high.

30

Maturitní ples

While Karel was away skiing, I also took up an invitation that came by letter from my gorgeous Sedlčany student Kamila to attend Maturitní ples. That was the Gymnázium Sedlčany 'graduation ball' for classes 4A and 4B.

Kamila described an evening of much pomp and ceremony, where starry-eyed school-leavers were sent out into the world, and students such as Kamila and Pavel entered their final year. I was excited. I hadn't seen my students for several months and if I was to head home in March I didn't want to miss the chance to say goodbye.

On the Friday afternoon I boarded the now familiar bus, remembering Headmaster Zdeněk and Young Maruška driving me along the same road many months before. Gazing at the enormous mound of white snow dropping away below me, it was hard to believe how much the countryside had changed within the space of one year. Bare trees lined the roads like a tangle of cobwebs against the snowy mountains in the distance, and yet I knew that in a few months they'd be alive with blossom. It was so different to my home. Alice Springs really only had two seasons—summer and winter. Spring and autumn skipped in for a couple of weeks and then vanished. Thinking about home brought on a wave of confused emotions, so I tried instead to focus on the happiness of the weekend to come.

—————⟫●⟪—————

Maturitní ples was, as Kamila had promised, a simply wonderful occasion. Her parents drove us to the large wood-panelled hall, which was strewn with streamers and banners, all handpainted and hand-decorated; the walls were lined with trestle tables of food, wine and beer. I did a double take. It was a complete step back in time, as if I'd walked into one of those old-fashioned country dances that existed right up until the 1970s and '80s across rural Australia and that I remembered so well.

Jak je to možné? How is it possible?

Sedlčany connected me to my past in a way nowhere else did. I couldn't explain it. Here I stood, behind the former Iron Curtain on the other side of the world, yet I was transported back to my childhood. How could I describe Sedlčany? If Prague was a place of dreams, Sedlčany was a place of hope and heart.

I'd been back to Sedlčany a number of times, including in early December for the highly anticipated St Mikuláš ball (the Czech version of Father Christmas or St Nicholas, who came with his very own Angel and Devil), and each time I stayed with Kamila and her family who welcomed me in as one of their own. Tonight was Kamila's big night and I was proud to be with her. She wore a long, fitted velvet gown made by her mother, with a black choker and gold-buckled shoes. With her long blonde hair curling down her back, she could well have been Guinevere heading off to a medieval dance.

I was filled with joy at seeing the teachers when I arrived at the ball. There were lots of hugs and catch-ups and Cinzanos in curved glasses. Male teachers and boys smart in shiny nylon suits with coloured bow ties came up to shake my hand; the women and girls twirled in front of me in their beautiful home-sewn garments. A local orchestra was already in full swing, playing some sort of polka or reel, and the dance floor was a swirling buzz of young and old. Nad'a and I ducked into the corner and tried to catch up over the noise.

'How is life in the Prague?'

'Wonderful. But I may have to go back to Australia in March. My ticket expires then.' Tears stung my eyes.

Nad'a looked sorrowful. 'I am sorry to hear this, my friend. We have all been so happy knowing you are teaching in Prague. Will you come back?'

'I hope so.'

But before Nad'a could respond, the local orchestra kicked off the ceremony with trumpets and a dramatic fanfare. We moved to one side and watched. To great applause, the final-year students processed towards the front of the hall where they were first presented with sashes by Headmaster Zdeněk. Next came a presentation from their form teachers: colourful carnations (even in winter), intricately wrapped in green fronds and ribbon, and a crystal glass of wine. The orchestra struck up again, the students tossed back the wine, and then all the families gathered in a wide, noisy circle to throw *haléře* (coins) all over the floor.

'This is ceremony for good luck,' Nad'a explained as grown men and women yelled their support while the students scrambled unceremoniously on the floor to grab coins and stuff them into the empty glasses. 'But I think the boys mostly enjoy looking at the girls' legs from the floor!'

She grinned conspiratorially and I laughed. I was so grateful in that moment to know Naďa—to know them all, to be part of the ceremony so rich with meaning and tradition. I was grateful for their friendship, grateful for this night.

But no evening with my students would be complete without music.

'Tanya, please sing for us!' Pavel said.

The crowd started clapping.

'You may borrow my guitar,' another favourite student, Michael, offered.

'Please,' Pavel cajoled. '"Waltzing Matilda"?'

I was easily persuaded. Truth was, I couldn't wait to sing— couldn't wait to sing along with all my bright-eyed students who pressed around and wanted to be part of it all.

Pavel led me to the stage and Michael followed with his guitar. I'd never sung with a Czech orchestra before and could not believe my luck. This was a dream come true.

'Waltzing Matilda! Waltzing Matilda! Waltzing Matilda!' the crowd yelled, stomping and clapping.

Michael put his guitar in my hands and then stood behind me, holding the strap in both hands to keep it from falling. The orchestra members didn't speak English but that didn't matter. I turned to them and we communicated with fingers on frets and sign language, and all the while the crowd cheered us on. I touched the strings on the guitar and leant towards the microphone.

'Thank you!' I said to the hundreds of faces below. 'Thank you for welcoming me back!'

The faces looked back, expectant, smiling, eyes shining. The students stomped their feet and shouted in a strange mixture of English and Czech. The orchestra waited for me to lead off. Then they swung in behind me. We filled the rafters. I sang like I'd never sung before. I felt I could drown in the warmth and acceptance of that room. Even if I never returned here, I knew I would never forget everything this place and all its people had given me.

———————

But it was not over yet.

'Before you go, we have present for you.' Zorka, a gorgeous curly-haired student from 4A, pulled me to one side.

A gaggle of students—Michel, Lenka, Petr, Honza, Štěpánka—watched as she handed me a small, roughly wrapped package in green-and-gold paper. The significance of the colours became clear when I pulled it open. Nestled inside was a large tea towel with 'Made in Czech' embroidered across the bottom and a picture of two kangaroos against a desert backdrop at the top. A box in the top left corner was headed 'My Country'. Inside the box was Dorothea Mackellar's famous Australian poem, carefully printed in English.

'I love a sunburnt country . . .'

I stared in disbelief; my heart somersaulted.

'We found this in souvenir shop in Prague,' Zorka told me, smiling shyly. 'You like?'

———————

All the way back to Prague I clutched the tea towel close to my chest. Dorothea Mackellar's poem surged through me in

unceasing, powerful waves, bringing up exquisitely deep feelings of belonging, of connection, of remembering my sunburnt
country so far away. Feelings separate to the world I lived in
here. Feelings I knew I could never share with Karel.

31

Petřín Hill

When Karel returned from skiing, I summoned my courage and said in a rush, 'Karel, I have decided to go home and see my family in March.'

He nodded slowly, pushed his hands into his pockets.

I plunged on. 'I've spoken to all my students and they are happy for me to have a break. They won't bring in a replacement teacher but will wait for a month or so for me to return.'

I was secretly chuffed that my students didn't want to replace me. And now I'd made the decision to return to Australia I was starting to feel excited about getting on that plane. My beloved home and family were finally within reach after such a long time. And I didn't feel it was goodbye to Prague—I was sure I would return because I wasn't ready to give it all up here. And I secretly hoped that absence might make the heart grow fonder for Karel.

I finished with my breathless pièce de résistance. 'And
Mrs Wurstová is confident she can get me extra hours at the
Ministry to make it worthwhile coming back.'

Karel sighed. 'Táničko, you must do what you must do. We
will all be still here if you wish to return to us. You know I have
always said that. You can come back forever. But you must
choose what is right for you.'

Then he saw my face fall and tried to distract me in his usual
way.

'*Prosím tě*, maybe you might like to join me in Malostranské
náměstí after the 6 p.m. tomorrow night? We can have *pivo* in
some nice pub and I will take you to Petřín Hill in the snow.
Then you will have some beautiful pictures in your mind to take
home to your family.'

I'd been with Karel to Petřín Hill numerous times—it
was one of the first places he'd mentioned to me on my first
day in Prague—and it offered glorious vistas over the city. I
agreed, relieved to be distracted and always glad to have time
alone with Karel, which was increasingly rare with our busy
and competing schedules. But it was freezing and dark as we
stomped our way through the snow up the hill the following
evening and I lost enthusiasm with each step. Karel, however,
wouldn't pause until we reached a huge monument, well-lit
with gas lamps.

'And now, we arrive at my most favourite place at Petřínské
sady.' He spread out his arms and gazed reverently up at the
structure, and then down at the slopes that spread below him
in waves of white and darkness. 'This is the monument to Karel
Hynek Mácha that I told you about on that first day I met you.
Do you remember?'

'Yes,' I said shortly, my breath coming out in gasps. My fingers and toes had surely grown chilblains. 'You've actually told me about him a number of times.'

He raised his eyebrows.

'Ah. Yes, well, he is our most famous romantic Czech poet. Many people come in the spring and the summer to lay flowers at the foot of his statue. They pay the tribute to his works on love.'

Love?

He turned and gazed at me very intently. Underfoot, the snow crunched beneath my boots. The sound matched our laboured breathing. Apart from that, there was silence. The trees below and above and around us were draped in blankets of white, enfolding Karel and me into our own private circle.

My mouth was suddenly dry. 'But you don't believe in love.'

'Mácha wrote about his love of the countryside and the beauty of the nature as well. I have told you about his poem "May", yes? He describes the loveliness of the dawn, the stars on the lake, the sky in rose light, the songs of the nightingale and turtle-dove, the pale moonlight over the dark hill. He uses most evocative of Czech words. Of course'—he laughed for a moment—'it is also tragic poem about tragic love. But, for the way he talks of our nature, there is no more romantic words or feeling.'

He paused, shuffled in the snow.

'So here, Táničko, right in Prague, under the snow and the stars and the moon, here is something more than words can say, but the heart can feel.'

The air itself felt almost frozen, swirling with white mist.

'I feel you understand us, our country, our soul.'

I started to feel giddy.

'*Jak je to možné?*' How is it possible?

One of Karel's favourite sayings.

I didn't know how it was possible either but I was confused. What was he doing? Meaning? Suddenly I was frantic—I didn't want to lose the moment.

'Karel,' I burst out, 'I *will* come back. But I also need some . . . hope. I just need you to . . .'

He rocked backwards and forwards on his feet. Then took my face in his hands and kissed me. But his eyes betrayed him. I could see that he thought that, like the snow, I too would soon be gone forever.

32

Žofín

Before I left I had one very important thing to do.

The Czechs enjoyed a season of balls to dispel the gloom of winter. From January to March, when the snow turned to slush and the short, dark days took their toll on the national spirit, the Czechs adopted one of the more stylish practices of their Austro-Hungarian rulers. The newspapers were crammed with photographs of glamorous Prague celebrities sweeping off to balls in grand palaces and Gothic halls. It reminded me of the bejewelled New Year's Eve concert broadcast every year from the Vienna Opera House.

Like Cinderella gazing at the castle in the distance, I longed to experience a ball. Indeed, I'd dreamt of this moment since my first day in the city, when Karel had danced with me on Slovanský ostrov by the Žofín palace. I remembered so well the white-and-yellow ball house with its impressive entrance pillars and high balconies. It sat on its island in the Vltava like a grand madam. When I saw it on my first day in Prague, I had thought everything was possible and dreams would come true.

Now I was desperate to go there and dance with Karel before I left. But when I proposed this, Karel looked as though I'd asked him how we might get into KGB headquarters.

'The balls there at present are full of our special communist friends, who are still in our system, simply in different disguise. They would throw us out before we even got to front door. We need to find a ball somewhere *else*.'

I was undeterred. It was the Žofín or nothing. I had to live out the dream for Mum and me if nothing else. I kept remembering Mum waltzing me up and down the kitchen, the *Blue Danube* album on her little record player, telling me we were both prin- cesses from Vienna. Mum would twirl me under her arm, her eyes alight. Outside, the heat of the desert summer stifled breath and crushed down upon the baked land, but such was the joy of the moment, we might as well have been waltzing in a palace under glittering chandeliers. I was going to find a way into the Žofín, even if Karel couldn't.

I went to my fairy godmother, Mrs Wurstová. Did she know of any upcoming balls at the Žofín?

Mrs Wurstová looked at me over the top of a mound of Top-Secret Documents that spilled from one end of her desk to the other.

'Yes, I do, as a matter of some facts. ODS have ball at the Žofín next week. Our very own Minister Novák will be present. It is Prague's most important—how you say—"who's who" affair.'

ODS was the leading coalition Czech party.

'*Really?*' I scrabbled for more information. 'Will you go, Mrs Wurstová?'

'Oh no, I am not important enough.' At my raised eyebrows, she said, '*Ne ne ne*, I am not political person. After communism time, I do not want politics. If it was legal ball, perhaps . . .'

I hugged my wonderful fairy godmother, then rushed home to tell Karel about Minister Novák and the ODS ball.

'And I've got a great idea how we can do it.' I paused for dramatic effect. 'Let's *gatecrash*!'

Karel was stunned. I might as well have suggested we both volunteer to go off to a Russian gulag.

But I was undeterred. 'We'll pretend that we are entitled to be there because I am part of the Ministry in some way. The only person who might recognise me is Minister Novák. But I could keep out of his way. My link with the Ministry gives us a chance. What do you think?'

Karel shook his head in disbelief. Then he went to the English dictionary to find a word to describe me. 'Yes, you are sooooo *audacious*, Táničko!' I couldn't tell whether he was exasperated or admiring, or both.

I was taking a gamble, but Karel was a natural free spirit at heart and loved a challenge. I just hoped the *Švejk*-like spirit of my suggestion would win him over.

After a lot more persuasion on my part, it did. He conceded he had promised to take me dancing, and although he hadn't expressly said it would be at the Žofín, now I'd raised the possibility he took to planning Operation Žofín with minute detail, as though it were one of his major reconstructions. 'Okay, Táničko, we go, we do!'

On the week of the ball, Karel suggested we have a back-up plan, 'just in case we do not get through the front door'.

I wasn't interested in a back-up plan. The hardest thing I'd faced to date was deciding to leave Karel and Prague, even if temporarily. Gatecrashing a ball and possibly being thrown out were surely nowhere near as difficult. But I didn't tell Mrs Wurstová of my plans. Caution and restraint were required there. I did not want to prematurely lose my job—especially if I was going to come back.

The big night arrived, finally.

As we dressed, I felt a strange sense of euphoria.

Neither Karel nor I had proper ball attire. He didn't have a tuxedo, nor did I have a ball gown. It would all be smoke and mirrors. Karel wore his 'dress suit', which was dated, but he looked distinguished. I also thought the expression 'dress suit' was rather romantic. I had an elegant black pantsuit that managed to do those things all girls want—it accentuated my cleavage, displayed my back and arms, flattened my tummy and swept out flatteringly over my hips until it touched the floor.

Karel looked at me with his blue, blue eyes and smiled, touching my cheek. 'You look beautiful, Táničko.' No matter how many times he looked at me with those eyes, they always had the same mesmerising, heart-fluttering effect.

I tried not to blush like a schoolgirl. Bedecked in enough fake jewels (generously loaned to me by Radka) to look the part, black high heels and bright-red lipstick, I wondered madly, crazily, whether this evening would be enough to give me that butterfly 'down' Karel deemed necessary for finding love. But I pushed the thought away as quickly as it arose. No point raising my hopes. Just enjoy the moment, as Karel always said; take it easy. We were Bonnie and Clyde (hopefully with a better ending), both of us sprinkled with Cinderella stardust, and we were off on the adventure of our lives.

'Taxi!' called Radka, peering over the balcony. A taxi was an almost unheard-of luxury for any Czech in any *panelák* suburb, but Karel deemed it a worthy chariot for the night's outing. I was grateful for his generosity. It would not have been much fun traipsing in high heels to the Žofín via Prague's public transport system. I would have arrived with sore, frozen feet before the ball had even begun. This way I would arrive instead like a princess.

We climbed into the taxi, which was fragrant with vanilla pods—a specialty of Czech drivers—and Karel gave directions. I listened to his lilting Czech and leant my head on his shoulder. He took my hand. It was all perfect—Cinderella in her carriage, heading to the ball, with Prince Charming by her side.

The Žofín was ablaze with lights, surrounded by long black cars and swarming with guests in evening attire. The sound of an orchestra tuning up floated down from an upstairs window. At ground level, the Žofín was ringed with big men in suits.

'Prime Minister's army,' Karel whispered to me as we alighted from the taxi.

Outside, the temperature had dropped to –10°C and our breath froze on the air. But I couldn't feel a thing. Fixing his eyes on the line of guards, Karel squared his shoulders, took my elbow and instructed me to hold my head up and walk confidently towards the door.

'Act as though you are someone important,' he murmured. No problem there. I was a glamorous spy on James Bond's arm, about to infiltrate a secret Cold War meeting. In my stilettos and Australian pantsuit, I was walking a tightrope between two worlds, the East and West . . . and *nobody knew*.

We passed the first set of guards and then the second. Karel held two thin slips of white cardboard in his hands that looked like tickets. He flashed them at the guards. Beyond them, I could see golden chandeliers glittering in the high hallway. Just out of reach, beyond the main doors, sparkling lights illuminated the grand entrance. We were so close. Another few steps and we would be in the antechamber. We crossed the threshold. Security people lined the room, examining tickets and ushering guests through the doors. An older man and woman with clipboards watched from the corner.

'Stay here, if you please,' Karel said.

Slipping the papers into his pocket, Karel relaxed the grip on my arm. He strode to the couple and bowed slightly. They appeared surprised but nodded back. Within seconds he was talking earnestly, gesturing towards me, gesturing towards them, looking like a politician himself. I caught snatches of the inflections in his voice and of shared laughter. The couple handed him two tickets, nodded and waved him on. He strode confidently back to my side.

'Yes, Miss Heaslip.' He bowed slightly. 'We have the opportunity to go in. Won't you come this way?' Almost as an afterthought, he added, 'Our hosts say they are delighted to welcome some special legal diplomat who teaches English to our most important Minister of Justice.'

Unable to speak, I took his proffered arm once more. Even in my high heels I barely came to his shoulder. We glided into the hall towards a magnificent marble staircase that rose before us. It gleamed golden brown, with rich red carpet leading up its centre. Pillars rose high under the vast ceilings. Ornate lamps and sparkling chandeliers lit our path as, high above us, four black-suited trumpeters heralded the arrival of the dignitaries with a Czech fanfare.

A waiter hovered on the landing. Karel took two glasses of Bohemian Sekt from him, turned to me and clinked my glass. My fingers trembled around the crystal stem. Then I collapsed into one of the gilded chairs lining the walls. 'What did you *say* to them?'

Karel waved his glass at me, impishly.

'Well, Táničko, I used all my special Švejk innocence and charm to tell them I accompany one certain VIP from Australia who was specially appointed to work with the Minister of Justice and that she wants to say hello to some Comrade Ministers she knows. I told them there had been some problem with her tickets and we needed new ones.'

'That was it? That was enough?'

'Táničko, you have to understand how special communist-trained system works. It is very important to, how you say, save face when confronted with someone very important. Nobody knew who we were but nobody dared to reject our presence because you are international VIP and we are here to see the Minister. They are not willing to make the fatal mistake of admitting they do not know us. You see?'

I didn't really, but I tried.

'We are presented with tickets from Special Representative for Prime Minister. That is the man I spoke to. It is also my game. To approach the most important person in charge of tickets because they will not dare to upset their ministers by refusing us entry.'

I laughed out loud. Really? Karel had just conned the Special Representative for the Prime Minister? And it was all because he knew how to work the system, where saving face was more important than rejecting a possible gatecrasher. My dream had come true. I was here—about to enter the ballroom, which looked exactly as I had imagined: gleaming wooden floors, beautiful decorations, glittering chandeliers, fresh flowers on white linen tablecloths, tables laid with heavy silver cutlery and crystal, waiters dispensing champagne, hundreds of people in their finery swarming around, and couples already waltzing to the strains of an orchestra.

'Can we dance?' I begged.

'No, not yet.' Karel was making the most of his success. 'No, first we must visit some of the ministers here. This will be great example to you of how Švejk is still alive and well in our society.'

With the aplomb of a high official accompanying a famous dignitary, he led me up to several ministers and introduced me. As none of these men knew either of us, they behaved precisely as Karel had predicted, nodding graciously, shaking my hand and appearing charmed to meet an English expert from Australia who had come to see Minister Novák.

'You see, they do not dare to reject our presence,' Karel said with glee. 'Every minister treats you most cordially so that they look as though they are on the same board as the other ministers.'

He hadn't finished yet. '*Tak*! Here ahead is your Minister Novák. Do you want to say hello to him too?'

Panic struck. 'But he knows me! He is the one person who will see through your scheme, Karel.'

'It is no problem! I have another trick. We have exercised one half of my clever plan. Now it is time for the second half. Listen to me carefully.'

I listened, hardly daring to breathe.

Trembling, but armed with Karel's advice, I tottered up to Minister Novák. Then I bowed slightly, as Karel had done earlier.

'Good evening, Minister Novák.' I gave him my most dazzling smile.

The Minister's eyes narrowed. His evening plans clearly did not include being confronted by a foreigner he could not quite place. Particularly one who addressed him in English. The security guards moved closer.

'Good evening,' he said curtly in English. 'Do I—'

'I am an Australian lawyer and teach English at your Ministry of Justice.' His group of onlookers moved closer, interested. 'I am delighted to see you again this evening.'

Minister Novák inclined his head. 'May I ask why you are here at this ball?'

'I am here with one of Prague's top engineers who is very involved with major reconstruction projects for the government,' I responded blithely, and turned to introduce Karel who was standing politely behind me.

The Minister nodded, at a loss as to where or how to take this line of questioning any further, and led the group in shaking Karel's hand. They all exchanged pleasantries.

'Someday soon I hope to see you in my class, Minister,' I added, with more cheek than was entirely necessary. 'I know that you speak English well and I would be pleased to work with you more closely should you find the time and inclination.'

The Minister was again at a loss for words. 'Well, thank you.'

As I knew perfectly well the Minister had no intention of studying English, and left all that to his deputy, Mr Svoboda, I retreated while I was ahead. Mission accomplished, I thanked him for his time, and he wished me a marvellous evening.

We took two more glasses from the nearest waiter and fell into chairs in the corner, laughing. Karel even kissed me. Adrenaline and bubbles fizzed through me from top to toe. The band leader interrupted with a tap on the microphone and Karel pointed to the stage.

'Aha, Czech Republic's most famous singer, Karel Gott. You are especially lucky to see him in the live.'

In the live? Well, Mr Gott certainly looked live alright: tall, dark and handsome, and attired in a dazzling white suit.

'He is great heart-throb in this country and women love him. But'—Karel lowered his voice further—'it is said he was on side of communists. He went against Mr Havel's charter in 1977. But perhaps he was forced to do so by the government. That was *normální* if you wanted to keep your job, your safety.'

The legacy of communism affected and muddied everything in this country. But one thing was clear: Mr Gott could sing. He kicked off the ball with some serious groin-gyrating (rather Tom Jones-esque), and the crowd went wild. Having finished his rousing first number, he launched straight into a waltz. A dreamy, old-fashioned waltz.

Karel took my hand. '*Tak*! Would you care to dance with me, Táničko?'

I wished Mum and Dad could have been there. They were beautiful dancers. They'd taught me all the steps I was now putting into practice. They would have loved it. But Karel was a wonderful dancer too and now I was in his arms, waltzing through the Žofín.

'Relax,' he repeated, hand against my back, breath warm on my cheek.

I enfolded myself into him, wanting this night to go on forever, wanting never to leave his arms.

———

Yet even Cinderella had to leave her handsome prince before midnight. She could not risk exposure of her rags and pumpkin.

Nor could Karel. At 11.45 p.m., he whispered, 'To use your expression, Táničko, it is best to leave while you are ahead.'

Touché.

With a last ecstatic look around the ballroom, knowing I might never see something as beautiful again, I followed Karel outside to the darkened driveway and a waiting taxi hailed for us by one of the undoubtedly frozen bodyguards.

As we swept away, I gazed at the magnificent Prague Castle, set high on its hill on the opposite bank. If only Václav Havel had been at the ball! Now that would have been *really* something. He was my real hero—the poet who became a president.

'Karel' I snuggled into him. 'Do you think there might be another ball where I could meet the President?'

His response was dry and to the point. '*Vymalováno.*'

It was painted. In other words, it was finished. Our ball season had ended as quickly as it had begun.

The sour smell of the driver's cigarette slowly brought me back to reality as we headed towards Prosek's *paneláky*. But it didn't matter. Given our success tonight, Karel told me that we might as well be driving home accompanied by three black cars adorned with the national flag and the President's personal emblem.

33

Alice Springs

March 1995

Central Australia greeted me with bright, bright light and endless sunshine.

I leapt back into life there with joy and relief; I was home at last, back in this strong, ancient landscape. I could hardly get enough of the light, the space, the clean air. Everything was hot and familiar, from the pungent smell of eucalyptus to the sound of cicadas at night, from the red dirt under my boots to the vivid blue of the sky reaching out beyond the hills. I walked for hours alone, soaking up the space and the solitude. I raised my face to the sun and started to thaw after the long winter I'd just left. My skin peeled after barely a day. Strands of light, fine hair crackled with electricity as I pulled my brush through them. I spent hours curled up with M'Lis and Mum, chatting endlessly to my brothers Brett and Benny, telling Dad all about the politics of the Czech Republic, and gabbling joyously in English.

Family and friends swept me back into a life that was much as I had left it twelve months before. I revelled in good wine and good food, caught up with all the latest legal gossip and reunited with colleagues from my old law firm as though I'd never been away. For the first few weeks I felt empowered, strong and happy, a far cry from the confused and anxious self I'd left behind in Prague. It was a strange scenario. I was like a bold and brave visitor and no one knew if I would stay or leave—including me.

But Prague was never far from my thoughts. The vast horizons of untouched bushland and rugged ranges rising out of the desert were stark reminders of how far I'd settled into my new Czech life. There I lived cheek by jowl with everyone else in ancient, bustling, crowded Prague, soaking up historic cultural experiences unimaginable in the bush—even unimaginable in our big cities.

There were challenges in returning home too. The first day back M'Lis took me to the nearest supermarket, I felt nausea bubble up and had to rush outside for fresh air. The rows and rows upon rows upon more rows of brightly coloured, shiny packaged goods of every possible variety were sickening. The trolleys overflowing with groceries seemed decadent. Everyone had so much. The place smacked of greed. So much unnecessary consumerism. So much waste. It was unbearable.

By the end of the second week I was aching for the morning light on the Vltava that greeted me every day as I headed to work. The dark span of Charles Bridge at night. The jangling sound of trams along narrow cobbled streets. The sweeping lines of Renaissance buildings on the riverfront. Art Nouveau cafés overflowing with scholars debating culture, history and politics. They were all a world away from me. I even forgot about my dread of Czech *paneláky*—or at least pushed it out of my mind. Absence definitely made my heart grow fonder. I talked to friends and family constantly about Prague—its beauty, mystery, magic—and in some strange way felt more connected to Prague than I did to Alice.

And, of course, there was Karel.

I'd told myself I'd be strong and not contact him but by the third week I succumbed, longing to hear his voice and reinforce the reality of the life I had woven back there. I spent hours trying to get through the unpredictable Czech telephone system before he answered.

'*Ahoj*, Táničko!' His voice sounded happy. 'How are you?'

But our conversation quickly became disjointed across the miles, punctuated with awkward pauses, my English now fast again, Karel unable to understand much of what I said. I realised how much I'd limited my vocabulary and slowed my conversation down to survive in Prague. For the first half of the call I wished I hadn't rung.

However, when Karel finished our conversation with a halting, 'Against my will, I must tell you something, Táničko'—pause— 'I miss you, very much.' I shivered all over. 'This is my truth. Nothing is the same since you've been gone. It is cold in my world.' Another pause. 'When are you coming back, Táničko?'

That was enough for me.

Karel had never said such things, or intimated that he ever would, and it was as close to 'love' as he'd ever come. I hung up, went to the bank, drew down on my already over-tight mortgage and booked a flight back to Prague for the following month.

I waited for the right moment to tell Mum and M'Lis about Karel and why I was going back. But they had already guessed. My constant references to him in letters home had been a giveaway.

'The fact is . . .' I hesitated, looking up into their earnest and worried eyes, struggling to find the right words. We were sitting out on the lawn in the sunny late afternoon with a glass of wine. Mitch crawled around our feet and gurgled happily. 'I want to be with him more than anything else.'

There was a long silence. I could see something glistening in Mum's eyes and she put a finger to her cheek as if rubbing something away. She didn't speak. Neither of them did.

'Look . . . I don't know where it's going between us . . . it's very difficult in many ways . . . I just know . . . he is the most wonderful man and I—I love him.'

For better or worse, that was my truth. And after our call, I thought it might, just might, be his too.

It was also a really hard thing to say to my beloved Mum and M'Lis. They both started crying; soon we were all crying, and we embraced with the pain of what this news might mean for the future. But I was propelled by a force beyond me. While I loved my family and my home with all my heart, and I would be desperately sad to leave them again, there was no doubt in my mind about my returning to Prague, at least for the foreseeable future.

Prague and Karel were unfinished business.

And I didn't want to prove Karel right by default.

34

Return to Prague

The Czech Republic did not disappoint. It greeted me with the fragrance of new spring, with wide, soft skies and green wooded hilltops. The fields shimmered with yellow flowers. The light and the air felt gentle and caressed my skin after the harshness of Central Australia.

Hurrying through Prague Ruzyně International Airport, I flashed my passport at the customs controller, feeling the confidence of returning to a place where I knew the system, where I was no longer a foreigner; indeed, I was almost a local. When the controller stared suspiciously at my permanent residence stamp, I responded in what sounded (to my ears) like flawless Czech. Retrieving my passport carelessly, I then bounced out into the waiting area and the pale light of the afternoon like an excitable puppy. I simply couldn't wait to see Karel. I thought my heart might burst out of my chest.

'*Ahoj*, Táničko.' I heard the lazily spoken words that had been missing from my life for eight weeks and my body tingled all over. Karel strolled towards me, his face creased in that familiar smile, his blue eyes alight, the familiar sight of a wilting carnation squashed into his right hand. Did I detect something else? Relief?

Šárka, Princess and Radka were outside with the family's little car and we headed for a traditional picnic in Horní Šárka, a gorgeous, sunlit valley bearing the same name as Karel's irrepressible daughter. I was thrilled to be welcomed back by the whole family. We cooked sausages over a fire and Karel brought out his guitar and we lay in the sunshine. I soaked up the Czech language and knew I'd made the right decision.

By the time we made it back to the *panelák*, my sense of Australian space was definitely a world away. Despite my jetlag, all I now wanted was time alone with Karel. I was aching to reconnect with him and make up for lost time. But Radka needed help with her homework. Šárka and Princess were staying for dinner. There was preparation required for an urgent meeting with British clients tomorrow. Phone messages to return. Faxes to send. And to top it all off, Karel was tired after making music with his friends until late the night before. But still, Czech *pivo* was best in the world, and would I like one?

It was definitely business as usual, I thought, folding my weary limbs into bed, pushing down the ache in my heart, and trying through the fog of fatigue to come to terms with the life I had returned to. It was not everything I wanted, but then again, could anything be as good as my hopes and dreams? Karel rolled in beside me at 2 a.m., cuddled up, and left again before daylight.

I returned to the workplace fired with energy and enthusiasm. This year I would be successful, I decided. Last year had been my entrance to this country, a time of feeling my way through a new culture and language, but this year I had experience and energy on my side, and I intended to secure my thirty hours here and stay on. My students were all delighted I was back and I had lots of Australian stories to tell them.

However, at the end of the first week, Headmistress Anne invited me to English House and dropped a bombshell. Dickie of The Exploding Buddhas had won her hand and she was returning to England to be with him. They would marry next year. Richard and Anne's partnership, and English House, would dissolve.

As Anne spoke I thought the floor would collapse beneath me. But I threw my arms around her and tried to be brave, tears blurring my eyes. 'I really am so happy for you, my darling Aničko. I can't believe I'm crying, I'm sorry, it's the most wonderful news—I just don't know what I'll do without you.'

Anne was my best friend, my English-speaking companion, and the only one who knew about the ups and downs of life with Karel. Her departure would leave a huge hole in my life. What would Prague be without her humour, her Scottish common sense and the bond we shared with this country? We'd even taken to calling each other Aničko and Táničko as a joke. It made us feel almost Czech.

'Táničko, I have a very important question to ask you,' she said, gravely. 'I would like you to be Best Woman at our wedding.'

I stared at her, laughing and crying properly now, lost for words.

'And guess what—we're getting married in Prague! Richard is going to help us organise the Czech side and I'll manage the English paperwork.'

She handed me her hanky.

'Perhaps May or June next year. Will you still be here?'

'I certainly hope so.' I took a deep breath and wiped my eyes. 'But if for any reason I am not, don't worry, I'll come back. Thank you so much for the honour of asking me to be part of something so . . . so . . . incredible, really.'

We headed arm in arm to the Obnoxious Pub to celebrate. From the Obnoxious waiters we then ordered little glasses of Cinzano (the best thing available there) and clinked glasses.

'So when will you leave us?' I finally asked the question that neither of us had yet broached.

'End of the school year,' said Anne. 'Yes, I know—July, not far away. But Dickie and I are longing to be together. We can't wait anymore. Besides, it makes sense to close everything down then. It will give Richard time to work out how he wants to proceed— whether to find another partner or shut up shop altogether.'

Heading home on the bus much later, I stared out at the long line of *paneláky* obliterating the horizon. The evening shadows had lengthened them into grotesque chunks, like abstract prison blocks, and I shivered. A dark sense of loss had lodged deep in my stomach. Anne's departure would change everything for me, especially in the expat and teaching world. But there was something else. Her news had hit a raw nerve. Deep within I longed for a future like hers: a joint commitment between two people, a joint declaration of love, a joint future together on equal terms, a joint lifestyle, and the joint desire to declare all of that to the world.

I'd come back hoping for that outcome too but it now felt a long way away. Karel might have spoken the words I wanted to hear on the phone but now I'd returned to Prague it was back to situation normal. He was constantly busy, I shared him with family and friends, and we were almost never alone. We were never going to be 'on the same board' in the same way that Anne and Dickie were. But I'd come back to be with him because I wanted a life here with him more than I wanted to stay in Australia and I had to do my best to make it work.

Forcing the deep, dark block of misery down, I tried to focus on what I did have. A Czech home, a Czech family, and a Prague life. I was lucky. Most of the expat English teachers envied me. Not everyone had those things.

———✦———

On the work front things did start to improve. True to her word, the wonderful Mrs Wurstová found me additional teaching within the Ministry. During our lessons I also began to help her with her Top-Secret Documents and started to assist at Very Important Diplomatic Meetings. It was like acting in my very own spy movie, whizzing around behind my boss like a faithful henchwoman.

I also met Mrs Wurstová's latest 'assistant', a glamorous Marilyn Monroe look-alike named Romana.

Rumours abounded. 'She is a spy,' Dana whispered.

'Special intelligence' was all Romana would concede, with a wink. We became friends immediately and she took me to numerous hidden Prague wine bars where we gossiped, giggled and spoke mainly about boys. She lived in an unidentified secret apartment and otherwise lived a mysterious life, all the while— as far as I could tell—avoiding real henchmen.

Networking Irena invited me to Women in Business dinners and even though they were really beyond my budget I knew I had to go. One night I met a new friend, Alyson.

A German IT specialist, Alyson was great company, charming and smart. Her clothes were beautifully tailored; she wore her straight light-blonde hair tucked behind her ears and topped off the professional look with serious round-shaped glasses. When she said, 'You have been here much longer than me. I would be very happy if you would show me around Prague,' I felt like an old hand. I was able to show her hidden galleries and Old World cafés and ancient theatres, and I realised with delight that I now knew a lot more about this beautiful city than I had ever thought I would.

Within a few weeks of our meeting, my networking outlays had paid off. Alyson found me translating work through her contacts with a young and vibrant law firm called Váňa, Oršula & Partners.

Actual translating work was still beyond my skill set, but I'd been madly studying Czech and Czech law at nights, and my working understanding of legal commercial Czech documents was now good enough to 'wing it' at this law firm; especially as I'd be working alongside a gorgeous young Czech guy, Milan, who'd studied law, spent time in America and was fluent in English. Milan and I proved to be a great team. Every day we pulled the firm's English and Czech documents apart until we were satisfied the translations reflected the legal intent behind them, and every night I swotted over the documents to teach myself more. It was fascinating to be at the 'coalface' of the firm's new dealings with the West.

I adored Milan. I'd never used a computer before, and he said, 'It is the luck that you could come here so we could teach you modern way of working, honey.'

I also became great friends with two of the young lawyers, Petr and Radek, and over drinks after work we would debate for hours the differences between the legal jurisdictions of the East and West. They treated me as one of their own and I realised, with a pang, how much I missed collegial work.

My advertisements paid off too. Soon I was teaching two glamorous Czech girls, Michaela and Eliška, at a Czech/French law firm called Gide.

Both girls spoke French, Czech and English and were dressed like fashion models whenever I turned up for their lessons, which was always after 5 p.m. I was astounded by this. By 5 p.m. in my former life, my lipstick would have faded, my hair would be standing on end (because I'd run my hands through it so many times during the day) and my suit creased. A day in a law firm always left me wrung out and exhausted. And I'd be desperately looking for a drink.

'How do you do it?' I asked them, in awe.

Michaela looked at me gravely. 'It is important for us to look as the firm wants us to look, to present to our clients in smart way. No more old-style dressing. We represent the future, an international world.'

Eliška smirked coquettishly. 'I must always look this way because I am married to French man. And when I go to French office in Paris, always I go shopping. It is very enjoyable.'

'*Mais oui*, most of our clothes are from Paris,' Michaela nodded.

They represented a new generation in every sense. I loved working with them and hoped their equally charming (and handsome) French boss Daniel would extend my hours and perhaps even tell other law firms about me.

Even Networking Irena was impressed.

Soon I was working incredibly long hours. I applied for a Czech Business Licence to give me greater rights and status.

Váňa, Oršula & Partners generously supported the process. I visited Sedlčany often. My network continued to expand. Karel said, 'You will become Czech girl yet' and started speaking to me more often in Czech. He seemed amazed and impressed at how much I was achieving.

But I had the bit between my teeth. If Anne was leaving, and my relationship with Karel was not exactly what I wanted, I was determined to make up for both with success at work. I couldn't bear the idea of being a failure, especially as I'd returned here on such a high, reassuring my family that Prague was the place for me.

But despite my best efforts, the mulga ache never went away. Each time my Australian home hurtled into my Czech home with a rattle and a whirl of the fax machine I found myself straddling two worlds. As I sat on the edge of my *panelák* bed in one, devouring the letters from another, I tried to visualise a third where I might live—whole, complete and happy.

35

Loss

Headmistress Anne's departure loomed.

Vera, Anne and I spent a lot of time talking about her wedding. It kept us from falling into the doldrums. Every time I thought about Anne leaving, a lump formed in my throat and my heart felt heavy and hard.

But the departure date did eventually arrive and Vera and I stood side by side, silent and morose, as we hugged her goodbye. As the large intercontinental bus, packed to the rafters with students and backpackers, lurched out of the bus stop—next stop London—it occurred to me that in less than one second a way of life can suddenly be over. While five minutes ago it might have been buzzing along, with a flash of a farewelling hand that life was gone, leaving behind nothing more than memories and a stab of loss.

'You must live every moment as though it's your last, because this time will never come again and we don't know how long we have our life for.' These were the wise words intoned by one of my Ministry students, Marek, who took me several days later to look through some of the magnificent headstones of Prague's most famous cemetery.

As I stumbled after him I wondered why I had agreed to this grim outing, but Marek was an enthusiastic historian and wanted to show me the beauty of Prague's headstones of former times. A trip to a cemetery seemed fairly in keeping with the nature of that week so I trailed through the collection of remembrances, and gazed in despair at the headstones of people who had once made such a phenomenal contribution to their country but were now no more.

'What is the point?' I finally burst out to Marek. 'These people gave their all and now they are barely remembered. They might as well have never existed.' I glared at him as though it was his fault. 'What on earth is the point of it all?'

Marek gazed back morosely, with the hangdog expression of the Czech melancholic, and agreed. His response was not what I was hoping for, but then again, what should I expect from someone who frequented graveyards as a hobby?

'You are right, Tanya. That is why all this stressing and striving of you people in the West is ultimately for nothing. You will all still end up here—or somewhere like it. That is why you must grasp every moment, enjoy it to the full, let it touch you . . .'

I froze. Although the day was warm, a chill ran down the back of my neck. How many times had I heard this sentiment, in one guise or another? In how many different voices and different settings had it been said to me? And what was it that I was still not learning or hearing?

I returned to Prosek confused and equally hangdog, realising with a greater profundity than ever before that the only certainty was death. My head ached. When Karel finally returned home that evening, I flew at him, buried myself in his shirt, hungry for reassurance, needing comfort.

It didn't come. What else had I expected?

'Take it easy, Táničko,' Karel drawled as he poured us both a *pivo*, the salve for any drama or untenable situation. 'You think too much. Just live the life.'

———— ✦ ————

Two weeks later my maternal grandmother died. My beloved Nana Parnell was a woman who had struggled and suffered much in her life. However, she read me some of my first Enid Blyton books and introduced me to the joy of the written word, the thrill of the blank page and the use of imagination to create stories. She always allowed me to stay up late to finish reading as I begged, 'Just one more chapter, Nana.' I remembered drinking cocoa in bed whenever I stayed at her old blue house with its big windows and wide verandahs.

With a shaking hand, I read Mum's fax about the funeral plans and recalled the last piece of advice Nana had given me, set out in her spidery handwritten Christmas card just six months before.

'Enjoy your experiences in Prague and write them all down, dearie,' she'd advised. 'One day you will need them all to put them in the book I know you are going to write.'

I wept inconsolably for days. Never before had I felt so far away from my family nor needed them so much. I managed to telephone Mum, and for those few moments felt her pain and that of M'Lis, who loved Nana Parnell with all her heart.

Karel watched me quietly. I tried to hide it from him, and it wasn't difficult, as our lives were increasingly busy and separate, but he knew. I wanted to get on a plane and fly home, to be part of the ritual to bless Nana on her way from this world. But I couldn't. The distance was like a raw wound. Instead, I climbed through Ďáblický les, a magnificent forest more than a half-hour bus trip away from Prosek, and spent a day there on my own. It was a place, a sanctuary, that I knew would give me space to grieve alone. A high wooded area, it had plenty of walkways for families, which was how I had first found it: Karel and Šárka had taken me there one afternoon. It was a place many Czechs went on the weekend to promenade and have picnics.

The day was hot, very hot, and I could hear the sounds of Czech families above me, their voices filtering through the trees. But in here I was enclosed by the thick, glossy oak trees of my childhood books—the kinds of books Nana had read to me as she helped to develop my imagination. I smoothed the bark of an oak trunk and picked up a handful of dirt, letting it trickle through my fingers and fall back to the earth under my feet.

Dust to dust.

Goodbye Nana, from Prague and from me.

36

Late autumn

End of October 1995

'*Ahoj*, Táničko, I will be near your law office in half an hour. Would you care to join me for the lunch? I know some nice little pub nearby.'

Karel's mellifluous tones floated down the telephone line of Váňa, Oršula & Partners and my heart skipped. It was rare to see or speak to Karel during the working day. Phone communication across the city remained unreliable and our timetables rarely coincided.

Running a brush through my hair, I excitedly escaped the office shortly after 1 p.m. Rain splashed down on the cobbled street and I hoped Karel wouldn't notice my wet stockings.

'Take it easy . . . you need not hurry. Would you like to share my umbrella?' Karel's lazy, lilting tones caressed my name and sent a rush of adrenaline through me.

I gazed up at his blue eyes through the rain. A rush of happiness filled my heart as it did every time I looked at him.

318

While I might not have exactly the life I wanted with Karel, it didn't stop the love I felt for him.

Taking my hand, he led me down a side street and in through a small unmarked door, beyond which was a cosy dining area filled with locals. Being with Karel was always a thrill. I'd never have known about this place much less have had the courage to go in on my own. He remained the source of my greatest adventures in this city.

We sat down and he ordered a large beer for himself and a small one for me.

'*Tak*! What is new, Táničko?' Karel leant forward, using his favourite Czech expression in English while downing the first *pivo*.

Buzzing from this unexpected lunchtime adventure, I dived right in. 'Karel, I have been thinking for some time about my next step here and now I know what I want to do next!'

'You do? That reminds me of our special joke about the Russian Minister of Defence who has some special plan for the people . . .'

I interrupted him. This was no time for Karel's humour. 'No, I'm being serious. I've spent so much time around lawyers over the last five months, seen the really interesting work they do, and it makes me want to be part of it all again. Not just as a translator, but as a lawyer here.'

Karel raised his eyebrows. 'But I thought you liked being a translator.'

'I do! It's fantastic work and really interesting, but I feel like I'm ready to move to the next step of working properly in law here. I know it won't be easy to do and I'm not sure how to do it but it feels like the next stage in my plan. *Proč ne*?'

Karel sat back in his chair. 'Táničko, can you not be satisfied with what you have achieved so far? In a few short months, you have managed to get a Business Licence. You have done more than most foreigners could have done in this time. You know more people in Prague than both my daughters! Can you not take it easy?'

'But the fact is I *am* a lawyer. I want to be back using the skills I've been trained to use—where I can do my best work.'

He sighed. 'And what about the advice from your Ministry expert, Dr Holub? Has he not told you many times that unless you speak Czech and have a Czech law degree, it will not be possible?'

I squirmed. Karel was possibly right. But I didn't want to hear such pessimism. Or, as Karel and Dr Holub would call it, 'Czech realism'. We'd had so many conversations of this nature and I was sick and tired of all the doomed predictions, the Czech passivity and negativity. *Why* wasn't shooting for the stars possible?

'Karel, if I accept your advice, I have no choice but to take second-best . . .' I spread my hands, frustrated. 'It's so defeatist! Why can't I live and work fully *here*?'

'You have so much passion,' Karel sighed, and touched my cheek. 'This country cannot meet it. We are former communist world and we are bound by so many old rules that will take many years to change. And you know it too.'

Silence fell. We both knew that if he was right, and if I was determined to practise law again, there was no other option but for me to return to Australia. Karel's words—*I always said this would happen*—hung between us, unspoken. I wanted to scream at him and at Dr Holub, too.

A waitress in a short skirt broke the silence by banging down two full plates of pork. Then the waiter arrived with the next round of beers. Karel drank his heavily and I stabbed the slice of pan-fried meat furiously.

'Karel, okay, can we talk about something else for a moment? I would really like to go away together, somewhere, for a weekend or maybe even a holiday. Somewhere you could relax, and we could have time alone, without anybody else—just us.'

Karel choked on his beer. 'Just us? What would we do? We would have nothing to talk about!' He gave a wan grin. 'That is old Czech joke about men and women.'

'This is not a joke.'

Normal couples *went away* together. *Without* their children and grandchildren. *Without* their friends. *Without* their next-door neighbours. They went to places where they did *not*, as a rule, know the chalet owner, the local publican, the people in the cottage up the road, the people in the cottage down the mountain slope. I was longing for intimacy and space. In all the time we had been together, we had never gone away without other people.

'That is insulting to me as a man.' His face was flushed. 'Any spare time I have is for my girls and my work and my friends. Also, I do not have that kind of money.'

'I have money now.'

'I will not take your money.'

'Look, it doesn't have to be expensive. Not a weekend, anyway. We can plan and save for it if necessary. But it's not about the money: I want time alone with you. I want the chance to relax and hang out together and *be* together. *It's what normal people do in a relationship.*'

There was something deeper too. I was increasingly missing intimacy, that time spent with someone close, sharing my feelings, hanging out. I didn't have my family here, nor the friendship of Anne, and the ache inside for a deeper connection was growing. Work and work colleagues couldn't fill all the gaps.

322 ALICE TO PRAGUE

But there was a long silence. Karel stared fixedly at the busy tables around him. Finally, he drew in a long breath. 'What I have here is what I can offer you, and you know it pretty well,' he said.

Yes, I did know. As Karel constantly reminded me, he came as a package. He came with his existing priorities: his two daughters and granddaughter, his friends, his work and his country. He'd had the chance, momentarily and briefly, to escape in 1968 with his friends, but he'd chosen not to leave. He was Prague and Prague was him.

He finished his beer and said, 'Please, Táničko, take it easy.'

'I don't *want* to take it easy,' I shouted, and the waiter arriving with more beers scuttled away. 'I *want* to make plans and create a future. Anne and Dickie are doing it,' I finished angrily.

'They are young, without children and a business here.' Karel replied tersely. 'Táničko, why do you make this so hard? For me and you?'

Why was I wrong for having needs? Why was I wrong for expressing them?

A scream rose inside my throat.

'*Because I want more! I love you, Karel, and I want more!*'

37

Tears

Later that afternoon, I dragged myself away from Váňa, Oršula & Partners and sat looking over the river. The late hour brought mist but a thin trail of pale light glinted off the water. I sat hunched up against a wall, staring at strands of hair that had fallen loose over my shoulder, and then back at the river. At the worn cobblestones, at my hair, at the wan sunlight over the water, at my fingers turning blue in the chill.

Several ducks swam to the edge, and a mother and daughter leant over them. The little girl pointed and chatted animatedly. Her mother smiled and encouraged her and they threw some bread. The ducks moved closer. I sat watching them as though they were a movie playing out frame by frame. Inside my bubble, I was paralysed and disconnected, while a toxic mixture of grief and paralysis spread through me, dark and heavy, like sludge.

The recriminations in my head were like a battlefield.

What had happened to the independent traveller I used to be? How had I got sidetracked? Why hadn't I done something a year ago, or even six months ago, when it was clear that Karel and I were not 'on the same board'?

Anne had shown me what to do and I'd ignored all the signs.

And then, across the water, as though it was written in the waves, the words came to me:

Not to go is just to postpone the inevitable.

The sky darkened, sending a trail of thin colour across the water, and eventually night enveloped me in its inky waves and extinguished the day.

Hours later, I turned the key in the front door. The face reflected back to me in the hall mirror was blotchy and pale. Huge black rings under my eyes made me look like Morticia from *The Addams Family*. But I didn't care. What did it matter?

Karel sat at the kitchen table, head bowed and propped up by his hands, glasses pushed high on his head and an empty table before him. No papers that he would normally be working on, no beer bottles, nothing.

'Where have you been?' His voice was harsh. '*Je mně špatné!* (I am bad!')

'*Co? Proč?*' What? Why?

'Because I've been waiting and worried. I have been nearly out of my mind with worry.'

Once those words would have made me feel wanted, hopeful. Now I felt empty.

'I'm sorry,' I said automatically, heading towards the stove to boil some water to make tea. I was freezing and hoped it would warm me up. 'Actually, I'm not sorry. Why should you care?'

He glared at me. 'You think you can treat people like this?'

I swung around, pulse pounding, voice heated. 'How dare you?'

'I dare because . . . because perhaps I love you more than you love me,' he said finally.

'*What?*'

Silence. Long, gripping, heart-stopping silence.

'What did you say?

'Perhaps that is my truth too, deep inside. But I cannot love you, I must not, and you know that too.'

'Are you trying to humiliate me even more?' I banged down the saucepan, spilling water. 'I don't understand this, or you, or anything anymore.'

I crumpled over the chair, exhausted, the fight draining out of me.

He came to me, hands spread.

'I've told you many times, I'm not interested in big words about making big plans for a life, because they are never the truth. They do not last. Táničko, I wish you could live with this moment that we have and enjoy it.'

'Sorry, Karel,' I said, looking away. 'I can't do this anymore. I can't survive it, as you would say. I'm going back to Australia.'

He blanched, pulled me against him. My tears blinded me, my hands pushed against his chest, but I couldn't resist any longer. I caved, rage and despair and my hunger for him reasserting themselves, a driving heat through our hot mouths offering relief and release, postponing reality, if only for the moment. My body arched under his, and I cried for the sweat of the passion to dissolve my mind altogether. And then it was over.

But how do you take the final steps to wrap up a life and a dream?

I needed help, and Anne was gone.

Some days later I blurted out to Mrs Wurstová that I needed advice—'of a personal nature'—and asked if she knew anyone I could talk to.

Mrs Wurstová's eyes were wide with shock. 'Have you—some baby inside?'

'No, no!' I almost laughed. 'It's more—psychological.'

She paused, looking right through me. 'Is it your heart? Your Karel?'

'Yes.' My eyes were blurred with tears.

'Tanya, my dear, you must see Doctor Jílek. He is a "modern-day" Czech psychologist and I think he will be very helpful. He speaks English.'

Without missing a beat, Mrs Wurstová bustled me into her office.

'We must use my telephone right now to call his secretary. I do not know if she speaks the English so I will help.' Before I knew it, she had arranged an appointment for me the next day, and even offered me a room at one of the courts if I wanted 'some space'.

The next afternoon, I headed towards a western part of Prague and found my way up several flights of stairs and along to the end of a narrow corridor where a tall, thin man waited. He had a short goatee beard and wore a white jacket. For a moment I had visions of a Cold War science experiment but he was gentle and kind, and invited me to talk. Once I started, I couldn't stop.

Eventually, he responded.

'You have to respect your needs, otherwise your partner won't, and you will lose him anyway.'

I rocked on his couch.

'Yes, it is normal and right and proper to believe that a man and woman can share a common goal for a life together. If your current partner doesn't or can't, that does not mean there is something wrong with you—or that you are unworthy of love—or unlovable.'

Tears: despairing, angry.

Finally, there was the clincher.

'Perhaps you could consider taking this step by step? Allow yourself to go away for a trial. Do not call leaving here "the end", if that is too distressing for you. Do not make absolutes for yourself. Give yourself six months back in your country and allow all your feelings to bubble up and come out. Then you will have a better idea of what is right for you. Allow the body to help and give you the answers in its own time.'

Ahhh.

I breathed out.

'The body always knows best, Tanya. But it cannot be rushed.'

Yes, yes. Six months was manageable.

Six months would take me up to Anne's wedding, which had been set for May next year. If I went away, the wedding would give me a legitimate reason to come back.

All I now had to do was find a way to explain my departure to my students and clients. I couldn't bear for anyone to think that I was giving up on the language and the culture—and on them.

In the end it was my beloved sister M'Lis who gave me the way out. M'Lis asked me to attend the birth of her second child (due in January) and I told everyone I wanted to be there. The family pull legitimised my departure. After all, family was what the Czechs knew best.

I sat down and wrote a fax to M'Lis.

———⊰⊱———

Šárka's eyes welled with tears when I told her and Radka I was leaving.

'You know you have gone to his core,' she said.

'His core?'

'Yes. But . . .' She paused, and there it was again—the inevitable 'but'.

'*But* I don't have the Czech "butterfly down",' I finished for her, not wanting to hear the words from anyone else. 'I'm not his type. And I'm not a Czech girl.' I wanted to cry.

Šárka simply sighed again. 'He is a fool. But what to do?'

She shrugged, knowing her father would take no notice of her views either. Then she explained to Radka, whose big eyes grew wide and dark. Radka held out her arms, tears brimming, and we all hugged.

Mrs Wurstová had the final word.

'Simply because you love someone does not mean it is right to be with them forever,' she said, with the wisdom of someone who had lived through more sadness than anyone else I could imagine. 'Perhaps life in our country is not to be your path anymore. Everything is in the timing. You must trust that if you are meant to return, you will. We will always be here for you.'

———⊰⊱———

December 1995

I spent my last day walking through the Old Town, soaking up images of the city, burning into my brain 'mind photos' to recall in later times. The day felt surreal. Christmas was just around the corner, the market stalls were bustling and everyone was in festive mode. Váňa, Oršula & Partners had given me a huge farewell party and I'd wept as I left them. My students and colleagues had been beautiful, sad, generous. They gave me gifts, hugged me, and wished me well for the birth of my sister's baby. They all told me to come back soon. I'd spoken to my Sedlčany friends by phone and Kamila in particular was inconsolable. 'But you love your Karel,' she cried down the unreliable phone line. 'Why you must leave?' There were no good answers to give, especially to a young and beautiful teenager who still believed that love would conquer everything. We hung up, promising to write.

Anne had already sent me plans for the wedding and I imagined it all while I drank my last coffee near Jan Hus's statue. The wedding ceremony was to be held in the Old Town Square, inside the beautiful Town Hall that boasted the Astronomical Clock. That was the place where several years before I'd first met Míša and Jarda and fallen in love with the city. The wedding party was later to walk along Charles Bridge and we would celebrate with champagne in an ancient hall under the castle. Karel would be invited as my partner, of course.

The wind whipped around my ankles as I clutched Mrs Wurstová's coat tight. The pain in my heart was savage, like it wanted to rip its way out of me, claw its way into the fresh air so it could breathe, so it could escape, so it could explode.

But there was nowhere for that pain to go and no release from its burn.

———————<>———————

On my last night Karel took me to Petřín Hill—well, where else would we go? We climbed the huge hill to Karel Mácha's monument. The poet of love looked down upon us solemnly, only too aware of the fickleness of love. Late twilight blanketed the city of spires and turrets with its soft web. Before long it had turned into a black velvet cushion studded as though with glittering diamonds. Prague Castle was floodlit, and the evening bells from St Vitus Cathedral pealed across the city.

My heart ached so badly it felt bruised and battered. Such an odd contradiction—so much beauty around me, so much pain inside me. To paraphrase Kafka: 'Prague has claws and does not let go.' He was right. My love for Karel and his city would last forever, no matter what followed over the years.

Karel cupped my chin and gazed with his intense blue eyes into mine.

'You must know I think you are most precious person I've ever met, Táničko,' he said. 'So I will say something to you because it is important and I don't think you always understand me. Tomorrow you will go, so now is the time to tell you before it's too late.'

Too late? Too late for what?

He smiled gently.

'Be glad of your life because there's always the other side, můj miláčku.'

Below us the lights spread out below like a jewelled necklace around the River Vltava.

'When you gain, you lose. When you lose, you gain. As we say in Czech, beware of something nice because it always has a sting. If you were married and had children with me, you could not live the life you are about to live. And you will see so much more of the world and live so much because you are courageous.'

My vision blurred with tears.

'To Czech friendship—the highest form of love. It never dies, Táničko. It lives always.'

Was that the lesson I'd come here to learn in the first place, the lesson that had taken me so long to understand?

There were no words left to say. My dream had dissolved with my last day in the Czech Republic. I'd done what I'd come to do.

38

2002

'*Ahoj*, Táničko. Here is Jarda, and I also have with me Míša.'

My heart leapt at hearing the gentle, lilting tones of my two Czech-Australian friends. It had been a while since I'd spoken to them. My life in Australia was busy.

Jarda got straight to the point.

'Táničko, I have bad news.'

Karel was dying.

Cancer.

He had cut off contact with everyone and it was only a matter of time.

Leaning over the desk, barely holding the phone up, I tried to keep my voice steady, but the words punched my stomach: hard, visceral. It couldn't be true.

I'd been back for Anne's magical wedding, and numerous times since. Karel and I had both managed to move on in our lives but I'd never stopped loving everything Czech.

Momentarily, selfishly, I felt cheated. I'd left Prague and Karel many times before but I'd always been able to return. They'd always *been* there.

After Jarda's phone call, I frantically scrabbled for numbers in my messy 'travelling' drawer and miraculously found what I was looking for: a slip of paper, stuck between my last two Prague plane tickets and a coffee receipt from the Old Town Square. On it was a mobile phone number. Karel had given it to me when I last visited. Would it still work? Tentatively, I dialled, praying Karel would answer, and praying I'd know what to say if he did.

I held my breath. The phone rang and rang. Would it ring out? Finally, '*Ano.*'

I'd recognise that gentle, accented voice anywhere.

'Karel,' I cried. 'It's me, Tanya.'

A painful silence crackled through the phone.

Then, in a disbelieving tone, he asked, 'Táničko? Is it really you?'

We exchanged an awkward, confused rush of words.

'Is it true, Karel?' I whispered.

There was a long silence. I'd caught him off guard and he seemed to have lost his sense of control. It was as though hearing me released a well of pent-up grief. Finally, he blurted out some words, disjointed and angry.

'Yes, Táničko, it is like some bad theatre. I do not believe it myself. *Je to špatné.*' ('It is bad'.)

I didn't know what to say. I wanted to help, to go to say goodbye, but my words became tangled. Mercifully, having recovered his own composure, he interrupted.

'So what is with you, Táničko? Are you yet married and do you yet have children?'

I was silent for a second.

'Yes, I am married. And'—I paused, wanting him to know— 'I am very happy. After I last saw you, I met someone in England. We live in Margaret River, a wine-growing region. My husband is in the wine industry and . . .' I stopped. I was babbling. 'But no children.'

There was a short laugh.

'You see, *moje* Táničko, I was right all along. Children or no, you always had your destiny in your own country and you are now living it.'

A long silence.

'Now, I will tell you something, Táničko,' he said. 'You are married and I am dying and I can now tell you this.'

He paused.

'I have always loved you.'

My world spun dizzily in front of me. I thought my heart would stop beating.

'And you know very well why I could not tell you at the time.'

A scream rose within my chest, like a trapped bird flapping frantically—a mad, hunted, grief-stricken scream. Tears streaked down my face, wretched tears, full of frustration and despair.

'Yes, I know it is hard for you to hear this now when you wanted me to say it all those years ago,' he said softly. 'And I am so sorry for all the pain I caused you, but as you know, I always did what I thought was best.'

He finished quietly.

'I was in love with you from the day you arrived in Prague and you knew it pretty well. Even though I fought it and I would not say it to you. But I could not follow you to Australia and let my daughters alone. Talking about friendship was very easy and talking about love was nearly impossible.'

———◦✦◦———

It was Jarda on the phone again. His voice sounded a long way away.

As Karel would have said himself: '*Vymalováno.* 'It is painted.'

Epilogue

Czech friendship

It is still hard to believe the man with the bright blue eyes has gone, swallowed up by one of those tiny, twisting alleyways overhung with lanterns and shadows and gabled roofs that he took me through on my first day in Prague. Taken far beyond the struggles he'd endured during decades of occupation by foreigners who captured his beloved soil by force, a repressive regime that stole his friends and much of his soul. He'd known only fourteen years of freedom.

I was lucky to be part of that time. In total it amounted to not more than about two years of my life but the impact that Karel and Prague had on me felt more like a century's worth of experience. Karel had made the Czech Republic possible for me—in every way.

When I first left, the grief at losing both Karel and his country felt too big for my body; it threatened to flatten me, extinguish my own breath, and I thought I'd never recover.

But Karel was right.

Home is not just where the heart is but where a person can live and work and love fully and openly. Returning to Australia wasn't the end but rather the beginning of a newer and more precious life for me. Building on all I'd learnt over those years, I finally found the work and love I was longing for, without the fear of being trapped or losing my independence—my own 'happily ever after'. The Czech world will be forever intertwined in my own world as a girl from the outback, making it forever bolder, brighter and more beautiful.

The Czech spirit continues to live on in my life, too, like an eternal flame.

I keep in contact with my Czech and English friends; my beloved Šárka and Radka; Kamila, Naďa, Pavel, Maruška from Sedlčany; Headmistress Anne, Czech Richard, Czech-English Vera, English Alistair, Canadian Carolyn from English House; Networking Irena and German Alyson; the wonderful judges, Romana and my adored Mrs Wurstová. Mr Svoboda and I have even exchanged emails! He remains as inspiring as ever, reminding me, 'we cannot give up our readiness to make our world better.'

The Czech Republic is now no longer hidden either, but accessible at the tap of a computer. On Google Earth I can fly over Prague and show my family the sights. I discovered during my last visit that the Czech *paneláky* have been painted pretty pastel colours. The Czechs couldn't get rid of the *paneláky* so came up with a solution that I thought was very 'them': turn something soul-destroying into something beautiful, through their special blend of creativity and art and colour. Sedlčany in particular has been transformed.

The Good Soldier Švejk would have approved.

My wonderful 'big brothers', the Czech-Australians Míša and Jarda, and the bubbly Naďa in Melbourne, have remained my soulmates. Many years earlier they'd come to terms with the contradictions of living in and loving two countries. They continued to share their wisdom with me as we camped in Central Australia and drank wine in Margaret River.

Their connection led me to the charming Zdeněk Jiránek from the South Australian Československý Klub. A tall, intelligent man with a cheeky grin, he brought Pilsner Urquell back into my life and I called him 'Mr President'. He read my first chapters on meeting Karel and clicked his tongue. 'That Karel sounds like trouble. Lucky you came home to us, Táničko.' Every time he used the diminutive of my name, I beamed from ear to ear.

The Klub is an oasis for homesick Czechs, a sanctuary in Adelaide that holds the culture and language of the Czech homelands. I was introduced to it by the wonderful Helena and Zdeněk (Danny) Kotásek, an older and courageous couple who'd fled the tyranny of Czech Republic decades earlier. Helena painstakingly corrected my Czech words and sighed, 'That Karel! Hopeless Czech man. What was wrong with him?' Her husband, on the other hand, read the draft and gripped my hand, tears in his eyes. 'Thank you. At last, someone has told our story.'

Our story.

Our story of the West's betrayal. Hitler. Stalin.

Danny's words, more than anyone's, gave purpose to my story and the journey of telling it here. Sadly, Danny passed away before I could show the story to him in print and recently I received yet another one of those phone calls. '*Ahoj*, Táničko. Here is Míša. Our Jarda has died.'

Once more my knees crumpled and my heart broke. It was impossible to believe. Jarda, still fit and energetic, had suffered a stroke while visiting Prague. He was playing guitar and singing Czech songs with his beloved wife Věra and friends in a pub beforehand. Through my grief I thought that if there was a good way for a Czech to go, perhaps there was no better way than that.

Míša is now fighting cancer. His wonderful wife Jari remains by his side. He continues to remind me to live in the moment. 'There is no point taking life too seriously. You won't get out of it alive, Táničko!'

Tak! In the spirit of the brave Czechs, this story can't end too seriously either.

I am reminded of Jarda's words after Karel's death. At the time we were fighting to hold fragments of a life together, to give it meaning, and Jarda did that for me.

'It is important to find something to remember Karel by, Táničko. I'll always remember him for his jokes. It's all summed up in his tram story.

'One night after a party Karel and I and some of the gang were going home on the night tram. It was a long trip at such a late hour so to pass the time Karel started telling a very long and very funny joke about a Russian general and a Czech soldier on their way to a military parade. It was so funny that all the people around us who were meant to get off before us did not get off, and stayed on the tram just so they could hear the end of his joke. They did this even though by now it was 3 a.m. and they had missed the chance to make it home before dawn. There were so many of them! And do you know, Táničko'—he paused—'they had never met Karel before in their lives.'

Acknowledgements

So many people have helped me on my fourteen-year journey to tell this story. Every step of the road has led to the kindness of strangers, support beyond my dreams, and the generosity of people who have become friends over this time. I feel incredibly lucky and grateful. I could never have written this book without you all—thank you!

It all began in Margaret River. The fabulous Karen McDonald believed in me and my story from the outset; Lorraine and Richard Firth generously invited me to write in their magical home, Merribrook; my beautiful writing soulmate Bernice Barry offered up her kitchen for the next draft and supported me along every step of this journey; clever gals Wendy Mitchell and Rosi Moore-Fiander gave early advice, as did the generous Keith McLeod; Margot Edwards held the best-ever workshops in her farmhouse; the inspiring Pat Negus never stopped believing in me; the brilliant Rebecca Scott painstakingly transcribed my tapes from afar when I couldn't write; the inspired healing work of Brad Mitchell, Debbi Wilson and Kym Walker helped me write again; and the wonderful Patti Miller mentored me through the Australian Society of Authors, encouraged me and believed I had a story worth publishing.

Then came the Adelaide crowd: the sensational Moggies writing group (and you all know who you are); Rob Grindstaff brilliantly edited from afar; and Penny McCann and Stephanie Mallen each worked tirelessly to create opportunities for my story to be heard.

Perth followed: I met the brilliant Kathryn Heyman at a workshop (thanks, again, to Bernice); Kathryn later mentored me with magic and generously assisted me towards publication. My beloved friends Jane Aberdeen and Kellie Hill encouraged me over glasses of wine and never let me give up. The all-round-simply-wonderful Martin Rooney kept me going—thank you in so many ways, Martin.

Alice Springs: Jo Dutton, Genevieve O'Loughlin and Leni Shilton offered helpful advice; and the sparkling Carolyn Lopes and Marg Bowman created the opportunities for me to meet the incomparable Bernadette Foley.

Bernadette's insight and wisdom and fabulous support led me to my publishing contract—truly a champagne moment! Thank you always and forever, Bernadette!

Throughout there were many helpful and wise eyes: Annette Every, Roxane Scott and Dani May advised on numerous versions of the manuscript; the inspiring Helena Kotasek from the South Australian Czech Club reviewed the first and last round of Czech words; the already busy Toni Tapp Coutts and Liz Harfull generously read and offered comments; and my beloved Andrea Davies supported me throughout.

An enormous thanks to my publishers Annette Barlow and Tom Gilliat who have given me this incredible opportunity; to the eagle eye of Samantha Kent—thank you, you are the best editor imaginable!; to Chloe Erlich for her beautiful photographs; and to everyone at Allen & Unwin who has brought my story to life. Thank you, thank you, thank you!

Then of course there are the wonderful people who made this whole journey possible. Darling Michael White helped set me on my adventure; the inimitable Peter Barr made it happen; the generous and extraordinary Czech people opened their homes and hearts to me; and course, the tremendous trio—Míša, Jarda and Karel—made *everything* possible. I will always be thankful I met you.

Finally, there is my beloved family without whom there would be no book: Mum, Dad, M'Lis and Chris, Brett and Fiona, Ben and Laura, and my cherished nieces and nephews—thank you, all.

In particular, I need to thank my precious Mum and sister, M'Lis, who supported me through many dark days of this journey and stood by me every step. My nephew Mitch inspired me to keep going too: 'I want to go to Prague because of you, Aunty Tan!' Niece Anna, at age thirteen, read the first half of the book and told me, with sparkling eyes, that she 'loved it'— encouragement beyond words for an aunty! And my talented niece Bonny took evocative and beautiful photographs of me in the horse yards—thank you, beautiful Bon! Finally, a special thanks to my wonderful cousin Fleur McDonald—you have been the most extraordinary support and it has been so much fun going through this process with you!

But the greatest thanks of all go to my darling husband, Steve. There aren't enough words to capture your encouragement, patience, love, and the fact you would 'never, ever' let me give up telling this story, as you knew how much it meant for me to tell it.

Thank you all and everyone. I am forever grateful!

The facts in this story are true in so far as my memory, diaries, letters and notes are an accurate recollection of my time in the Czech Republic although certain events, timeframes and travels have been compressed. Some names and events have been changed out of respect for people's privacy. Any factual, language, spelling and style inaccuracies are mine and mine alone—*promiňte*.